72.95

S0-ATF-090

Gandhi, Mao,
Mandela, and Gorbachev

GANDHI, MAO, MANDELA, AND GORBACHEV

$\blacklozenge\blacklozenge\blacklozenge$

Studies in
Personality, Power, and Politics

ANTHONY R. DeLUCA

PRAEGER

Westport, Connecticut
London

Colorado Christian University
Library
180 S. Garrison
Lakewood, Colorado 80226

Library of Congress Cataloging-in-Publication Data

DeLuca, Anthony R.
    Gandhi, Mao, Mandela, and Gorbachev:
    studies in personality, power, and politics / Anthony R. DeLuca.
        p.   cm.
    Includes bibliographical references and index.
    ISBN 0–275–95969–4 (alk. paper)
        1. World politics—20th century.   2. Gandhi, Mahatma, 1869–1948.   3. Mao, Tse-tung,
    1893–1976.   4. Mandela, Nelson, 1918–   5. Gorbachev, Mikhail Sergeevich, 1931–
    I. Title.
    D443.D437 2000
    909.82'5—dc21   99–046619

British Library Cataloguing in Publication Data is available.

Copyright © 2000 by Anthony R. DeLuca

All rights reserved. No portion of this book may be
reproduced, by any process or technique, without
the express written consent of the publisher.

Library of Congress Catalog Card Number: 99–046619
ISBN: 0–275–95969–4

First published in 2000

Praeger Publishers, 88 Post Road West, Westport, CT 06881
An imprint of Greenwood Publishing Group, Inc.
www.praeger.com

Printed in the United States of America

The paper used in this book complies with the
Permanent Paper Standard issued by the National
Information Standards Organization (Z39.48–1984).

10 9 8 7 6 5 4 3 2 1

To My Students

CONTENTS

Preface   ix

Chapter 1.   Gandhi and the Struggle for India's Independence   1

Chapter 2.   Mao and the Communist Revolution in China   31

Chapter 3.   Mandela and Freedom in South Africa   63

Chapter 4.   Gorbachev and the Collapse of the Soviet Union   99

Conclusion   163

Suggestions for Further Reading   173

Index   177

PREFACE

In preparing a study on prominent political figures and historical personalities of the twentieth century, I have sought, as I did in my earlier book on Napoleon, Bismarck, Lenin, and Hitler, to emphasize the relationship between the individual personality and the expectations, opportunities, and challenges of the historical setting. Since the case of each of these individuals was strongly influenced by the theme of war and revolution, their responses to the forces of colonialism, racism, and totalitarianism have figured prominently in my account. The political debate concerning the extended role of nationalism as a feature of global development also produced a struggle within these figures, who had to wrestle with the attraction of nativism and westernization, the development of a political identity, and the formation of a new political consciousness. With the exception of Mikhail Gorbachev, who tried to reform the system from within, the others—Mahatma Gandhi, Mao Zedong, and Nelson Mandela—came from outside the system and sought to wrest power and authority from the political establishment.

From the perspective of Mahatma Gandhi's political odyssey, the anti-Imperial struggle against Great Britain represented the only path to achieve Indian independence, although the attraction of European culture remained strong among members of India's anglophile elite. Gandhi is an example of someone who was drawn to English culture in London and South Africa where he trained and practiced as a lawyer, but who also experienced a profound internal transformation upon his return to India and discovery of the mystique of India's native soul and culture. His life then became a living testimony to how to use the ingredients of Indian culture to establish a popular movement and achieve freedom and independence from British rule. In the eyes of the world his heroic, yet peaceful, victory and emphasis on religious commitment, nonviolence, and compassion provided a new definition of nationalism and transformed him into a holy man and a martyr worthy of the world's respect and admiration.

On his long and tortuous road to political power, Mao Zedong began with drawing lessons from his peasant background while remaining open to insights from the West. And his adaptation of Marxist thought to the Chinese setting enabled him to promote social revolution through a radical realignment of China's political and economic forces. In addition to his "Sinification" of Marxism, Mao also had to build a military force capable of winning a civil war against the Nationalist Chinese and liberating China from the grip of an aggressive, expansionist Japan. Much like Otto von Bismarck, who unified imperial Germany, Mao also benefited from a long period of power following the creation of the People's Republic of China, which earned for him the title of "the Great Helmsman." But in Mao's case the outlines and dimensions of the new China were not as clearly defined as had been the case with Bismarck's Germany. As a consequence Mao chose to experiment with various forms of communist construction and popular motivational campaigns, including his "Hundred Flowers Speech" and "The Cultural Revolution," which eventually led to a break with the Soviet "revisionists" and to the struggle between pragmatists and revolutionary purists within the party. In Mao's case, I have relied heavily on contemporary source materials to capture his political energy and the spirit of the movement he led.

Like Gandhi, Nelson Mandela had to confront the issues of personal humiliation, identity, persecution, and above all racism in a land where white colonial oppression had for centuries dominated the lives of South Africa's majority black population and other nonwhite minority populations as well. And it is no accident that Gandhi's time spent in Mandela's homeland contributed to Gandhi's awareness of the need for the black and Indian populations of South Africa to make common cause against the Dutch and the English. What was different, however, was the less than human treatment of South Africa's blacks and the ways in which racism and color poisoned the South African political environment. In that regard Mandela's search for his own political identity, his views on revolution and political change, communism, violence, his espousal of Marxist principles, his long imprisonment, and his ultimate political victory were a testament to his strength of character in the pursuit of his own identity, the political identity of his people, and their common struggle for freedom.

In Mikhail Gorbachev's case, it is important to confront the discrepancy between political symbolism and political reality. For example, during his early years as Soviet head of state, Gorbachev's charismatic personality and innovative programs of *perestroika* and *glasnost* generated an enthusiastic response around the world. But the charismatic quality of Gorbachev's appeal also revealed the disruptive circumstances and pressures that confronted the Soviet Union, once Gorbachev had set the policy of reform from above into motion. But his attempt at revolution from above was a failure, which led to his own political demise and to the sudden collapse of the Soviet Union. In terms of Gorbachev's larger historical significance, it is also important to analyze his role as the most mediagenic and commanding international political figure of the period. As the last Soviet head of state, he presided over the triumph of nationalism and the collapse of an empire; as ideologue, he also inherited a Leninist revolutionary doctrine that no longer met the needs of the people.

There are some interesting parallels between and among the four individuals. Gandhi, Mao, and Mandela all believed in a rigorous routine of physical exercise, be it walking or swimming or some other form of physical fitness. Three of them, Mandela, Gandhi, and Gorbachev were all trained as lawyers. In the case of Gandhi and Mandela the law provided them with a means to defend themselves and obtain limited access to the workings of the white European political system. In Gorbachev's case the motivation is less clear, although he may have viewed the study of law as part of some mythic connection with Lenin, who was also trained as a lawyer. The study of the law also left a formative stylistic impression upon Gorbachev by providing him with greater access to western political thought and values. In the Marxist context Mao and Gorbachev both fought against the emergence of a new class in their respective countries, although in obviously different ways and for clearly different reasons. Both also referred to the fundamental importance of concrete political situations. Mao, for example, highlighted the Leninist emphasis on a "concrete analysis of concrete conditions," while Gorbachev was fond of quoting Hegel's dictum "the truth is concrete." They also sought to change Marxism: Gorbachev by reform from above and Mao by revolution from below.

All four struggled against political legitimacy but in different ways: Gorbachev by appealing to the reformist element in the party and reinvigorating the Soviet system through *glasnost* and *perestroika*, Mao by appealing to the tradition of peasant revolution and the popular urge for freedom from all forms of domestic and foreign oppression. Gandhi and Mandela searched for their own identities within by combining the native traditions of their own respective cultures and elements of Anglo-European culture that appealed to them, including the pursuit of a British education and lessons in ballroom dancing and western music. Their European outlooks, however, also led them to struggle, albeit in different ways, against the traditional notion of arranged marriages in their respective cultures. While Gandhi made peace with it personally and preached against it publicly, Mandela quickly fled his tribal court for Johannesburg before the prospect of such a union. In addition to their fascination with elegantly tailored suits, Gorbachev and Mandela also shared an interest in drama and performance, while Mao favored military tunics and promoted the more radical practice of guerrilla theater as a form of political enlightenment.

Events played an important role in determining the outcomes of all four careers. While the collapse of communism in Eastern Europe in 1989 obviously influenced developments in the Soviet Union, it also enabled the white South African government to transcend its obsession with international communist control and accept the indigenous reality of the African freedom movement. Two of the four won the Nobel Peace Prize: Gorbachev in 1991 and Mandela in 1993. In both cases, however, the ceremonies were clouded: in Gorbachev's case by domestic discontent and political turmoil in the Soviet Union, and in Mandela's case by having awkwardly to share the podium with F. W. de Klerk at a time when the early constructive collaboration between the two men had deteriorated into distrust.

Chapter 1

GANDHI

AND THE STRUGGLE FOR INDIA'S INDEPENDENCE

BRITISH RULE

Beginning in the eighteenth century, the British encountered only marginal resistance to their military conquest of the Indian subcontinent. The divisions separating the native Mughal princes, the rival claims of the Hindu and Muslim religious communities, the "mass acquiescence" of the Indian people, and the collaboration of India's ruling elite made it easy for the British Raj to assert its power and dominate India culturally and economically. To secure their control of the Indian government and create a lucrative career path for British subjects, the British excluded Indians from high positions in the army and the civil service. Reflecting as it did the cultural preferences of the English and the primacy of the English language, The Indian Civil Service or I.C.S. encouraged widespread feelings of inferiority within the native population by discriminating in favor of British applicants and candidates for promotion. For those members of the Indian elite who had been coopted by years of British education and devoted service to the British Empire, Britain's presence in India had provided an attractive but frequently unattainable menu of cultural alternatives. Moreover, the fascination with British taste and manners rendered them incapable of providing inspirational political leadership.[1] Recognizing the symptoms of this identity crisis and the ambivalent nature of the West's attraction, Gandhi carefully admonished his followers not to "mistake the glamour for true light."[2] British rule, however, was a two-edged sword, since exposure to British ways and education also brought westernization, a belief in progress, and an emerging sense of national identity among the Indian people after centuries of cultural and political torpor.

When Indian troops rebelled against the imperial command during the Sepoy Mutiny in 1857, the British encountered the first real challenge to their authority in India. The mutiny was provoked by long campaigns, un-

Mahatma Gandhi. Reproduced from the collections of the Library of Congress.

received back pay, and the practice of distributing cartridges that were greased with the fat of cows and pigs. The act was offensive to both the Hindu and Muslim populations, because the cartridges had to be bitten off at the ends. The British response to the rebellion was severe. In the town of Crawnpore where there had been a massacre of European women, British troops ravaged the entire population. In the aftermath of the mutiny Parliament passed the Act for the Better Government of India in 1858, which rendered the East India government a quaint anachronism. In its place India came under the direct rule of the British Empire, and Queen Victoria was proclaimed Empress of India. But the imposition of imperial authority did not exorcise the nightmare of "mutiny-phobia"[3] that periodically haunted the British. To cope with this fear, the British undertook a program of legal and administrative reforms, including the limited participation of Indians in legislative councils and an extensive program of public works. These initiatives, however, slid into the familiar pattern of British control, as Whitehall would propose a discussion of self-rule measures, while at the same time working surreptitiously to prevent their implementation. By the turn of the century India had clearly become the commercial and defensive "linchpin" of the Empire, and no British government so much as "dare[d] to tinker" with the sacred notion of imperial rule.[4]

As a largely backward and impoverished India entered the twentieth century, a nationalist wave of independence swept across Hindus and Muslims alike. In the case of the Hindus, the movement dated back to the nineteenth century and the formation of the Indian National Congress, which had split into two contradictory camps composed of westernizers and nativists. Westernizers tended to be moderate in their political views and solicitous of British manners and styles as a means of gaining admission into the Indian Civil Service. Intelligent, upwardly mobile in their thinking, they trusted the British notions of fair play and justice. More important, however, the westernizers were willing to collaborate and share the responsibility of governing with the British. Militants, however, led by B. G. Tilak, criticized the moderates for their spiritual and moral weakness and challenged the moderates' faith in British justice. Instead of administrative reforms, the nativists preferred to extol the virtues of heroic national resistance. The result of the split, however, was to render the congress ineffective. Testifying to the fractured, feckless nature of its activities, Gandhi once observed: "The Congress would meet three days every year and then go to sleep." His early accounts of congress sessions stressed the listless, ineffective character of the proceedings, featuring an elaborate ritual of "lengthy speeches."[5] The congress also provided Gandhi with greater exposure to the thought of his political elders, and, in particular, to the moderate positions of Gopal Krishna Gokhale and the more radical views of Tilak.[6]

With Gandhi's appearance on the Indian political scene in 1919, he presented the British with a threat to the perpetuation of their privileged position.

He did so through his disarming candor, independence, unpredictability, and uncanny ability to draw the masses around him and embarrass high-ranking government officials.[7] When Gandhi assumed leadership of the congress in 1920, he addressed the organization's unwieldy structure, its listless inactivity, and even its lack of a full-time secretary.[8] Setting out to strengthen the organizational basis of India's fragmented political life and address the split between westernizers and nativists, Gandhi emerged as a "reformer and [an] activist" and not as a political "theorist."[9]

Fearing the spread of violent political movements after World War I, the British passed the Rowlatt Acts in 1919 authorizing government officials to detain anyone suspected of sedition without regard for due process. The action infuriated Gandhi, who had loyally supported the British cause during the war. In April, when British troops in the town of Amritsar fired upon demonstrators marching in support of two leaders who had been jailed for opposing the Rowlatt Acts, the seemingly random act of political repression came as a bloody shock to the population of India. In reaction to the shooting, members of the crowd ran amok, burning government buildings and killing four Europeans. As public tension increased, General Reginald Dyer, the British officer in charge, insisted on imposing martial law and broke up a public meeting in which hundreds of people were killed and as many as three times that number were injured. Once martial law had been imposed, Dyer quickly extended it to the entire Punjab region and subjected the Indian population to a regime of public humiliations. Indians were forced to crawl on their bellies at the spot where a European woman had been assaulted, others had to alight from cars and salute passing Europeans, while a group of college students had to suffer by marching four times a day in the scorching heat of the Indian sun.[10]

A subsequent British inquiry into the affair revealed that Dyer troop's had fired without warning and continued to fire upon the crowd as it dispersed. This information notwithstanding, a heroic version of the massacre quickly emerged, portraying Dyer as the "saviour of India" for suppressing the Punjab rebellion and putting an end to a conspiracy to undermine British rule. For Gandhi and the Indian nationalists, Amritsar was hardly heroic. What most upset the nationalists was the British government's cold-hearted refusal to rectify the injustice as well as the attitude of the British upper classes, who showed little if any concern for the slaughter of innocent protesters. The massacre also reinforced the perception among the Indian people that Britain believed it had a special birthright to rule by decree and treat the Indian subjects as inferior subjects.[11] Moreover, like the Sepoy Mutiny, the bloody reality of Amritsar demonstrated once again that force remained "the ultimate sanction" for one country's rule over another.[12] Gandhi would later write in a somewhat elliptical voice that he did not blame the British for the sorry state of affairs in India, since "Englishmen lose in character after residence in India and . . . Indians lose in courage and manliness by contact with Englishmen."[13] Nor did he hesitate to tell his countrymen in 1925 that "their enslavement was the result of their weaknesses, not of British might."[14]

POLITICS AND IDENTITY

Born into comfortable economic circumstances on October 2, 1869, Mohandas Gandhi was a rather conventional youth who exhibited little, if any, of the intelligence and charisma that characterized his political career. He was, however, profoundly influenced by his mother's deep religious faith,[15] which undoubtedly served as a model for his own spirituality and saintly behavior. As a small, frail, polite, and diffident youth, who often recalled how he was afraid of the dark, Gandhi suffered from an inferiority complex, which manifested itself in his reluctance to speak in public. Maintaining that this anxiety taught him to appreciate the value of an "economy of words," he would later describe his shyness as a form of protection that enabled him to grow and learn how to discern the truth.[16]

At age thirteen he married his child bride, Kasturbai. Though they remained together throughout their lives, Gandhi regretted what he described as "the cruel custom of child marriages"[17] predicated primarily upon economic convenience.[18] From the arranged union sprang four boys—three of whom succeeded in life, while the eldest, Harilal, rejected his father's stern, exacting authority and led a "profligate" life as a "drunkard." Much has been made of Gandhi's failure as a father: his stern, disciplinary manner; and his unwillingness, despite the entreaties of Kasturbai, to give his sons a proper education.[19] Although Gandhi freely admitted the errors of his paternal experiments, he conscientiously stressed the primary importance of spiritual training and the need to place the education of the heart over that of the intellect. In keeping with these views, he openly stated his preference for "vocational training" over "literary training" and his belief that the teacher should take precedence over the textbook.[20] As a teacher, Gandhi also believed that he had to serve as "an eternal object lesson" in matters of self-discipline and self-restraint[21] and willingly assume "responsibility for the errors of his pupil[s]."[22]

Kasturbai for her part resented the household chores and communal lifestyle she was forced to lead and Gandhi's lack of interest in money, jewelry, and other material possessions. Finding it difficult to live according to Gandhi's spartan standards, Kasturbai protested her having to clean chamber pots and at one point challenged Gandhi, asking to be let go. Gandhi in his own oxymoronic fashion acknowledged that he "was a cruelly kind husband," although he claimed that "with the gradual disappearance . . . of the carnal appetite," their domestic life became more peaceful and happy.[23] He even maintained that they had evolved into "a model couple, she the acme of service, he the paragon of consideration." But his transcendent nature and commitment to the larger cause of forging a new India also enabled him to distance himself from the more immediate concerns of his own family circle and earnestly declare: "All of India is my family."[24]

At the age of sixteen Gandhi cared for his dying father and recalled how much he enjoyed rendering service as his father's nurse and massaging his legs. The night his father died, however, Gandhi had gone to bed and began making love to his wife, assuming as did other members of his family that his father's life was not in immediate danger. When stunned by a knock on the bedroom door and informed of his father's passing, Gandhi suddenly experienced enormous guilt for having been unable to escape "the shackles of lust" and be with his father during his final moments.[25] The noted psychologist Erik Erikson argues that unresolved traumatic experiences such as Gandhi's frequently occur among "religious innovators" possessed with a demanding conscience. Erikson does point out, however, that a single experience of this nature does not by and of itself constitute what might be described as a "curse" in an individual's life.[26]

Perhaps the single most formative experience shaping Gandhi's identity were the two years and eight months he spent studying law in London. Just one month shy of his twentieth year, Gandhi left his native Rajkot for Bombay, where he undertook his own version of a foreign subject's passage to England. For Gandhi this passage served as "a period of apprenticeship" on the road to shaping his cultural identity and fulfilling his leadership role in Indian politics.[27] At the outset Gandhi tried to mirror the lifestyle and taste of the British, particularly in his adoption of stiff British business dress and Victorian manners. Although he would later condemn the "tyranny of [the] English"[28] language and English culture, early photographs of Gandhi during his stay in London reveal something of an awkward dandy ill-suited to his new surroundings in his top hat and tailored Bond street attire. He also studied French; took dancing, violin, and elocution lessons;[29] and cultivated his passion for long walks, which enabled him to husband the energy and stamina he exhibited throughout his life.[30] While in London, he also learned to be frugal and pursued his interest in the benefits of a vegetarian diet, which distanced him from the world of the British "meat-eaters" he envied as a youth.[31] As a boy Gandhi had secretly conducted his own experiment in eating meat with his Muslim friend Sheik Mehtab, only to recoil in guilt from his deception and swear that he would not eat meat until his parents had died.[32] During his stay in London he even ventured to the Paris Exhibition in 1890 to see its newest attraction, the Eiffel Tower. But Gandhi was not impressed, since he viewed the tower as a children's toy and more of a "monument [to] man's folly" than to "his wisdom."[33]

Though he freely experimented with western ways during his stay in London, he remained faithful to the Hindu beliefs of renunciation and selflessness, which served as a formative moral and ethical matrix throughout his life.[34] These virtues also contributed to his identity as both a spiritual and a political figure and reflected his perception of his own development as a process of "self-realization" gained through "deep, self-introspection."[35] Following his return to India and his failure as a barrister in his native land, the painful process of self-discovery continued. When he tried, for example, to intercede with a British agent on behalf of his brother, he experienced the direct impact of British arrogance. The official, who according to Gandhi had been friendly to him during his stay in London, summarily rejected Gandhi's request and had him unceremoniously dismissed from his office. Disgusted with the "intrigue" and "petty politics"[36] he had encountered, Gandhi decided to leave India and set sail to represent his firm in South Africa, only to encounter a new form of discrimination when he was labeled a "coolie barrister." Another incident aboard a South African train reinforced the pattern of discrimination, when Gandhi was told to move to the baggage car despite the fact that he had purchased a first-class ticket. When he indignantly refused to do so, he was forced off the train at the next station and left alone on the platform. Deeply incensed by the injustice, Gandhi began to undertake a different journey in pursuit of his own personal path of political resistance that would keep him in South Africa from 1893 to 1914. During that period he spearheaded the fight against physical abuse, racial insults, "colour prejudice," and the detested "disability laws," which imposed strict curfews and restrictions on property rights based solely on color.[37] Gandhi would later encounter a similar attitude in India, where railroad officials regarded third-class passengers as just "so many sheep."[38]

From these experiences with discrimination sprang Gandhi's interest in politics, which he cleverly compared to the ubiquitous "coil of a snake."[39] While practicing law, he also discovered that the real "function of a lawyer was to unite parties riven asunder,"[40] an insight that would serve him well in his years as a conciliator and peacemaker. Moreover, his uncompromising candor earned the trust and affection of his colleagues and clients and enabled him to refute the notion that "the lawyer's profession was a liar's profession."[41] Over time he also learned to "pocket . . . the insult [and] become inured" to the sting of racism and political prejudice.[42]

The Dutch and the British derisively referred to the Indians who came to South Africa as "coolies." In his *Autobiography* Gandhi explains that in India the term referred only to "a porter or hired workman," whereas in South Africa it had acquired a more "contemptuous connotation."[43] Gandhi's desire to reverse the discriminatory pattern and campaign for law and human justice, however, angered local Europeans, who threatened and beat him. But their actions only confirmed Gandhi's resolve, as he continued to write, organize, and labor politically to extend the franchise to Indians. Although the campaign failed to secure the all-important right to vote, it did bring Indians of all backgrounds together in a common cause. To fight the "colour bar" in South Africa, Gandhi petitioned for admission to the Supreme Court. In a metaphorical gesture that reflected his willingness to compromise to achieve his political objectives, he reversed his previously symbolic position and took off his turban

in order to refrain from antagonizing the members of the high court.[44] His political campaign fought against the imposition of a burdensome poll tax and
embraced the cause of formerly indentured laborers, who threatened to out-
produce the whites and undercut their market.[45] In 1904 Gandhi's political
evolution took another turn when Indian activists in South Africa approached
Gandhi about starting a journal, *Indian Opinion*. Gandhi supported the idea,
and for nearly a decade he contributed to the journal. In his *Autobiography* he
recalled how writing in "the journal became . . . a training in self-restraint" and
emphasized, as he did with so many aspects of his personal and public life, that
"the sole aim of journalism should be service," because "an uncontrolled pen
serves but to destroy."[46] Although critics would accuse him of being more concerned with the plight of Indian immigrants than with the larger issue of
racism in South Africa, it is interesting to note that a later generation of black
South African militants, including Nelson Mandela, adopted the tactics of passive resistance, boycotts, hunger strikes, and acts of civil disobedience in their
struggle against the white South African government after World War II.[47]
And despite Mandela's reluctance to accept nonviolence as a political principle,
he did credit Gandhi with developing a strategy of "nonviolence that seeks to
conquer through conversion."[48]

When the Boer war broke out in 1899 between the British and the Dutch
Afrikaners, Gandhi enrolled a contingent of Indians to serve as ambulance dri-
vers for the British. Believing in Britain's sense of justice and fair play, he
hoped that his action would create greater sympathy among the British for the
Indian cause. He also hoped to demonstrate to the English that Indians were
not by nature cowardly.[49] Though decorated, the Indian contingent failed to
improve the Indians' lot. Nonetheless, Gandhi pursued the same strategy of
cooperation with the British during the 1906 Zulu "rebellion" and throughout
World War I. The 1906 endeavor, however, had presented Gandhi with a powerful contradiction, as his volunteers came to the aid of the British government
engaged in the slaughter of black South Africans. Openly admitting that he
"vied with Englishmen in loyalty to the throne,"[50] Gandhi attributed his actions to his personal commitment to the empire and his belief that the empire
"existed for the welfare of the world."[51] Though admittedly welcome, if not
somewhat perplexing in light of his avowedly pro-British position, his later
claim that his "heart" and work rested "with the Zulus" and "nursing [their]
wounded" remains consistent with his commitment to render service and alle-
viate all forms of human suffering for those in need. Less ambiguous is his assertion that his reflections on the Zulu rebellion caused him to search deeply in
his heart and take the vow of *brahmacharya,* or celibacy, which represented a
commitment to higher spiritual pursuits.[52] Eight years later, when the issues
during World War I were far less complicated, Gandhi felt no need to apolo-
gize for helping the British "in their hour of need" and thereby improve the Indians' status.[53] He also hoped, and again somewhat naively, that in return for
its support Britain would reward India politically after the war was over.[54]

While in South Africa, Gandhi read John Ruskin's *Unto This Last,* which transformed him into a devotee of physical labor and the back-to-nature movement.[55] His search for the simple life led him to buy a farm and establish the Phoenix settlement in South Africa in 1904, where he developed his selfless, ascetic lifestyle and furthered his commitment to social change. Here he read books on washing clothes, experimented with various forms of "self-help," and began to avoid the barber and cut his own hair.[56] Five years later he established Tolstoy farm, which was modeled on the similar principles of communal social organization, as a haven for South African Indians, who resisted the South African ban on immigration.[57] Gandhi's preoccupation with the quality of community life also transformed his concerns over sanitation into a lifelong preoccupation. During his 1896 visit to India to organize support for Indians in South Africa, plague broke out in Bombay. Gandhi immediately involved himself in cleaning latrines and introducing sanitary practices to combat the "foul smell" that afflicted all layers of society, including India's upper crust.[58] When he returned home to India for another visit in 1901 he again condemned "the stink, . . . the stench and the dirt" and vigilantly pursued his public cleanliness campaign.[59] Gandhi was so ashamed of the conditions in India that he came to the realization that it was more important to change the hygienic standards of the Indian people than it was to foster the spread of literacy.[60]

Gandhi's political activism had made him the leading figure of the Indian cause in South Africa and the primary target of government officials. As early as 1896 he experienced the wrath of the white community, when an angry mob greeted him with a beating and threatened to kill him upon his return to South Africa.[61] Gandhi, however, was not intimidated by violence. When the government of Transvaal required Indians to be fingerprinted and "carry identification certificates around like dogs wearing license tags," the public mood stiffened.[62] Continuing to preach the gospel of "militant non-violence,"[63] Gandhi took an oath of "passive resistance" in 1907 and led his fellow Indians in protest against the Asiatic Registration Act that restricted internal immigration. He was arrested and pleaded "for a heavy sentence as agitator and ringleader" before he was unceremoniously sent to jail.[64] Undeterred by the court's verdict, Gandhi and two thousand of his followers burned their registration cards on the grounds of a Johannesburg mosque as an act of public protest, an event that one British journalist compared to the impact of the Boston Tea Party on American colonial public opinion.[65]

During this period Gandhi drew inspiration from Henry David Thoreau's theories of civil disobedience, which made a powerful impression on him.[66] Of particular significance was Thoreau's insistence that "it was every man's right—indeed, his duty—to resist a tyrannical government."[67] Gandhi later reinforced his nonviolent thinking and moral perspective through his correspondence with the like-minded Russian author and visionary, Leo Tolstoy. Gandhi credited Tolstoy with helping him to overcome his skepticism, to rely on the singular pursuit of truth, and to embrace "passive resistance" as the only way to "counter [the] evils [of] war and violence."[68] Gandhi and Tolstoy did, however, differ in personal temperament and outlook, with Tolstoy a proud, tempestuous soul and Gandhi a serene and compassionate holy man.[69]

In 1909 Gandhi set sail for England to plead the Indian cause and transform the status of colored Asiatics into "a major imperial headache." When the British government insisted on collecting unjust taxes, imposing a ban on immigration, and withholding recognition for non-Christian marriages, the resistance intensified. Gandhi actively supported striking miners and led a march into Transvaal. Years later, in 1914, as the pressure intensified, the Boer general and prominent government official in the Union of South Africa, Jan Christiaan Smuts, met with Gandhi and agreed to lift the special taxes on former indentured Indian laborers; recognize Hindu, Muslim, and Parsi marriages; and lift the ban on immigration, although restrictions on movement remained. Smuts later paid Gandhi the following tribute: "It was my fate to be the antagonist of a man for whom even then I had the highest respect." In the words of Louis Fischer, Gandhi's biographer, "Smuts helped to make Gandhi by not destroying him," while Gandhi's actions served to enhance Smuts's "stature" as a statesman.[70]

Gandhi's 1909 pamphlet, *Hind Swaraj* or *Indian Home Rule,* mirrored his internal spiritual transformation from Bond Street suits to the Indian dhoti or loincloth. In what Erikson describes as an "incendiary manifesto," Gandhi attacks the British Parliament for political "prostitution" and rails against the evils of machinery and modern civilization.[71] Moreover, he criticizes the West for "propagat[ing] immorality," and extolls the tendency of "Indian civilization . . . to elevate the moral being."[72] In the *Hind Swaraj* Gandhi also addressed the violent wing of the Indian independence movement, insisting that "true democracy" can be achieved only through nonviolent means and stressed that parliamentary power flows directly from the people.[73] By the time Gandhi left South Africa in 1914 after twenty-one years serving his Indian countrymen abroad, he had experienced genuine moments of bitter frustration as well as the surge of hard-won success. His experience had also caused him to grow "somewhat disenchanted with the British Empire."[74] But despite his reservations, he was still unwilling to break with the empire and chose, instead, to draw upon his inward strength and search for a spiritual and political solution to India's problems.

Gandhi's discovery of an inner spiritual dimension to his personal identity also informed his perspective on the political struggle for Indian independence and the need to achieve *swaraj* or "self-rule." But for Gandhi *swaraj* did not simply mean the acquisition of home rule or political independence from England, it also meant achieving "inward freedom" and an "outward freedom" to think, and feel, and move about freely and independently.[75] To achieve this freedom, Gandhi emphasized the need to look back and rediscover the true meaning of Indian culture as a means of charting a new course for India's spiritual and social revolution. Since Gandhi believed that the instrument for social transformation would be the Indian peasant farmer, his populist politics enabled him to make contact with the masses. Consistent with his principles, Gandhi chose to lead by example and established an *ashram*, a village commune or community, in which his ascetic example rejected untouchability, practiced social equality, took pride in Indian culture, and served as a beacon for national revival.[76]

His intense preoccupation with "mastering" the details of his daily life not only served as an industrious, self-sufficient example for his followers, it also served as a vehicle for "mastering his spiritual self"[77] and molding his political strategy and tactics. Describing his commitment to the poor as his "heart's desire,"[78] Gandhi was also able to identify directly with the suffering masses. To rectify their plight, he engaged in acts of civil disobedience or "non-violent non-co-operation"[79] and set out rules of noncooperation for resisters to guide their political conduct, including the use of "the *minimum force necessary to reach a defined goal*," the need to "*rely on themselves*" and "*keep the initiative*," and the capacity to be "*willing to persuade*" and "*be persuaded*."[80] Erikson believed that "if Satyagraha [meaning the way of truth through nonviolence and civil disobedience] had in it the stuff to rival Lenin's liberation of labor" and challenge other twentieth-century political creeds, it would do so on the "success or failure [of] its inner purity."[81]

Gandhi's actions frequently led to conflicts and to his arrest and imprisonment. He did, however, put his time behind bars to good use. In his own words: "Most of my reading since 1893 has been done in jail."[82] In 1917 he shouldered the burdens of the peasant poor and fought openly for the indigo tenant farmers of Champaran, who were ordered not to grow indigo by their landlords at a time when synthetic indigo was dominating the English market. When Gandhi arrived in Champaran in 1917 to champion the peasants' cause, he received a hero's welcome, prompting local officials to issue an order for him to leave the district. When he refused, he used the opportunity to plead the peasants' case before the court. His presentation convinced the justices that the planting system was unjust, enabling them to rule in favor of the peasants.[83]

Gandhi's social commitment also extended to factory workers. In *Gandhi's Truth*, Erikson cites Gandhi's "first fast" and his role in organizing the textile workers in Ahmedabad in 1918 as his initial act of *satyagraha* or civil disobedience. Erikson maintains that this experience resolved Gandhi's lingering identity crisis[84] and paved the way for a life committed to the practice of "militant nonviolence."[85] In the Ahmedabad dispute Gandhi did not remain passive. He began by telling "the workers not to demand more than what was fair and right but also to be prepared to *die* rather than demand less." But while he took the initiative by confronting his opponent directly with the workers grievances, he also strove to create a climate that would make it possible to reach a solution by "*giving the opponent the courage to change*."[86] Although the "moral straight-jacket of satyagraha" irritated some of Gandhi's followers,[87] the creativity exhibited in its mischievous tactics benefited directly from Gandhi's inventive playfulness.[88]

Through his acts of civil disobedience Gandhi was also able to preach the gospel of pride and self-reliance—two of his major themes in reshaping the cultural identity of the Indian people. In his dealings with the British, Gandhi always emphasized that the British would do right by the Indian people if the Indian people convinced the British that their cause was just. But Gandhi's faith in human nature did not prevent him from acknowledging the racist attitudes of the British, who continued to maintain that "Force is the only thing an Asiatic has any respect for." Nor did he delude himself into thinking that British officers would ever view their Indian counterparts as equals. However, when the British wavered on their commitment to grant "self-governing institutions" to pave the way for dominion status following World War I, Gandhi altered his strategy and engaged in more direct political action.[89] For example, when the British reneged on their proposals, Gandhi launched a *hartal*, calling for a suspension of all business activity to bring the economy to a halt. He also introduced a spiritual dimension into the campaign in the form of *satyagraha*, which contained what has variously been described as "Soul Force"[90] or "Truth force"[91] in the sense of an all-abiding commitment to pursue the way of the truth. In his *Autobiography: The Story of My Experiments with Truth*, Gandhi explained the meaning of *satyagraha* as a combination of "*Sat* = truth" and "*Agraha* = firmness," comparing it to the English term "passive resistance."[92] For Gandhi, passive resistance meant "securing rights by personal suffering" rather than resorting to the force of arms,[93] and he viewed his life's mission as dedicated to the spread of the principles of nonviolence throughout the world.[94]

Assuming the epic significance of a "Great March,"[95] the Salt March of 1930 served as one of the most dramatic examples of *satyagraha* in practice and of Gandhi's use of civil disobedience as a political weapon. As with all forms of direct taxation on everyday commodities, the salt tax weighed most heavily on the poor and the destitute. When Gandhi's appeals to address the burdensome nature of the tax went unanswered by the British, Gandhi began his march to the sea. Quickly swelling by the thousands, Gandhi's peaceful procession clearly demonstrated that he knew how to "employ mass mobilization techniques to maximum effect."[96] When they reached the coast, Gandhi took some water from the sea, spilled it on the ground, and picked up the remaining tiny grains of salt, thus violating the preserve of Britain's salt monopoly. Gandhi's act of defiance quickly spread throughout India, as peasants took to the sea with pans to harvest their own salt. But even when Gandhi was arrested for violating the law, his followers sustained the political momentum and staged a peaceful march on the Dharsana saltworks north of Bombay. In keeping with Gandhi's example, the protesters advanced and took the bloody blows of the native police force without offering any resistance. This act of public civil disobedience instilled in Indians a new confidence that they could stand up to British rule. It also caused the British to rethink their position and develop a different strategy to manage India's future.[97]

The march had clearly confirmed Gandhi's status as a prominent international political figure. According to Dennis Dalton's analysis of Gandhi's public persona, the trek to the sea also revealed Gandhi's impact as a mass political leader. His ability to combine his "use of the media" with "a performer's sense of his audience" in orchestrating events betrayed his "uncanny sensitivity to the mood and temper of those around him."[98] None other than Jawaharlal Nehru recalled Gandhi's presence and how, in Nehru's words, "we marvelled at the amazing knack of the man to impress the multitude."[99] He also exhibited a profound awareness of international public opinion, as he promoted his message of nonviolence and issued the following appeal from Dandi at the end of the march: "I want world sympathy in this battle of Right against Might."[100]

In his quest for justice, Gandhi declared "Truth . . . the sovereign principle"[101] and proclaimed himself "a worshipper of Truth."[102] For him "truth was the substance of all morality,"[103] and he would later confess how eager he was to "catch a glimpse of . . . Certainty and hitch [his] waggon to it."[104] Ironically, it was during his stay in London that Gandhi had begun to read the *Bhagavad Gita*, describing it "as the book *par excellence* for the knowledge of Truth" and comparing it to the Sermon on the Mount.[105] The *Gita* also led him to discover the importance of duty over personal gain and the insight that "any action is better than no action" at all.[106] Later in life he explored the mystical meanings of the *Gita* and developed an inner sensitivity that led him to believe that "When he listened to his inner voice, he often thought he heard what the masses were" prepared to accept.[107]

The *Gita* also became for Gandhi a guide along the nonviolent path of *satyagraha*. Terms such as *aparigraha* [nonpossession] and *samabhava* [equability] provided comfort and insight into the need to renounce earthly possessions in one's search for peace and equanimity.[108] For Gandhi the renunciation of earthly possessions reinforced the practice of self-discipline and the importance of humility, sacrifice, and nonviolence. To set an example, he openly divested himself of the burdensome, troublesome material possessions he believed denied one access to the real "treasures of the world."[109] As a political figure who always preferred simplicity to grandiosity, he also looked askance at the maharajas, who ostentatiously flaunted their "costly jewels" as emblems of their royal standing.[110]

In framing his code of nonviolent conduct, Gandhi also believed that "a Satyagrahi [should] obey the laws of society intelligently and of his own free will, because he considers it to be his sacred duty to do so."[111] With this commitment came the emphasis on "combining civility with fearlessness" and the realization that "civility is the most important part of Satyagraha,"[112] which is why leaders of a campaign must carefully educate the public on the values and goals of *satyagraha*. In this way *satyagraha* would be able to bear witness to ethical principles in politics and serve as a healing statement of human compassion, because in Gandhi's words: "*Satyagraha* is gentle, it never wounds."[113]

Gandhi's appeal to moral authority was tested in the aftermath of the 1919 Amritsar massacre. The "blood bath," which decisively altered Gandhi's view of

the British Empire, forced him to question the values of the British government. True to his principles, however, he did not adopt violent political methods and opted instead for an economic boycott and a strategy of
noncooperation. On a separate occasion, in 1922, when Indians slaughtered
British constables who interfered and fired on a passing procession, Gandhi,
fearing the brutal consequences of government repression, refused to "purchase independence at the price of national blood-drenching." Nonetheless, for
his opposition to the government and his seditious acts he was arrested and
sent to jail. In his statement to the court he recorded his disaffection with
British rule, which had "emasculated the people and induced in them the habit
of simulation." Moreover, considering it "an honor to be disaffected," he asked
characteristically for "the severest penalty" the court could impose.[114]

While in prison (Gandhi served only twenty-two months of a six-year sentence), he came to the full realization that the future of India depended on
Hindu–Muslim relations. To emphasize his commitment to a peaceful solution to India's religious divisions, he launched a fast for Hindu-Muslim unity
in October 1924 to serve as a testament to religious tolerance and mutual respect. For Gandhi fasting had become a powerful means of political communication, and to underscore his symbolic plea for brotherhood and "unity in
diversity" he entered and completed his twenty-one day fast in the home of a
Muslim friend. In an expression of religious unity, Gandhi invited a local imam
to recite verses from the Koran on the last day of the fast, which was followed
by the singing of both a Christian and a Hindu hymn. But prayers alone could
not transcend deep-seated differences in education, language, and social practices—differences that divided the Hindu and Muslim communities and contributed to a Hindu sense of superiority that forbade interfaith marriages and
condemned the simple act of dining with Muslims.[115]

In his search for personal direction, Gandhi also turned to the roots of popular culture for inspiration. The symbol of this renewal was the use of the spin-
ning wheel and the making and wearing of *khadi* or native cloth, which
generated enormous ridicule from opposition members within the Congress
Party.[116] Gandhi, however, was not deterred by their criticism and spent much
of his time at the wheel, preaching the virtue of homespun *khadi*. Gandhi's
message was twofold. First, he believed that to preserve the village community
by promoting self-reliance and overcoming seasonal idleness provided a virtuous alternative to urban society and the vicissitudes of the Industrial Revolution. Second, he believed that demand for homespun clothing could provide
Indians with labor and employment to meet the needs of the Indian market.
Gandhi also feared that technological innovation and the spread of mecha-
nization and mass production as the tools of Britain's economic exploitation
would undermine the village and lead to the further dehumanization, "moral
degradation," and "social fragmentation" of India's impoverished population.[117] In Gandhi's words: "The *kisan* or peasant comes first."[118] As an alternative to the march of Western industrialization, Gandhi placed greater

emphasis on agricultural communities than on the growth and development of urban industrial centers.[119] Moreover, he championed the "self-governing," self-sufficient village[120] with its emphasis on individual dignity and collective values as a model of communal organization.

PERSONALITY, VIRTUE, AND SAINTLINESS

Gandhi's greatest contribution to India's political life was his ability to provide Indians with a sense of national identity rooted in Indian history and cultural traditions. He did so by restoring pride in Indian culture and reaching out to the alienated members of India's educated westernized elite. Both the goal and the manner in which he pursued it account for much of his politically unorthodox style as well as his reputation and success. Furthermore, this approach made it possible for him to cast himself in the role of "a man engaged in politics but aspiring to saintliness,"[121] while at the same time capitalizing on his charismatic leadership, his communication skills, and his ability to employ "symbols and images" that were readily accessible to an Indian audience.[122] When properly orchestrated, the popular enthusiasm and genuine support generated by one of his campaigns could extend, as it did in South Africa, for more than six years without the benefit of a steady stream of financial support.[123]

Gandhi's reputation in large part evolved through the saintly behavior of a gentle, diminutive man, who made his way through the world clad in a loincloth and sandals and armed with nothing more than a walking stick in his hand. Not all his reviewers, however, were of the same mind. For example, when Gandhi succeeded in obtaining an interview with the British viceroy of India in February 1931, Winston Churchill—who remained a stalwart defender of the British Empire and a "relentless opponent of Gandhi and India nationalism"[124]—Churchill described Gandhi, making his way up the steps of the viceroy's palace clad in his loincloth, as a "half-naked fakir." Churchill's remarks were designed to cast Gandhi in the unsavory role of an ascetic Hindu monk or common mendicant. But the result of Gandhi's encounter with the viceroy was that future meetings of the Round Table Conference in London would include the congress, with Gandhi serving as a representative.[125] While in London, he gave numerous public lectures and addresses outlining his desire to see India achieve dominion status within the empire.[126] The political outcome, however, was not exactly what he had envisioned. Returning from London, in his words, "empty-handed," he and other members of the congress leadership were imprisoned for obstructing the writ of the British government and trying to set up an alternative political authority.[127]

Ever true to his inner self, Gandhi insisted that in discarding European dress and manners "we all feel the freer and lighter for having cast off the tinsel of civilization."[128] His simplicity, saintly manner, and democratic instincts contributed to his personal appeal in the same way his courage and commitment magnified his public personality. Gandhi's followers frequently recalled the "mystical," "godlike" quality of a man who was able to control vast crowds simply by raising his finger.[129] In many ways his courage was also his most distinguishing characteristic, since its strength lay not in force but in love and conscientious civil disobedience.

Standing only five feet, five inches, tall, Gandhi's big ears and, later in life, his naked gums accentuated the unattractive aspects of his face. His meticulous attention to his diet, his devout commitment to daily exercise, and his staunch advocacy of nature cures and home remedies[130] also contributed to his eccentric image. As regimented and disciplined as he was on the inside, he was equally and totally committed both internally and externally to peace and the peaceful pursuit of India's independence. He also condemned "the mad race for armaments" around the globe[131] and insisted that his message of peace and love was by no means passive, but assertive in its truth. As an activist who found both frustration and comfort in trying to turn his message into political reality, he held firmly to his commitment to his fellow man and to his belief that "God could be realized only though service" to all humanity.[132]

At the root of Gandhi's beliefs stood the unremitting, unforgiving practice of *brahmacharya,* meaning self-control or "conduct that leads one to God" through sexual self-restraint and self-denial.[133] In Gandhi's words: "*Brahmacharya* means control of the senses in thought, word and deed."[134] The most provocative form of this practice was the vow of celibacy, which Gandhi took at age thirty-seven and observed for forty-two years until his death,[135] contributing in large measure to the public's perception of his ambivalent attitudes toward sex. Gandhi even reflected upon his own ambivalence in his *Autobiography* when he described how a friend once took him to a brothel, which turned out to be less than a pleasurable encounter for a young man of Gandhi's sensitivity, preoccupied as he was with "carnal desire," lust, and feelings of his own guilt and moral depravity.[136] Gandhi also believed that sexual intercourse was purely a religious duty, whose sole purpose was to provide for the procreation of the human race.[137] He did, however, confess in his *Autobiography* to being "wedded to a monogamous ideal" and committed to marital fidelity as "part of the love of truth."[138] Having declared his commitment to sexual abstinence, Gandhi's life became "an open book" in which he mingled freely and openly among his friends and disciples wherever he worked, ate, and slept.[139]

When he took the vow of *brahmacharya* in South Africa in 1906, Gandhi, who also suffered from chronic constipation, began his dietary experiments with fruit, nuts, goat's milk, and simple spiceless foods. His wholehearted embrace of self-denial and self-renunciation led to his adoption of fasting as an additional form of rigorous "self-restraint"[140] and as a means to curb "the carnal mind['s] . . . lust for delicacies and luxuries."[141] Although the internal personal struggle was intense and "the path of purification . . . hard and steep,"[142] Gandhi openly described how he slept surrounded by women who felt safe in his presence. In attempting to capture the impact of Gandhi's exceptional personality, Ved Mehta recalls how Gandhi on one occasion invited his distant cousin,

Manu, to test their ultimate purity by sleeping naked together.[143] As late as 1939 he proudly professed that if he "were sexually attracted towards women," he would "have courage enough, even at this time of life, to become a polygamist."[144] His critics, however, viewed his long massages and daily baths administered by young women as but "a cloak to hide his sensuality."[145] Nonetheless, drawing from his rigid sense of social justice and his own sexually abstemious perspective, Gandhi did condemn the notion that women were born to serve merely as "a plaything" for men,[146] and he viewed any reference to women as "the weaker sex" as patently libelous.[147] He even called upon American women to lead by example by activating their potential power and "ceas[ing] to be the toys of men's idle hours."[148] He also viewed women as "altogether nobler than men" because of what he viewed as their greater giving, self-sacrificing nature.[149] As a "champion" of social justice, he wrote as early as 1918 in favor of the "political and social emancipation of women" and supported the attempts of Indian women to secure equal status before the law and the right to vote.[150] His traditionalist values, however, led him to condemn abortion as a crime and to oppose granting women the right to own property, since property had already "led to the spread of immorality among men."[151]

Closely aligned with self-discipline and self-denial was the practice of *ahimsa*, which stressed nonviolence and the force of love in human relations. As the architect of a new political message, Gandhi was the first to extend the doctrine of nonviolence to the level of human and social relations.[152] For Gandhi, *ahimsa* and truth were inextricably intertwined, with nonviolence serving as the means and truth as the end. He even restated the Machiavellian proposition that the ends justify the means by asserting that "the means are after all everything" and declared his own uncompromising opposition to the use of violent methods in human and political relations.[153] Gandhi would later describe nonviolence as "the greatest force at the disposal of mankind."[154] He did not, however, view nonviolence as passivity or cowardice but rather as the soulful manifestation of courage in the face of tyranny. He also maintained that the armed man is more of a coward than the man who rejects the use of force, because "Possession of arms implies an element of fear, if not cowardice," while "true non-violence" is unequivocally fearless.[155] His political goal was "to convert the British people through nonviolence, and thus make them see the wrong they have done to India."[156] To do so, however, meant that "as one must learn the art of killing in the training of violence, one must learn the art of dying in the training for nonviolence."[157] Ironically, it was Gandhi's quest for truth and justice through nonviolence that led him to politics and his contention that "those who say that religion has nothing to do with politics do not know what religion means."[158] It is also what led him to believe that "the religion of nonviolence," which stood at "the root of Hinduism," would enable India to discard the European model based on force of arms and embrace a form of liberty in keeping with its own cultural traditions.[159]

In India, Gandhi's kind, caring manner led his followers, and later almost an entire nation, to call him *Bapu* (father). His deep religious convictions reflected his belief that "religion was simply an ethical framework for the conduct of daily life."[160] His spiritual outlook also inspired his personal piety and tolerance for all religions, which are all "at the bottom . . . one and . . . helpful to one another."[161] He believed in his search for truth that "Truth is God"[162] and that man could combat despair and achieve internal peace through faith and love.[163] Gandhi also attributed his "irrepressible" optimism to his religion and to the power of God,[164] which enabled him to overcome his personal doubts and find meaning in his struggle for truth and justice. Although he clearly understood the nature of poverty and human suffering in India, he could not move beyond general references to the need for equal and equitable distribution of India's wealth and resources.[165] Nor could he embrace socialism and the idea of class warfare, preferring instead to promote nonviolence and envision a trusteeship of the rich who would learn to act on behalf of the poor.[166]

Of the many divisions plaguing Hindu society, the caste system in particular constituted the single most pervasive form of social injustice and the main barrier to progress and reform. The system was made up of four principal castes containing myriads of subdivisions, with Brahmans at the top and the untouchables or "outcastes"[167] relegated to a nonstatus outside the system. The boundaries of social stratification within the system were rigid; the lines of admission carefully drawn; and once born into a caste, one remained within that caste for life. The first caste, the Brahman caste, was made up of priests and scholars; the second, the Kshatriya caste, of warriors and nobles; the third, the Vaisya caste, of farmers and traders; and the fourth, the Sudra caste, of manual laborers.[168] In Gandhi's case the name Gandhi, which means grocer, indicates that he was a member of the Modh-Bania subcaste of the third or Vaisya caste made up of farmers and traders.[169] Gandhi's own personal odyssey led him to move from his initial ambivalence toward the caste system and his upholding of in-caste marriages to his complete break with the system in 1935, when he published a piece entitled "Caste Has to Go" and accepted intercaste marriages and eventually the more explosive practice of caste–outcaste marriages. Unlike his early, ambiguous stand vis-à-vis the caste system, Gandhi remained "unequivocally" opposed to untouchability, which offended his moral sensibilities.[170] He also condemned the social practices of child marriage and child widowhood as examples of "ancient horrible belief[s] and superstitious practice" that he "would sweep" away "if [he] had the power."[171]

When the British attempted to introduce separate caste electorates in 1932, Gandhi rose in protest, seeing the proposal as an attempt to divide Hindu India in the same way they had divided the Hindu and Muslim communities within India. At the time of the announcement, Gandhi was still in prison in Yeravda jail after his arrest returning from the second London Round Table discussion. Gandhi's circumstances hardly diminished the strength of his conviction, and he protested directly to Downing street against the "statutory separation . . . of the

Depressed Classes . . . from the Hindu fold."[172] Receiving no satisfaction, Gandhi, whose acquired name Mahatma means Great Soul (his birth name was Mohandas), unleashed what he described as his "fiery weapon" of choice and began to fast for the soul of India.[173] When asked by an American missionary if his fasting constituted a form of coercion, Gandhi replied, "Yes . . . the same kind of coercion which Jesus exercises upon you from the cross."[174] Gandhi's sublime presence prompted Nehru to describe Gandhi as "a magician . . . [a] little man sitting in . . . prison," who "knew [how] to pull the strings that move people's hearts."[175] Through his fast Gandhi managed to stalemate British policy, address the impasse between Brahmans and the untouchables, whom Gandhi referred to as "Harijans or children of God,"[176] and promote his social message of improving the pitiable conditions of India's impoverished masses. His actions also lent new meaning to his publicly professed desire to return as an untouchable, if he were to be reborn.[177]

As a leader Gandhi freely admitted that he drew inspiration from great spiritual and historical figures such as Buddha, Jesus, and Muhammad.[178] In the West his gentle personality and reputation as a holy man inevitably led to comparisons with Jesus Christ, whom Gandhi admired as "a great world teacher."[179] Gandhi, who described himself as "a poor mendicant,"[180] was by no means immune to such religious comparisons, and he freely identified with the trials of such saintly figures as Francis of Assisi.[181] It is, however, interesting to note that in 1927 he wanted to support "a Bill to make it criminal for any one to call me mahatma and . . . touch my feet."[182] As late as 1946, he spoke with similar disdain of a project to build a statue in his honor as "a gross form of idolatry."[183] Nonetheless, despite his protests, his desire to be "always in the service of somebody or something that *needed* him" contributed to his holy image.[184] And while he enthusiastically embraced Jesus Christ as a religious figure, he rejected orthodox Christianity for abandoning the message of the Sermon on the Mount and becoming "the religion of kings" and war in the West.[185] He also extended that perception to all of Western civilization which, unlike the East, was "predominantly based on force."[186] When he received news of the atomic blast at Hiroshima, he recalled that he did not move a muscle and "said to himself 'Unless . . . the world adopts nonviolence, it will spell certain suicide for mankind.'"[187] Nehru later recalled, when he apprised Gandhi of the enormity of the blasts in Hiroshima and Nagasaki and the deadly capacity of the nuclear bomb, that it appeared as if Gandhi resolved to make it his holy, God-given "mission to fight and outlaw the bomb."[188]

PARTITION, BETRAYAL, AND SACRIFICE

At the outbreak of World War II Gandhi gave Britain and its allies his moral support. Churchill, however, did not mask his disdain for Gandhi, who in Churchill's view professed love for the British Empire while working to destroy it. In his stentorian declarations to preserve the integrity of the British

Empire[189] Churchill steadfastly opposed Indian independence—a position Gandhi maintained compromised the moral standing of the allied democracies. Faced with British intransigence, Gandhi felt compelled in the summer of 1942 to launch a campaign to force the British to "quit India." To strengthen his case, he asked the British to transfer power to the Indians so they could engage in the defense of their own country and protect India from Japanese invasion.[190] On the home front, he continued his oppositionist tactics and pursued the familiar path of civil disobedience despite militant resistance within the Congress. Fearful of an independence movement, the British arrested Gandhi and other leaders of the All-India National Congress during their August 1942 meeting. With the prophet of nonviolence once again confined behind prison walls, violence erupted throughout India. When the British attempted to place responsibility for the violence and killing on Gandhi's shoulders, he became irate and announced his intention to undertake another fast. He even refused a British offer to release him from prison and declared the fast a means of appealing, in his own words, "to the Highest Tribunal for justice which I have failed to secure from you."[191] With Britain's military victory and Churchill's electoral defeat marking the end of the war, India's internal situation assumed center stage.

At the core of the struggle stood the conflict between Hindus and Muslims. At the same time as the Hindu population of India was asserting its sense of national identity, so too were the Muslims pressing their own demands for national recognition. Making up one-third of the population, the Muslims constituted a powerful minority within India, and they were led by the inspirational and demanding figure of Mohammed Ali Jinnah. Jinnah was a separatist who wanted to put an end to the political cohabitation between Muslims and Hindus. His fierce commitment to the Muslim cause in India enabled him to defeat Gandhi's view of a free and united India and to emerge as the founder of modern Pakistan in the aftermath of World War II. Gandhi's conversations with Jinnah, who served as the president of the Moslem League, were fruitless, since Gandhi viewed the partition or "vivisection of India as blasphemy."[192] Jinnah, who was a "brilliant lawyer," "a superb tactician," and a gifted political leader,[193] stressed the views of Indian Muslims, who were fearful of their minority status in a predominantly Hindu Indian state. But Jinnah's "worldly" manner and "haughty" and "punctilious" style made collaboration between the two men difficult.[194] Still, despite Jinnah's dogged opposition to the perpetuation of a unified state, Gandhi continued to express his commitment to the goal of Hindu–Muslim unity. Gandhi also realized, however, that his passion for Hindu–Muslim unity would again put his belief in *ahimsa* to the test.[195]

When efforts to form a government composed of Hindus and Muslims failed, centuries of pent-up passions, rage, and religious hatred erupted into waves of mass hysteria, fierce rioting, and sectarian killing. Suddenly it seemed as if the country was bent on its own internal destruction[196] and that the violence would be transformed into a war of extermination.[197] Making his way on foot through difficult terrain from village to village, Gandhi drew upon his enormous compassion and self-discipline to visit the sites of the massacres in East Bengal and call for an end to the Hindu–Muslim conflict in an effort to preserve the notion of Indian unity. His pilgrimage for peace extended to Delhi, Calcutta, and other cities ravaged by the deadly mayhem. In the case of Calcutta, rampant "mob violence" had led to the death of nearly 4,000 people, transforming the former capital of British India into the grisly image of a "Paralyzed City." To counter the bloodshed, "the magician [Gandhi] . . . performed the Calcutta miracle" by fasting to bring about peace between Hindus and Muslims.[198] But the calm that settled over Calcutta did not eliminate the bloody specter of partition. Faced with the prospect of continuous internal turmoil amidst the vestiges of colonial rule, the British chose to withdraw their forces from India and sanction its partition into two separate and independent states, India and Pakistan, on August 15, 1947.[199] For Gandhi, who had worked all his life for a free, democratic, and united India, partition came as a deep personal disappointment. In his own words: "The partition has come in spite of me. It has hurt me. But it is the way in which the partition has come that has hurt me more. I have pledged myself to do or die in the attempt to put down the present conflagration."[200]

Although he did not know it, Gandhi's final mission was to try to quell a new wave of religious massacres and heal the wounds of partition through prayer and fasting. Waves of Hindu refugees in the millions fleeing from Pakistan added to the suffering and poverty. But Gandhi did not flinch in the face of the exodus. He continued to pursue the path of nonviolence and preach "the gospel of love and peace" throughout the cities and villages of India. Nor did he give up on his commitment to religious tolerance. He even made it a point to include special readings from the Koran in his prayer meetings.[201] He undertook his last fast on January 13, 1948, when out of concern for "minorities and those in need," he dedicated himself to a "cleansing of hearts" and "self-purification." Later in the day he gave a radio address in which he spoke of death not as a source of fear but as "a friend who brings deliverance from suffering."[202]

Prophetically, Gandhi had on numerous occasions anticipated his own death, when he spoke of being shot by an assassin's bullet, the nature of his unwanted martyrdom, and his desire to die with a prayer for his assassin on his lips.[203] On January 30, 1948, as he was making his way to his wooden platform for evening prayer services, Nathuram Vinayak Godse, a young right-wing Hindu extremist, who held Gandhi accountable for the partition of India, fired three bullets from a pistol. Gandhi, the man of peace who had fought to maintain Indian unity, suddenly became the victim of the very passions he had attempted to tame.[204]

The task of informing the Indian people of Gandhi's death fell upon the shoulders of Nehru, his devoted follower and heir, who announced on Indian

Radio: "The light has gone out of our lives and there is darkness everywhere. . . . Our beloved leader, Bapu, . . . the father of our nation is no more."[205] It is interesting to note that Indira Gandhi, Nehru's daughter, when speaking of the need to cherish Gandhi's image, stressed that "More than his words, his life was his message."[206] It is also doubly ironic that both she and her son, Rajiv, were sacrificed on the altar of Indian politics by extremist assassins.

In the end Gandhi was not just a holy man. He was also a statesman who cared deeply about global political issues. For example, in his role as a world figure he confronted the nuclear dilemma head-on and took it upon himself to visualize an alternative to the production, development, and use of weapons of mass destruction.[207] However, he was so holy in his mien and manner, and so diminutive in stature, that one cannot forget how his spiritual presence added enormously to his political significance and international stature during the most pivotal period of the twentieth century. In the words of his biographer, Louis Fischer, "Gandhi's on-the-earth simplicity . . . emphasized his authority." Though his "power was nil, his authority [was] enormous."[208]

For an American audience the parallels between Gandhi and Martin Luther King are self-evident. Both suffered as men of color under the yoke of white oppression. Like Gandhi, King valued the power of nonviolent political action in keeping with the spirit of Gandhi's *satyagraha*. King's role in orchestrating the Montgomery bus boycott in 1955–1956 enabled him to emerge as the architect of a strategy of civil disobedience that earned for the civil-rights movement in the United States unprecedented media coverage, new forms of public recognition, and greater access to political power.[209]

In his assessment of Gandhi's standing in history, Dennis Dalton discusses Gandhi's role as a transformational leader. Dalton specifically cites Gandhi's "therapeutic influence" on his followers and his ability to "repair wounds in self-esteem," accumulated over decades of colonial repression. Dalton also credits Gandhi's tactics, which were grounded in "truthfulness and trust," for lending dignity to his movement. And even his person, his message, and his futile struggle to keep Hindus and Muslims together in one tolerant, unified, and independent state reflected the virtues of the gospel of inclusion. Gandhi also believed in the universality of the human condition and held to the same views that King would later elicit in a moving letter he wrote from a Birmingham jail, that: "Injustice anywhere is a threat to justice everywhere."[210]

However, many of Gandhi's critics, particularly those in the West, who were steeped in the elitist assumptions of European supremacy, viewed Gandhi as "a barbarian, . . . and a dreamer."[211] Among the most acerbic was Archibald Percival Wavell, Lord Wavell, who served as viceroy for India from 1943 to 1947. Offering no praise for Gandhi, Wavell viewed him as "an unscrupulous old hypocrite," given to "chicanery and a false show of mildness and friendship."[212] Yet despite what others have described as his "moral absolutism," ascetic demeanor, and saintly aura, Gandhi's winning, genial personality and meek disposition[213] contributed enormously to his emergence as one of the truly prominent political figures of the twentieth century and a major architect of the struggle against racism, colonialism, and oppression. But the revolution he preached was founded upon "the *mantra* of non-violence" and the pursuit of universal peace through reconciliation. His message extended far beyond the borders of India and earned for him the reputation of one who remained a committed nationalist, while becoming a dedicated internationalist in his pursuit of peace, harmony, and the creation of a global "federation of friendly, interdependent states."[214]

NOTES

1. B. R. Nanda, *Gandhi and His Critics* (Oxford, Eng.: Oxford University Press, 1996), pp. 45–48.

2. As quoted from *Harijan*, Jan. 13, 1940, in Krishna Kripalani, ed., *Gandhi: All Men Are Brothers: Autobiographical Reflections* (New York: Continuum, 1992), p. 158.

3. Nanda, *Gandhi and His Critics*, p. 44.

4. Ibid., p. 50.

5. Mohandas K. Gandhi, *Autobiography: The Story of My Experiments with Truth*, translated by Mahadev Desai (New York: Dover Publications, 1983), pp. 196, 198–201.

6. Erik H. Erikson, *Gandhi's Truth: On the Origins of Militant Nonviolence* (New York: W.W. Norton, 1993), pp. 186–88.

7. Nanda, *Gandhi and His Critics*, pp. 57, 59.

8. Gandhi, *Autobiography*, p. 440.

9. Dennis Dalton, *Mahatma Gandhi: Nonviolent Power in Action* (New York: Columbia University Press, 1993), p. 1.

10. Nanda, *Gandhi and His Critics*, p. 37.

11. Ibid., pp. 38–41.

12. Nanda, *Gandhi and His Critics*, p. 43.

13. As quoted from *Young India*, Sept. 22, 1920, in Kripalani, ed., *Gandhi: All Men Are Brothers*, p. 134.

14. Ved Mehta, *Mahatma Gandhi and His Apostles* (New Haven, Conn.: Yale University Press, 1993), p. 159.

15. Louis Fischer, *Gandhi: His Life and Message for the World* (New York: Mentor, 1982), p. 9. See also Gandhi, *Autobiography*, p. 2.

16. Ibid., p. 55.

17. Gandhi, *Autobiography*, p. 10. See also Fischer, *Gandhi*, p. 10.

18. Gandhi, *Autobiography*, p. 6.

19. Fischer, *Gandhi*, p. 128. See also Nanda, *Gandhi and His Critics*, pp. 150–52.

20. Gandhi, *Autobiography*, pp. 299–301.

21. Ibid., p. 303.

22. Ibid., p. 307.

23. Gandhi, *Autobiography*, pp. 242–44.

24. Fischer, *Gandhi*, p. 127.

25. Gandhi, *Autobiography*, pp. 25–27.

26. Erikson, *Gandhi's Truth*, p. 128.

27. Ibid., pp. 139–40.

28. As quoted from *Harijan,* July 9, 1938, in Kripalani, ed., *Gandhi: All Men Are Brothers*, p. 140.

29. See Fischer, *Gandhi,* pp. 13–14, Gandhi, *Autobiography,* pp. 44–46, and Erikson, *Gandhi's Truth,* pp. 141–42.

30. Gandhi, *Autobiography,* pp. 48–49, and Erikson, *Gandhi's Truth,* p. 108.

31. Gandhi, *Autobiography,* pp. 17–18, 43.

32. Mehta, *Mahatma Gandhi,* p. 81.

33. Gandhi, *Autobiography,* pp. 68–69.

34. Fischer, *Gandhi,* pp. 14–20.

35. As quoted from Gandhi, *An Autobiography,* in Kripalani, ed., *Gandhi: All Men Are Brothers*, p. 4.

36. Gandhi, *Autobiography,* p. 87.

37. For a discussion of these experiences see Gandhi, *Autobiography,* pp. 97–102; Fischer, *Gandhi,* pp. 20–22; and Mehta, *Mahatma Gandhi,* pp. 101–2.

38. Gandhi, *Autobiography,* p. 338.

39. As quoted from *Young India,* May 12, 1920, in Kripalani, ed. *Gandhi: All Men Are Brothers,* p. 154.

40. Gandhi, *Autobiography,* p. 117.

41. Ibid., pp. 324, 328–29.

42. Ibid., p. 228.

43. Ibid., p. 254.

44. Ibid., pp. 127–30.

45. Ibid., pp. 136–38.

46. Ibid., pp. 252–53.

47. Nanda, *Gandhi and His Critics,* pp. 27, 32.

48. Nelson Mandela, *Long Walk to Freedom* (Boston: Little, Brown, 1994), p. 127.

49. Gandhi, *Autobiography,* p. 188.

50. Ibid., p. 151.

51. Fischer, *Gandhi,* p. 28.

52. Gandhi, *Autobiography,* pp. 278–83.

53. Ibid., p. 310.

54. Nanda, *Gandhi and His Critics,* p. 116.

55. Gandhi, *Autobiography,* p. 265.

56. Ibid., pp. 186–87.

57. Fischer, *Gandhi,* p. 41.

58. Gandhi, *Autobiography,* pp. 148–50.

59. Ibid., pp. 196–97.

60. Mehta, *Mahatma Gandhi,* pp. 243–45.

61. Erikson, *Gandhi's Truth,* p. 179.

62. Mehta, *Mahatma Gandhi,* p. 119.

63. Erikson, *Gandhi's Truth,* p. 181.

64. Ibid., pp. 198–203.

65. Mehta, *Mahatma Gandhi,* p. 121.

66. Fischer, *Gandhi,* p. 38.

67. Mehta, *Mahatma Gandhi,* p. 122.

68. Ibid., p. 115.

69. Fischer, *Gandhi,* pp. 39–40.

70. Ibid., pp. 40–49.

71. Erikson, *Gandhi's Truth,* pp. 217–25.

72. Dalton, *Mahatma Gandhi,* p. 20.

73. For a discussion of these principles see *Harijan,* May 27, 1939, and *Mahatma,* vol., 6, "Constructive Programme," Dec. 1941, as quoted in Kripalani, ed., *Gandhi: All Men Are Brothers,* pp. 126, 129, as well as Dalton, *Mahatma Gandhi,* 16.

74. Mehta, *Mahatma Gandhi,* p. 130.

75. Dalton, *Mahatma Gandhi,* pp. 2–3, 7, 9.

76. Fischer, *Gandhi,* pp. 54–56. See also Gandhi, *Autobiography,* pp. 357–58.

77. Mehta, *Mahatma Gandhi,* p. 193.

78. Gandhi, *Autobiography,* p. 134.

79. Ibid., p. 448.

80. Erikson, *Gandhi's Truth,* pp. 415–16.

81. Ibid., p. 421.

82. Gandhi, *Autobiography,* p. 146.

83. Ibid., pp. 363–83.

84. Erikson, *Gandhi's Truth,* pp. 45–47.

85. Ibid., p. 97.

86. Ibid., pp. 434–35.

87. Nanda, *Gandhi and His Critics,* p. 67.

88. Erikson, *Gandhi's Truth,* p. 133.

89. Fischer, *Gandhi,* pp. 60–62.

90. Ibid., p. 35.

91. Erikson, *Gandhi's Truth,* p. 198.

92. Gandhi, *Autobiography,* p. 284.

93. As quoted from *Indian Home Rule,* 1909, in Kripalani, ed., *Gandhi: All Men Are Brothers,* p. 81.

94. As quoted from *Harijan,* July 6, 1940, in Kripalani, ed., *Gandhi: All Men Are Brothers,* p. 87.

95. Dalton, *Mahatma Gandhi,* p. 101.

96. Ibid., p. 137.

97. See Fischer, *Gandhi,* pp. 93–102 and Mehta, *Mahatma Gandhi,* p. 148.

98. Dalton, *Mahatma Gandhi,* 108.

99. As quoted from Jawaharlal Nehru, *Mahatma Gandhi* (Bombay: Asia Publishing House, 1965), pp. 61, 63, in Dalton, *Mahatma Gandhi,* p. 113.

100. As quoted from M. K. Gandhi, *The Collected Works of Mahatma Gandhi* 43:180, in Dalton, *Mahatma Gandhi,* p. 114.

101. Gandhi, *Autobiography,* p. ix.

102. Ibid., p. 6.

103. Ibid., p. 30.

104. Ibid., p. 223.

105. Ibid., pp. 59–60.

106. Mehta, *Mahatma Gandhi,* pp. 93–94.

107. Erikson, *Gandhi's Truth,* p. 412.

108. Gandhi, *Autobiography,* p. 233.

109. Gandhi, Speech at the Guild Hall, London, Sept. 27, 1931, as quoted in Kripalani, ed., *Gandhi: All Men Are Brothers,* p. 41.

110. Gandhi, *Autobiography,* p. 203.

111. Ibid., p. 424.

112. Ibid., p. 394.

113. As quoted from M. K. Gandhi, *The Collected Works of Mahatma Gandhi* 54:416–17, in Dalton, *Mahatma Gandhi,* p. 37.

114. Fischer, *Gandhi,* pp. 67–73.

115. Ibid., pp. 73–81.

116. Dalton, *Mahatma Gandhi,* p. 61.

117. Nanda, *Gandhi and His Critics,* pp. 124–30. For a discussion of Gandhi's views on mass production, the advent of machinery, and the importance of sustaining the "character of . . . village industry" in India, see selections from *Young India* and *Harijan* as quoted in Kripalani, ed., *Gandhi: All Men Are Brothers*, pp. 113–17. For further discussion of Gandhi's related views on modernization and the self-sustaining village, see Fischer, *Gandhi,* pp. 81–93.

118. As quoted from B. N. Ganguli, *Gandhi's Social Philosophy*, (New Dehli: 1973), p. 245, in Nanda, *Gandhi and His Critics,* p. 135.

119. Mehta, *Mahatma Gandhi,* p. 214.

120. Fischer, *Gandhi,* p. 87.

121. Erikson, *Gandhi's Truth,* p. 401.

122. Dalton, *Mahatma Gandhi,* pp. 32, 108.

123. Gandhi, *Autobiography,* p. 173.

124. Nanda, *Gandhi and His Critics,* p. 62.

125. Fischer, *Gandhi,* pp. 102–4.

126. Ibid., pp. 104–7.

127. Ibid., pp. 107–8.

128. Gandhi, *Autobiography,* p. 162.

129. Mehta, *Mahatma Gandhi,* pp. 218, 216.

130. Mehta, *Mahatma Gandhi,* p. 60.

131. As quoted from *Harijan,* Nov. 12, 1938, in Kripalani, ed., *Gandhi: All Men Are Brothers,* p. 112.

132. Gandhi, *Autobiography,* p. 139.

133. Ibid., p. 21.

134. Ibid., p. 184.

135. Fischer, *Gandhi,* pp. 124–27.

136. Gandhi, *Autobiography,* pp. 20–22.

137. Mehta, *Mahatma Gandhi,* p. 204.

138. Gandhi, *Autobiography,* pp. 179–81.

139. Nanda, *Gandhi and His Critics,* p. 12.

140. Gandhi, *Autobiography,* pp. 182–85, 296.

141. Ibid., p. 294.

142. Ibid., p. 454.

143. Mehta, *Gandhi,* p. 203.

144. As quoted from Mahatma, vol. 5., "My Life," Oct.–Nov. 1939, in Kripalani, ed., *Gandhi, All Men Are Brothers,* p. 44.

145. Mehta, *Mahatma Gandhi,* p. 195.

146. As quoted from *Young India,* Dec. 8, 1927, in Kripalani, ed., *Gandhi: All Men Are Brothers,* p. 147.

147. As quoted from *Young India,* Apr. 10, 1930, in Kripalani, ed., *Gandhi: All Men Are Brothers,* p. 148.

148. As quoted from Mahatma Gandhi, *The Last Phase,* vol. 2, circa 1947, in Kripalani, ed., *Gandhi: All Men Are Brothers,* p. 152.

149. Mehta, *Mahatma Gandhi,* p. 182.

150. For a discussion of these topics, see Nanda, *Gandhi and His Critics,* p. 15, 141.

151. As quoted from *Women and Social Justice,* published in 1942, in Kripalani, ed., *Gandhi: All Men Are Brothers,* p. 150.

152. Sarvepalli Radhakrishan, "Introduction," in Kripalani, ed. *Gandhi: All Men Are Brothers,* p. viii.

153. As quoted from *Young India,* July 17, 1924, and Dec. 11, 1924, in Kripalani, ed., *Gandhi: All Men Are Brothers,* p. 74.

154. As quoted from *Harijan,* July 20, 1931, in Kripalani, ed., *Gandhi: All Men Are Brothers,* p. 77.

155. As quoted from *Harijan* (n.d.) in Kripalani, ed., *Gandhi: All Men Are Brothers,* p. 92.

156. As quoted from Louis Fischer, *The Life of Mahatma Gandhi* (New York: Harper & Brothers, 1950), p. 266, in Erikson, *Gandhi's Truth,* p. 444.

157. As quoted from *Harijan,* Sept. 1, 1940, in Kripalani, ed., *Gandhi: All Men Are Brothers,* p. 77.

158. Gandhi, *Autobiography,* p. 454.

159. As quoted from *Young India,* Aug. 11, 1920, and *Mahatma,* vol. 2, in Kripalani, ed., *Gandhi: All Men Are Brothers,* p. 96.

160. Nanda, *Gandhi and His Critics,* p. 72.

161. As quoted from *Harijan,* Feb. 16, 1934, in Kripalani, ed., *Gandhi: All Men Are Brothers,* p. 55.

162. For multiple references to Truth and God in Gandhi's writings, see Kripalani, ed., *Gandhi: All Men Are Brothers,* pp. 61–68.

163. As quoted from *Mahatma,* vol. 3, 1931, in Kripalani, ed., *Gandhi: All Men Are Brothers,* pp. 56–57.

164. As quoted from *Young India,* Aug. 13, 1925, in Kripalani, ed., *Gandhi: All Men Are Brothers,* p. 71.

165. As quoted from *Young India,* Mar. 17, 1927, in Kripalani, ed., *Gandhi: All Men Are Brothers,* p. 118.

166. As quoted from *Amrita Bazar Patrika,* Aug. 3, 1934, and *Mahatma,* vol. 4., 1934, in Kripalani, ed., *Gandhi: All Men Are Brothers,* pp. 124–25.

167. Nanda, *Gandhi and His Critics,* p. 19.

168. Mehta, *Mahatma Gandhi,* p. 73.

169. Fischer, *Gandhi,* p. 110.

170. Dalton, *Mahatma Gandhi,* pp. 52–53.

171. As quoted from *Young India,* Sept. 22, 1927, in Kripalani, ed., *Gandhi: All Men Are Brothers,* p. 69.

172. Fischer, *Gandhi: His Life and Message for the World,* pp. 115–16.

173. See *Collected Works of Mahatma Gandhi* 63:91 and 83:401, as quoted in Dalton, *Mahatma Gandhi,* p. 163.

174. E. Stanley Jones, *Mahatma Gandhi* (London, 1948), p. 143, as quoted in Nanda, *Gandhi and His Critics,* p. 21.

175. Jawaharlal Nehru, *An Autobiography* (London: Bodley Head 1958), pp. 370–71, as quoted in Nanda, *Gandhi and His Critics,* p. 76.

176. For a discussion of the term *Harijan,* see Mehta, *Mahatma Gandhi,* p. 59.

177. As quoted from *Young India,* May 4, 1921, in Kripalani, ed., *Gandhi: All Men Are Brothers,* p. 50.

178. As quoted from *Young India,* Oct. 10, 1929, in Kripalani, ed., *Gandhi: All Men Are Brothers,* p. 157.

179. As quoted from *Harijan,* Apr. 18, 1936, in Kripalani, ed., *Gandhi: All Men Are Brothers,* p. 41.

180. As quoted from *Mahatma,* vol. 3, Sept. 11, 1931, in Kripalani, ed., *Gandhi: All Men Are Brothers,* p. 39.

181. Fischer, *Gandhi,* p. 177.

182. As quoted from *Young India,* Mar. 27, 1927, in Kripalani, ed., *Gandhi: All Men Are Brothers,* p. 35.

183. See "A Temple to Gandhiji," as quoted from *Harijan,* July 1940, in Kripalani, ed., *Gandhi: All Men Are Brothers,* p. 45.

184. Erikson, *Gandhi's Truth,* p. 116.

185. For a discussion of these issues, see Fischer, *Gandhi,* pp. 129–33, and *Mahatma,* vol. 3, "Conversation with Sir C. V. Raman and Professor Rahm," May, 1936, as quoted in Kripalani, ed., *Gandhi: All Men Are Brothers,* p. 42.

186. Gandhi, *Autobiography,* p. 166.

187. As cited in *Mahatma Gandhi, The Last Phase,* 1945, in Kripalani, ed., *Gandhi: All Men Are Brothers,* p. 46.

188. Nanda, *Gandhi and His Critics,* pp. 158–59.

189. Fischer, *Gandhi,* pp. 133–35.

190. Mehta, *Mahatma Gandhi,* p. 153, and Nanda, *Gandhi and His Critics,* pp. 120–21.

191. Fischer, *Gandhi,* pp. 145–48.

192. Ibid., p. 149.

193. Nanda, *Gandhi and His Critics,* pp. 84, 86.

194. Mehta, *Mahatma Gandhi,* p. 167.

195. Gandhi, *Autobiography,* p. 398.

196. Fischer, *Gandhi,* pp. 161–63.

197. Mehta, *Mahatma Gandhi,* p. 171.

198. See Dalton, *Mahatma Gandhi,* pp. 140–59.

199. Fischer, *Gandhi,* pp. 163–77.

200. As quoted from *Mahatma Gandhi, The Last Phase,* June 9, 1947, in Kripalani, ed., *Gandhi,* p. 48.

201. Fischer, *Gandhi,* pp. 177–82.

202. Ibid., pp. 183–84.

203. For numerous references on this topic, see Kripalani, ed., *Gandhi: All Men Are Brothers,* pp. 49–50.

204. Fischer, *Gandhi,* pp. 187–89. Godse and his principal accomplice, Narayan Apte, were convicted of Gandhi's murder and executed by hanging according to the terms of the court's sentence. Mehta, *Mahatma Gandhi,* p. 176.

205. Mehta, *Mahatma Gandhi,* p. 173.

206. Ibid., p. 251.

207. Erikson, *Gandhi's Truth,* p. 51.

208. Fischer, *Gandhi,* p. 142.

209. Dalton, *Mahatma Gandhi,* pp. 176–83.

210. Ibid., pp. 188–200. Passage quoted from Martin Luther King, Jr., in Martin Luther King, Jr., "Letter from Birmingham Jail," in *Why We Can't Wait* (New York: Mentor Books, 1964), p. 77.

211. Nanda, *Gandhi and His Critics,* p. 143.

212. Penderel Moon, ed., *Wavell: The Viceroy's Journal* (London: Oxford University Press, 1973), p. 353, as quoted in Dalton, *Mahatma Gandhi,* p. 65.

213. See Erikson, *Gandhi's Truth,* p. 250, as quoted in Nanda, *Gandhi and His Critics,* pp. 151, 148.

214. Gandhi's presidential address at the Belgaum Congress in *Congress Presidential Addresses, From the Silver to the Golden Jubilee,* 2d ser. (Madras, 1934), p. 745, as quoted in Nanda, *Gandhi and His Critics,* p. 153.

Mao Zedong. Photo by China photo service. Reproduced from the collections of the Library of Congress.

Chapter 2

MAO

AND THE COMMUNIST
REVOLUTION IN CHINA

YOUTH AND POLITICAL FORMATION

As China entered the twentieth century, it too confronted the familiar challenge of a backward, agricultural nation struggling with overpopulation in an age of rapid technological change and economic expansion. The problem was rooted in Chinese history and the legacy of imperialism, which had reduced the once proud Chinese Empire to the status of a slave state at the mercy of foreign, and in Chinese eyes, barbarian conquerors. China's humiliating defeat during the Opium War of 1839–42, the burning of the Summer Palace by an Anglo-French expeditionary force in 1860, and the repression of the Boxer Rebellion in 1900 at the hands of the Europeans chronicled the decline of the empire, as did China's military defeat at the hands of a more modernized and westernized Japan in 1895.[1] By the end of the nineteenth century it had become clear that if China were to succeed in shielding its people from the yoke of foreign domination and the threat of military aggression, it would have to modernize its institutional structures and mobilize the nation's resources to better serve the entire population. What remained at issue, however, was whether China could undergo such a transformation without experiencing the intrusive, destabilizing effects of westernization.

As relations with the outside world continued to deteriorate, so too did the political and social conditions within China. Rival warlords ruled at will in the absence of any central authority. The bloody Taiping Rebellion (1850–1865), which was responsible for the death of 20 million peasants, reinforced the powerful tradition of peasant revolt.[2] The revolt's antitraditional impulses and the popular passion it unleashed were also important in the formation of a new "iconoclastic intelligentsia," which challenged the formal assumptions of Chinese society and culture and paved the way for the emergence of more radical twentieth-century political movements.[3] The combination of this "cultural iconoclasm" and Chinese nationalism led to a total rejection of the cultural past and to Mao Zedong's call for a "complete cultural and moral transformation" of Chinese society.[4] It also produced a truly "remarkable and illustrious" example of a revolutionary intelligentsia, which was able by the sheer dint of its will and determination to build a powerful state in the shadow of socio-economic failure and stagnation.[5]

Born on December 26, 1893, in Hunan province, Mao Zedong was a product of rural China. Lacking access to a telephone, a telegraph system, or even a local newspaper, he had to rely on his own devices in shaping his own impressions of the outside world.[6] In keeping with his maverick image, he later recalled how as a youth he enjoyed reading historical romances, featuring "tales of heroic bandits" who fought against social injustice, callous bureaucrats, and court corruption.[7] His father, who had become a fairly wealthy farmer and grain dealer, was a stern, autocratic disciplinarian, who contributed, albeit unintentionally, to Mao's identification "with the great rebels of the past."[8] Raised in the tradition of the Confucian classics and influenced by his own "romantic sense of self and history,"[9] Mao describes how at the age of thirteen he staged "a strike" against his father and later made an alliance with his mother—a devout Buddhist—his brother, and a household laborer to form "the Opposition" or a "United Front" and challenge his father's authority as "the Ruling Power" within the family. His personal rebellion enabled him to attend a newer, more modern school, where he was exposed to more "radical" Western educational thinking and methods.[10] He then entered the Hunan Normal School, where he developed his interest in Western ideas, the social sciences,[11] and such historical figures as Peter the Great, Napoleon, and George Washington in their roles as "warriors and nationbuilders."[12] In keeping with the formation of his new political outlook, he also familiarized himself with the burgeoning national revolutionary movement within China, led by Sun Yat-sen, who espoused the principles of nationalism, democracy, and socialism.

As Mao continued to grow politically, he soon discovered the world of newspapers and acquired what he described as "the newspaper reading habit."[13] He even admitted to having engaged as a student in some of his own "muddled" exercises in political journalism. Instinctively attuned to the politics of his time, he was deeply moved by the outbreak of the 1911 revolution and joined the ranks of the revolutionary army, which enabled him, under obviously exceptional circumstances, to savor the excitement of a military conflict and further his political education.[14] The revolution succeeded in overthrowing the Manchu dynasty and establishing a Chinese Republic with Sun Yat-sen as president in 1912.

Mao, who was now imbued with the revolutionary spirit, was nonetheless at a loss for political direction. "Confused, looking for a road,"[15] and lacking a firm political foundation, he spent the next four or five years searching for his own political identity, reading independently, and participating in student organizations and study groups, the most important of which was the New People's Study Society. In this more experimental environment he read the works of such leading Western social critics, economic theorists, and political thinkers as Jean-Jacques Rousseau, Adam Smith, John Stuart Mill, and Herbert Spencer. In this setting he was also able to discover his calling as a teacher and develop his own pedagogical approach to politics, which would profoundly shape the future tone and character of Chinese communism.[16] Mao shared with Gandhi a reverence for physical exercise and long walks to promote strength and stamina, and he took great pride in describing himself and his followers as "ardent physical culturalists,"[17] who shared a common belief that strength, prowess, and courage would breed "military heroism" and help the Chinese resist foreign invasion.[18]

Mao's peripatetic travels also took him to Beijing, where he served briefly as a librarian's assistant before returning to his native Hunan to participate in the dramatic events known as the May 4th movement of 1919. The movement arose in popular opposition to the decision of the Versailles peacemakers to award the German concession in the Shantung peninsula to Japan. Instead of returning the concessions to China, their transfer to Japan was a direct violation of China's national sovereignty, and it made a mockery of Wilson's principle of national self-determination. Denouncing "the Allied leaders as a gang of robbers,"[19] Mao joined other young revolutionaries, who took to the streets of China's cities to protest the Versailles decision. The novel experience and unprecedented union of students and workers engaging in a joint political action provided Mao with the beginnings of his own political "style."[20] After the movement failed to reverse the Allied decision, Mao immersed himself in his work as editor of the Hunan student newspaper and committed himself to revolutionary politics. Ideologically, he capitalized on the movement's abandonment of liberalism in favor of Marxist theory and its emphasis on cooperation between students and workers in promoting a socialist revolution. His exposure to Marxist thought also convinced him that scientific socialism provided him with the most reliable basis for the study of social conflict.[21]

Stemming in part from intellectual dialectics, political polemics, native cultural traditions, and the dynamics of Sino-Soviet politics, Mao's relationship to Marxism has always been a complex issue. For example, it was only after the Bolshevik Revolution that Marxism became an important political force in China.[22] And it was only in 1920 that Mao was able to read a complete translation of *The Communist Manifesto*.[23] Once he accepted the Marxist perspective, however, his conversion was complete, and he would later celebrate communism as "the most complete, progressive, revolutionary and rational system in human history."[24] As one who had flirted at times with anarchism and grappled with the tenets of permanent revolution,[25] he also felt strongly that Chinese nationalism needed to balance the goals of the international proletariat with the needs of the Chinese people and their revolution.

Though his acquaintance with Marxism was in many respects limited, his commitment to the pursuit of a liberating revolutionary ideal was total. He based his expansive revolutionary outlook on the following assumption: "change people's thoughts and you change them, change the Chinese people and China changes, and a changed China could change the world."[26] In time he would develop his own form of revolutionary Marxism, which transcended the elitist tenets of Confucian intellectuals, who viewed the peasants as dirty and ignorant, and the industrial bias of western Marxists, who favored the urban proletariat. He did so by drawing upon China's feudal tradition of peasant wars and uprisings[27] and by capitalizing on his ability to transform the revolutionary potential of the peasantry into a massive agricultural proletariat. Mao's revolutionary ideas also produced a new social and intellectual reconfiguration among China's educated elite. By challenging the rigorous intellectual assumptions of the past, it spawned a new cultural phenomenon wherein many of "the literate men" of China, who had always sought "to rise above the people," were now willing "to share [their] knowledge with the 'dark masses'" and in some cases "even idealize them."[28]

THE CHINESE COMMUNIST PARTY

For now, however, Mao turned his attention to the formation of the Chinese Communist Party. He attended the founding congress of the party in Shanghai in July 1921 and became active in its organizational structure. Although the Soviets played a major role in providing theoretical guidance, instructional aid, and advisers to the Chinese communists, the party remained primarily an "indigenous" political "phenomenon."[29] Its leadership, however, did not question the political wisdom of the Soviet line, nor did it challenge the responsibility of communist parties to adhere to the policies put forth by the Third International in Moscow, which Lenin had created to promote the cause of worldwide proletarian revolution.

Given the momentous significance of the Bolshevik revolution and the uneven development of Marxist revolution around the world, it did not come as a surprise that revolutionary Marxists routinely deferred to the Soviet Union as the model of proletarian revolution and looked to Moscow for political guidance and direction. In keeping with these new historical developments, Chinese communists celebrated Lenin's revolutionary leadership, respected Stalin's prominent position within the revolutionary movement, and drew hope and ideological inspiration from the Bolshevik Revolution.[30] In the early 1920s this outlook translated into the Chinese communists' acceptance of Moscow's policy of "collaboration with the bourgeois nationalists"[31] and their decision to join with the Kuomintang in pursuit of a national revolution—a policy that precipitated a series of political setbacks and contributed to the deterioration of "the party's urban base."[32] Though costly, these early reverses were by no means fatal. They did, however, stem in large measure from the Comintern's insistence on policies that put the interests of the Soviet Union first[33] and the dispatch of any substantial financial aid or military assistance to the Chinese communists on the political back burner.[34] Though materially disadvantaged and fighting "with less foreign help than any army in modern Chinese history,"[35] the communists would ultimately prevail through a policy of tenacious self-reliance and a strategy of basing their political and military effort on the support of the people.

One of the key components of the emerging national revolution was the desire to free China from the weight of the European and Japanese imperialists. Mao frequently exhibited his own abiding contempt for the foreigners, who routinely humiliated the Chinese people and rudely posted signs such as the one outside a park in Shanghai that read "Chinese and dogs not allowed." In his desire to wage a campaign against foreign oppression and exploitation, Mao enthusiastically embraced Moscow's policy of a "united front" and endorsed the attempt to promote cooperation between communist and nationalist forces.[36] When Sun Yat-sen, the father of modern China, died in March 1925, his legacy passed to his successor, Chiang Kai-shek, whose sober, decorous manner and abstemious lifestyle contrasted with Mao's chain-smoking, scruffy, rough-and-tumble character. For now, however, the differences between them, their prolonged confrontation, and the tortured history of their failed attempts at collaboration lay in the future.

For his part, Mao spent the years of 1924 and 1925 in his native Hunan, where his discovery of the revolutionary potential of the peasantry transformed his political consciousness and enabled him to develop his theory of mass revolution based upon the will of the people and the need to resolve the land question.[37] Armed with a Marxist, populist conviction that the land belonged to those who till it,[38] Mao was able to use his role as director of the Peasant Movement Training Institute to plant the seeds for "the agrarian revolution." Comprising detailed reading assignments for the peasants, political instruction, and a rigorous program of physical exercise, the style of organization clearly bore his stamp. The same can be said of the importance he attached to the formation of new, unified cadres[39] and his commitment to train them as "successors to the revolutionary cause."[40] Occupying crucial intermediary positions within the party structure, the cadres, who both taught and learned from the people, constituted the ideological backbone of the movement. But when Mao judged that they had begun to lose their revolutionary edge, he openly challenged their effectiveness and called for the training and continuous development of new, more reliable cadres within the party's rank and file.[41] Ever the organizational motivator, Mao loved to admonish party members to master the complexities of committee work by learning how to "play the piano" and grasp the movement of the fingers, as they dance across the keyboard.[42]

Though Mao's early organizational efforts reflected his innovative, structurally creative nature, it would be a mistake to conclude that he had already embarked on his own course of revolutionary Marxism. As Stuart Schram observed, Mao, who was still but "an apprentice" in the study of Marxist-Leninist thought, did not acquire "an adequate grasp of Marxist theory" until his "power had crystallized in practice."[43] But no one could doubt his "revolutionary passion [and] energy." As a modernist he sought to root out all forms of superstition and social conventions that held the peasants back.[44] As an advocate of direct peasant revolutionary action and the leading author of an early Draft Resolution on the Land Question commissioned by the Kuomintang, Mao championed the confiscation of all land from undesirable elements of the "gentry, corrupt officials, militarists and all counter-revolutionary elements in the villages."[45] But the opposition to the revolution among military commanders and officials, who wanted to protect their own landed interests within the Kuomintang, made it impossible to implement the terms of the declaration.

When nationalist Chinese forces massacred approximately 5,000 workers and communists in Shanghai in the spring of 1927, other issues quickly supplanted the land question.[46] Divided as it was into one world of elegant homes, expensive cars, and lavish wardrobes and another world of factories, malnutrition, and child labor,[47] Shanghai served as the quintessential example of a "foreign-dominated" city[48] and as the perfect backdrop for the violent confrontation between Chinese Nationalists and communists. When the Reds called for a general strike, truckloads of thugs, armed "with a license to kill," descended upon the strikers and slaughtered thousands, even feeding some of the "victims . . . live into the boilers of locomotives." The Shanghai massacre was followed in turn by "a nationwide reign of terror," which accumulated approximately 300,000 victims, sparing neither age nor gender.[49] Suddenly, it seemed as if Soviet insistence on cooperation with the Chinese nationalists was a bankrupt policy that sacrificed Chinese communists at the expense of Moscow's political ambitions. Moreover, in the wake of the Shanghai massacre, the more radical idea that Chinese communism should actually pursue its own independent path began to take root.[50] For example, while Mao continued to favor the creation of soviets (councils) and the land redistribution policy, he began to militarize the dialogue by highlighting the need "to arm the masses" and accelerate the process of change[51] through the creation of a "wave-like or tidal" revolutionary movement throughout China.[52]

What followed the Shanghai massacre was a twenty-seven-year period of civil war between the Chinese communists and the Nationalist forces of Chiang Kai-shek. Despite Mao's initial support of the united front and his adherence to the Moscow line, he set out to build his own base among the peasants and formulate his theory of a peasant-based revolution. In 1927 he returned to Hunan, where he organized a small military band of guerrillas and developed his idea that military units would be the best means of "striking a blow on behalf of the revolution."[53] Predicated upon a pattern of continuous peasant uprisings to generate and sustain popular enthusiasm for the revolution,[54] his strategy relied almost exclusively on the poor peasants and sanctioned the execution of wealthier peasants to reinforce the class character of his revolutionary message.[55] But by opening his ranks to "soldiers, bandits, robbers, beggars, and prostitutes" and praising their contribution to the class struggle, he did not restrict the composition of his armies exclusively to peasants.[56]

Mao also spent his time in the countryside developing his military strategy, which blended stealth, mobility, "tactical flexibility,"[57] and swift military maneuvers. As a self-sustaining military entity Mao's army also learned how to procure arms and material from a defeated enemy.[58] In time the pattern of tactical engagement took on a character of its own. Relying on distractions, decoys, diversionary feints, and ambushes to irritate the enemy,[59] Mao's forces learned how to tack quickly, retreat surreptitiously, and zigzag with uncanny dexterity.[60]

For now, however, as the Red Army grew under Mao's direction, it became more than just "a catalyst" for revolutionary upheaval. It also became the national "repository" for a new "ethos of struggle and sacrifice."[61] But the transitional process was fraught with political maneuvering and ideological adjustments. For example, given Moscow's rigid insistence on the theoretical preeminence of the urban proletariat, it was virtually unheard of during the late 1920s to think of the peasants and not party as the vanguard of the revolution.[62] Mao, however, placed his "populist faith" in the peasantry and continued to view them, not the party, as the real foundation of the revolution.[63] Confronted with the realities of guerrilla warfare and the merits of his own political insights, he developed his concept of "base areas,"[64] where the peasants would provide sustenance and material support,[65] including food and shelter for the army, as well as a vast network of tunnels dug by soldiers, which enabled them to hide in cellars and slither undetected from house to house and out of the village. Some were so large that they even contained supply depots and hospitals.[66]

Mao, who came to view war as "the highest form of struggle for resolving contradictions . . . between classes, nations, states, or political groups,"[67] stressed the role of the Red Army as "an armed body for carrying out the political tasks of the revolution."[68] Underscoring the importance of the movement's organizational structure, he also emphasized "self-criticism,"[69] "party discipline,"[70] and the ability "to live symbiotically" with the people "in order to conquer [them] ideologically and progressively assimilate them."[71] In keeping with his goal of social immersion and his desire to set a high standard of ethical behavior for his troops, he banned the smoking of opium, condemned the taking of liberties with women, and outlawed the presence of "camp followers [and] prostitutes." In the end, the sober, disciplined, almost puritanical behavior of the Red Army troops served them well,[72] particularly when contrasted with that of the Nationalist army, whose brutal and inhumane practices included murder, rape, the taking of young children as prisoners, the selling of young girls into slave labor, prostitution, and the maiming and mutilating of victims' bodies.[73]

Within the ranks of the army he pursued similar goals of socialist reconstruction by sharing a common, spartan lifestyle with his troops and introducing new democratic values by abolishing "the feudal practice of bullying and beating" troops of inferior rank.[74] The youthful composition and democratic character of the army[75] reinforced the unconventional image of happy, ener-

getic soldiers radiating self-confidence, marching in unison, and singing enthusiastically to maintain the pace and sustain their revolutionary morale. Indeed, what emerged from this unorthodox approach was not the image of an
army sparkling in spit and polish but an impression better suited to "a prep
school on a holiday excursion."[76] The Red Army Academy was further testament to this enthusiasm and to Mao's commitment to pursue his egalitarian
beliefs, as young students of both sexes spent their time living and studying together in caves, eating simple meals, ingesting the principles of communism,
and internalizing the values of a communal lifestyle.[77] Within the army, Lenin
clubs became the center of education, enabling soldiers, for example, to study
geography or hygiene, while others practiced writing characters.[78]

It was also during this period that Mao developed his combined strategy of
war and revolution and revealed the maverick side of his personality, when he
disobeyed orders of high-ranking party officials to relocate his troops for fear
of jeopardizing his army and the fate of the revolution.[79] Drawing from the
celebrated fifth-century writer Sun Zu, Mao stressed the importance of con-
centrating one's troops against the enemy, maintaining numerical superiority
in battle, engaging in surprise attacks, luring one's enemy into one's territory,
practicing secrecy and deception, and seizing smaller towns and villages before
attacking the cities.[80] The following passage from Mao captures the essence of
his views on the art of warfare:

1. When the enemy advances, we retreat!
2. When the enemy camps, we harass!
3. When the enemy tires, we attack!
4. When the enemy retreats, we pursue![81]

Mao also furnished his troops with a code of conduct to prevent them from
alienating the peasants and forfeiting their support. In addition to prohibitions
on looting, plundering, and social abuse,[82] his list included the need to be hon-
est and polite in dealing with the peasants, to pay for all that is purchased, to replace damaged articles, to maintain sanitary conditions, and to put all doors used
for bedding back in place when leaving a house.[83] Alongside his gentle, almost
hagiographic side, Mao demonstrated that he could also be ruthless. For example, in 1930 he ordered the execution of more than 2,000 officers and men who
had unsuccessfully rebelled against his authority in the southern part of Jiangxi
province. The bloody fighting between communists and nationalists during the
Civil War had also taken its toll on both sides of the conflict. During the war
Mao's first wife, Yang K'ai-hui, and his younger sister were killed by Kuomintang
forces in Mao's native Changsha. But in typically deliberate fashion, Mao understood that violence and death were part of the calculus of civil war, which is why,
in Stuart Schram's words, "he gave no quarter, and . . . asked for none."[84]

Having won control over large areas of the countryside, Mao emerged in
1931 as a part of a rival faction within the party leadership.[85] However, in an

attempt to emphasize the military rather than the military-revolutionary strategy advocated by Mao, the party leadership appointed Chou Enlai as political commissar for the Red Army in 1933.[86] But the Japanese invasion of the Chinese mainland beginning with the conquest of Manchuria in 1932 solidified Mao's control over the army and accelerated his rise to power.[87] In retrospect, these events gave new meaning to his provocative maxim: "Political power grows out of the barrel of a gun."[88] Since the communists and the nationalists spent more time fighting one another than they did their common enemy, Mao now became convinced that the only way to defeat the Japanese was to defeat the Kuomintang. In fact, both sides had already come to the conclusion that what mattered most was not the defeat of Japan, but the future disposition and control of China after Japan's defeat.

With his vision of a combined victory over Chiang and the Japanese firmly in place, Mao turned to a resolution of the land question to win the Chinese people to his side. His goal was to introduce the class struggle into the countryside and elevate the revolutionary consciousness of the masses by depicting "the landlord class [as] the principal enemy of the revolution." The goal was to mobilize the peasants in the countryside, lend them support, and secure a revolutionary victory for the people.[89] To sustain the struggle, he would frequently send bands of raiders into Chinese villages to dispossess the landlords and wealthy peasants of their holdings. These "fund-raising" ventures not only helped to finance the struggle, they also helped to reinforce his revolutionary message.[90] Through the Red Army's program of confiscating goods and supplies from the rich and distributing these "surpluses" to the poor, the peasants instinctively understood that unlike armies in the past or the Kuomintang forces under Chiang Kai-shek, the Red Army was "a poor man's army" allied to the needs of the people.[91]

Throughout his life Mao never deviated in his commitment to learn from the masses;[92] nor did he ever compromise his respect for their revolutionary spirit or underestimate the risk of isolating the leadership from their support.[93] Viewing the masses as "the real heroes" of the revolution,[94] he stressed the need to engage them in regular consultations and have the army become "one with the people" to ensure its invincibility[95] and the defeat of Japan.[96] In the summer of 1934, Mao had an opportunity to test the army's bond with the people, when, surrounded by nationalist forces, he decided that his beleaguered troops would have to slip through enemy lines and make their way to a more secure area. What followed was the Long March, perhaps the single most epic undertaking of the Civil War period and a major element in the formation of Mao's mythical revolutionary career. It served both as a heroic undertaking in its own right and also as a model of success for the Red Army and its ability to draw support from the people.

The Long March was also full of extraordinary examples of individual courage and sacrifice. When the Red Army, numbering approximately 100,000, left Jiangxi on its 6,000-mile trek to northwestern China, a detachment of partisans and a few Red Army regulars stayed behind in what one commentator later described as an act of "self-immolation." Fighting to the death to prevent nationalist troops from destroying the Red Army, they sacrificed themselves to let the army elude the grasp of Chiang's forces.[97] What followed was a multicolumn march with soldiers bearing their own clothes, weapons, and ammunition upon their backs, while horse-drawn carts carried everything from military shells to printing presses and stacks of office files.[98] Resembling an enormous piece of embroidery that wove its way across the contours of the Chinese landscape, the soldiers, with Chiang's troops sniping at their heels, struggled against all forms of disease, discomfort, and lack of food, which forced them to eat roots, grass, and small animals—even rats—in order to survive.[99]

The dramatic crossing of the Tatu river bridge, which consisted at the time of iron chains and wooden planks extending across a deep gorge, is perhaps the best-chronicled act of courage and sacrifice on the entire march. With half the wooden planks removed at one end of the bridge and enemy fire greeting them as they advanced, volunteers made their way across the chains at great peril, many of whom were shot and fell to their death. Their exploits set a courageous example of youths' willing "to commit suicide to win." When Red Army troops eventually succeeded in taking the opposite side, they were able to pave the way for the rest of the army to cross a hastily rebuilt bridge. But their perilous journey was far from over, as they still had to negotiate formidable mountain ranges and the dreaded swamp of the Great Grasslands, which literally swallowed up tired, inattentive soldiers who mindlessly strayed from the path. Of the original 100,000, fewer than half survived the march and settled in Yenan in the northwest corner of Shensi province, which became a communist stronghold and center for military training.[100]

Mao, who obviously understood the mythical significance of their heroic trek, also viewed the march as "a seeding machine" that enabled him and his comrades to plant the idea of communism in the minds of the people.[101] But as Maurice Meisner astutely reminds us, despite its heroics, compelling drama, and epic proportions, the Long March was the product of a politically defunct alliance with Chiang Kai-shek and the stepchild of a near fatal "military disaster."[102] These realities did not, however, detract from the political and psychological significance of the Long March and its ability to reinforce the revolutionary values of hope, confidence, and determination within the party and the Chinese people as a whole.

When Mao became chairman of the newly constituted Politburo in January 1935, he moved quickly to consolidate his control over the party apparatus[103] and assert his new role as party chief by calling for the construction of a Soviet-style economy in Yenan[104] and outlining the future of Chinese communism through "sinification."[105] Under Mao's guidance, the new leadership set out to build the foundations of a socialist community, based upon a strict code of "ascetic values" and inspired by what later became known as "Yenan spirit."[106] The setting, though austere, produced a rare sense of political community and social identity. Edgar Snow, a distinguished American journalist, who became a lifelong champion of the cause of Chinese communism, captured the spirit of the Yen-an community when he recalled the primitive living conditions he encountered during his early visits with Mao in northwest China. He vividly described the "cave-houses with earthen floors" and the absence of showers, baths, movies, and electricity.[107] With these plebeian quarters serving as a backdrop, Snow was able to detect a "solid elemental vitality" in Mao and his movement, which enabled him to synthesize and express the demands of the Chinese people.[108] His political vision and his charismatic personality also enabled him to forge a mutually protective, "rock-like solidarity" linking the people, the party, and the army in the pursuit of a bold new social experiment.[109]

His approach was both simple and effective. He fully understood the land hunger and burdensome tax obligations of the peasants. He also recognized the need to reduce land rents, promote a program of land redistribution, rectify the unjust system of taxation, and use these programs to broaden the popular revolutionary base of the army. Although he emphasized the importance of "widespread propaganda" to mobilize the political support of the people, his ideas concerning the creation of a "democratic dictatorship of the 'rural proletariat'" to guide the revolution remained at this early juncture at best elusive.[110] His economic policies included confiscating and redistributing the land "to the land-hungry peasants"; abolishing usury; eliminating the tax burden on the poor, while imposing heavy taxes on the rich; and introducing a cooperative movement based on the revolutionary principle of "collective effort."[111] The goals of his social policies were equally impressive. By supporting the formation of schools, colleges, hospitals, public health facilities, and industrial cooperatives and cracking down on drug users, looters, beggars, and prostitutes, Mao created a social blueprint for constructing a new communist society.[112] He also provided Yenan with a new political identity as the communist capital of China and a new historical legacy as the "mother of the Chinese partisans."[113]

Safely ensconced in his base in Yenan, Mao developed his views on the sinification of Marxism and established his reputation as a revolutionary figure and political theorist. By outlining his thoughts on the future development of China, he was able to emphasize the "class nature" of "dialectical materialism" and its practical applications. He also took this opportunity to put his own ideological stamp on Chinese communism by adapting Marxism with its fundamental Western orientation to the needs of Chinese people.[114] In so doing he emphasized the importance of achieving "a real grasp of Marxism" through practical involvement in the class struggle and direct "contact with the masses."[115] He made Marxism fit the needs of China's evolving political culture, the revolutionary character of its people, and the role of the peasantry in overthrowing the antiquated vestiges of feudalism.[116] As Mao ultimately refused to engage in a slavish imitation of the Soviet model, his independent, original views set the stage for the future autonomous development of Chinese communism[117] and the eventual break with the Soviet Union. In his efforts to tap into the wellspring of Chinese nationalism, however, he did not abandon the overarching view of international proletarian revolution. What emerged instead was a blend of social revolt and nationalism that gripped the people in the countryside, who lent their support to the Red Army in a common struggle against their wealthy landlords and the Japanese invaders.[118]

Mao also continued to influence the progress of the Civil War. Despite his reluctance to deal with Chiang Kai-shek, who, after the Japanese invasion of China in 1937, was infamously depicted as a "traitor to the nation,"[119] his elaborate dance around the concept of the united front continued. At one point the Communists even agreed to dispense with the name of the Red Army, abandon the term "soviet," and suspend further land confiscation[120] in order to strengthen the military effort against the Japanese. They also indicated that they would entertain the notion of an "armed truce,"[121] including a suspension of anti-Kuomintang propaganda[122] and participation "in the peaceful unification of the country," if Chiang would define "a policy of positive armed" struggle against Japan.[123] They now hoped that Chiang would, as he had promised in the past, support "freedom of the press," release political prisoners, and "halt his annihilation campaign" against the communists.[124]

The uneasy alliance, however, suffered a fatal blow when Chiang's troops attacked communist forces, killing approximately 9,000 men in January 1941. Coming at the height of the struggle with the Japanese, the attack constituted the *de facto* end of any cooperation between the two armies. From that point on, both men "fought separate wars," as they prepared for their own ultimate military and political confrontation.[125] Chiang for his part had never been genuinely interested in cooperating with the Chinese communists. In a remark that betrayed his true feelings about collaboration with Mao's forces, he had tersely observed, "The Japanese are a disease of the skin, but the Communists are a disease of the heart." His immediate aim was not to seek an alliance with the communists but to eliminate their power and then lead a national struggle for freedom and independence. What he failed to appreciate, however, was the extent to which the Chinese communists had already become associated with the national struggle in the eyes of the Chinese people.[126]

Meanwhile Mao, who was paying only lip service to the directives of the Kuomintang, now concentrated on strengthening his support among the peasants and forging his image as China's true national hero.[127] Despite, or perhaps on account of, the combined threat posed by the Japanese and the Kuomintang army, the communists were able to secure their hard-won advantage in the countryside, as artfully revealed in Mao's simple but compelling metaphor: "The people are a pond and the Red soldiers are fish swimming among them."[128] The Kuomintang intensified their economic blockade of areas under communist control, prompting Mao to call for greater production in the base areas, which reinforced his message of economic self-sufficiency and political independence.[129] Conditions between the two camps continued to deteriorate throughout the war. And despite lengthy negotiations aimed at achieving a *modus vivendi* between the two groups at the end of World War II, it became clear that neither side was interested in sharing power, nor did they have any intention of relinquishing any authority or territorial control. In the end, as the Japanese withdrew from China in 1944, the Reds were well positioned to fill the "temporary vacuum . . . with arms, . . . teachers, and . . . faith in the people's strength."[130]

To build and sustain that strength, however, Mao had to construct his own forms of political edification and propaganda to reach a vast audience and spread his revolutionary message of peasant revolution, social equality, and character formation. Moreover, the lack of anything resembling an information infrastructure forced Mao to create simple but effective mechanisms to coordinate the flow of information, political education, information, and indoctrination.[131] The absence of conventional mass media, including newspapers, radio, film, and later television prompted Mao to turn to such alternate modes of communication as wall newspapers and posters to applaud courage, bravery, and sacrifice. In an effort to reinforce democratic principles, he even provided soldiers with a column in their military newspapers where they could openly criticize one another and the failings of their officers.[132]

Mao, of course, held party members equally accountable to exemplary standards of behavior, requiring them to go through a process of "remolding" the individual.[133] He admonished them to observe "democratic method[s] of persuasion and education,"[134] to be "prudent"[135] and earnest in their pursuit of "modesty" as a progressive virtue,[136] and to avoid becoming impetuous,[137] greedy, egotistical, "arrogant," and "conceited" in their attitude and demeanor.[138] To guard against the suffocation of popular democracy, Mao insisted on "the principle of 'Don't blame the speaker,'" thereby encouraging individual speakers to express their views and opinions without fear of reprisals.[139] Moreover, he insisted that party members must never "resort to commandism, . . . coercion," or "compulsion," since the process of "ideological remoulding" is and must remain a slow, deliberate, and patient undertaking.[140] The same held true for his desire to blend military strategy, political conviction, and revolutionary tactics into a coherent ideological message.

The post–World War II military stalemate set the stage for the ultimate bloody struggle between Mao and Chiang over China's political future. According to the terms of the surrender, Japan was obligated to transfer territories to the Chinese government. But the bifurcated presence of two separate armies and two political authorities with conflicting claims to political legitimacy called into question the nature of any postwar settlement and the viability of any form of coalition government. Moreover, since the communists had been the first to declare war on the Japanese, they resented the Allies' exclusive support of Chiang's government as the legitimate expression of the political will of the Chinese people. The fact that Mao had named his Red Army troops and guerrillas the People's Liberation Army infuriated Chiang. Chiang also rejected out of hand Mao's proposal of a coalition government because Chiang had no intentions of sharing power with anyone, let alone Mao and his communist revolutionaries.[141]

What followed was a brutal, bloody civil war, which Mao named the War of Liberation.[142] Though outnumbered, as had always been the case, and out-supplied by the Americans, who sent vast amounts of aid to Chiang Kai-shek with virtually no strings attached,[143] Mao's highly motivated troops were able to rout Chiang's army. Since the Americans had openly and publicly extolled Chiang as the national leader of the legitimate, noncommunist, democratic government of China, Mao's victory represented a startling triumph for inter-national communism over the citadel of Western capitalism and bourgeois democracy. His strategy was simple yet effective, as he was able to win over the countryside, encircle the cities, and ultimately seize them in the name of the people's revolution.[144] As his military strategy had been clear and concise, so too were his political initiatives. He quickly introduced "people's courts" in the countryside, urging the peasants to come forward and denounce their land-lords and participate directly in the government's land distribution program.[145] In keeping with the words of one of Mao's commanders, it seemed as if the Red Army had lived up to his early prophecy by demonstrating that it was "a people's army" and that "We are nothing but the fist of the people beating their oppressors!"[146] In the spring of 1949, with his portrait hanging everywhere throughout a liberated China, Mao launched the final battle from across the north bank of the Yangtze river. Virtually unimpeded, his forces advanced rapidly,[147] securing a victory for the Red Army and its now celebrated leader Mao Zedong.

THE GREAT EXPERIMENT

With the Nationalist Chinese huddled in retreat on the island of Taiwan, Mao stood triumphantly atop the Gate of Heavenly Peace in Tien An'Mien Square and proclaimed the creation of the People's Republic of China on October 1, 1949.[148] Hailed by millions as the "nation's savior,"[149] he embarked on a new twenty-seven-year journey to complete the process of "national unification and national independence"[150] and protect the revolution against enemies from within and the threat of intervention from abroad.[151] After decades of civil war and struggle against the Japanese, the social and economic conditions were bleak. They were further compounded by the drain on economic resources cre-ated by the Korean War (which began in June 1950) and the drain it imposed on China's scarce economic resources. Though costly in terms of lives and ma-teriel, it did provide Mao with another political triumph and an opportunity to proclaim Korea China's first military victory over a Western state.[152]

On the domestic front, the new government introduced a system of ra-tioning cards to purchase food, clothing, and other scarce commodities essen-tial for everyday living.[153] With the assistance of Soviet advisers, the government also undertook much larger projects as part of its overall modernization campaign. The construction of power stations, dams, and sewage systems reflected the regime's desire to strengthen the nation economically, while at the same time promoting public health and a more tolerable standard of living for all China's people.[154] Curbing and eliminating social ills also loomed large on the agenda, prompting government officials to crack down on blackmarketeering, religion, and the sale of opium. In the case of opium, the government imposed stiff criminal penalties, including the execution of suppliers and dealers. By 1951 addiction to opium had fallen off sharply, enabling the government to focus more on the social consequences of drug abuse and on educational and rehabilitation programs for victims and users.[155]

In keeping with the populist, revolutionary commitment that the land belonged to those who till it, Mao continued to pursue his land redistribution policies. Conscious of the need to maintain productivity, the government chose, however, to refrain from an excessively aggressive approach to land reform, which might have proven debilitating. The peasants, nonetheless, found the pace of land reform liberating. It also had a powerful political and psychological impact on their collective identity, injecting them with a new sense of hope and political power.[156] Mao reinforced this new level of political consciousness by inviting the peasants to participate in "speak bitterness meetings" against landlords and wealthy peasants, whose most notorious offenders were pilloried or executed, in effect putting an end to what remained of the hated "landlord class."[157]

Government intervention, however, did lead to greater administrative supervision in the workplace in the form of "strict codes of labor discipline,"[158] internal passports, restrictions on travel, and the restructuring of unions to serve as "transmissions belts" for government instructions. Despite previous admonitions to avoid the use of compulsive measures in the formation of the public's political consciousness, conventional and unconventional forms of compulsion reinforced the practice of party oversight and the monitoring of political reliability. "Denunciation Boxes," propaganda campaigns, the ubiquitous presence of party slogans, loudspeakers, and the censorship of the written and the printed word, which "Mao controlled . . . with an iron hand" continued to assure mass levels of political compliance. Over time, however, the combination of ideological fervor and Mao's enormous individual authority ultimately led to the emergence of a cult of personality. The intensity of the cult manifested itself in the ubiquitous display of portraits and badges of Mao throughout China; weddings that turned into toasts and declarations in support of his leadership and the future of the revolution; and images of Chinese youth reciting from memory sections of Mao's writings and publicly proclaiming: "Long Live Chairman Mao."[159]

As a revolutionary nationalist, Mao also realized the need to modernize and strengthen the theoretical foundations and structural components of the communist system in China. As a young revolutionary Marxist, he had first borrowed from the Soviet model as a historical example of how a socialist state could "industrialize a backward country."[160] In his own words: "The Communist Party of the Soviet Union is our best teacher and we must learn from it."[161] In keeping with the spirit of these remarks, he assiduously emphasized the doctrine of centralized planning, rapid industrialization, the collectivization of agriculture, and the introduction of a Soviet-style five-year plan. Unlike the situation in Russia, however, collectivization in China proceeded without much violence and without "economic chaos." Moreover, in stark contrast to Joseph Stalin's methods of collectivization, which had widened the chasm separating the party and the state from the people, the Chinese people trusted the regime and its leadership and openly accepted the collectivization process. The contrasting reactions also underscored the fundamental differences between Leninism—with its elitist, authoritarian character and organizational distance from the peasantry—and Maoism—with its deep agrarian roots and close political proximity to the peasants.[162]

Differences in levels of economic and technological development further complicated the Sino-Soviet relationship. Fearful of a potential threat to their leadership within the international communist movement and of the sudden emergence of a powerful state along their southeastern border, the Soviets were reluctant to provide technical and economic assistance to China. For obvious reasons pertaining to the Soviet Union's superpower status, the conflict over the transfer of knowledge and technology related to the nuclear bomb became particularly acute. And as Mao's revolutionary stature continued to grow and the competing claims of Beijing and Moscow over the future of the revolution intensified, a personal rivalry developed between Mao and Stalin. Although Mao was careful to create the impression that he had absolutely no desire to displace Stalin's privileged position within the ranks of the communist movement,[163] his willingness to experiment with alternative forms of political and economic organization challenged the Soviet model and threatened to wrest Marxism away from its exclusively European framework and provide it with an alternative Asian format.[164]

His own theoretical orientation, however, reinforced his commitment to educate the peasants in the political process by making them aware of their political power and encouraging them to seize the land and kill their landlords. In fact, estimates of the number of counterrevolutionaries executed during the early period of Mao's domestic revolution range between 1 and 3 million people, figures that raised the specter of a government-sanctioned reign of terror.[165] And while the bloody campaign against reactionary forces in Chinese society did, in fact, enhance Mao's dictatorial image, it did so by portraying him not as an agent of evil, but as a "dictator for good."[166]

Mao looked beyond the land question into other areas of social inequality, including the role and status of women in Chinese society. One incident, in particular, seems to have deeply moved Mao. It involved the suicide of a young woman, who slit her throat on her wedding day because her parents had insisted on an arranged marriage.[167] Recognizing the basic injustice within a system that accorded "men . . . rights and women . . . duties,"[168] he set out to destroy the patriarchal order of Chinese society[169] and put an end to arranged marriages, the selling of wives, and the abusive treatment of women. True to his Marxist perspective, he also maintained that "genuine equality between the sexes" could be achieved only through a complete "socialist transformation of society,"[170] in which women were allowed "to own property, use their own names, . . . sue for divorce," and enter the professions.[171] He also regarded women as a "vast reserve of labor power," embraced "the principle of equal pay for equal work,"[172] and sought to weaken the traditional bonds of the family as a means of modernizing the Chinese economy and encouraging greater geographical and social mobility within the workforce.[173] He would later use his ideas on women and social justice to introduce a ban on the primitive practices of infanticide and footbinding and update conditions in Chinese factories by providing women with access to free medical care and nurseries for their children.[174]

Mao also stressed the importance of raising the public's political consciousness through thought reform, attitudinal transformation, and a carefully articulated "'anti-God' propaganda" campaign.[175] To achieve his ideological objectives, Mao called upon the party and its agents to educate China's intellectuals[176] and initiate programs of social restructuring through marches, banners, public denunciations, and mass political confessions. Taken together, the sheer magnitude of these activities, framed as they were within the imposing backdrop of mass political drama and government-sponsored spectacle, created an awe-inspiring sense of revolutionary truth and power.[177] For Mao, all aspects of social education were political and had to be practical in their application,[178] which is why he stressed that all forms of literature and art must serve the masses and become an integrated, well-coordinated part of the revolutionary message.[179] For these reasons, free democratic theater performances, which were staged in open air settings and which were free of the social trappings of reserved boxes and preferred seating, played an important role in reshaping the values of the Chinese people. Despite the scarcity of costumes and sets, the players were able to celebrate the common struggle and victory over the Japanese and the importance of their revolution. Between acts, the festive mood would often lead to spontaneous outbursts of song by members of the audience. The entire experience underscored the importance of "propaganda in art," where "illusions of life" embraced political meaning[180] and theater served as the revolution's "education-through-entertainment department."[181]

By the mid-1950s changes outside China opened new vistas for Mao at home. The specific catalyst was Nikita Khrushchev's famous, or infamous, denunciation of Stalin at the Twentieth Congress of the Communist Party of the Soviet Union in 1956. The attack on Stalin enabled Mao to unveil a new political approach and chart a course independent of the Soviet Union. The tone was set in his famous "Hundred Flowers Speech," which he delivered in the

spring of 1957 as part of his effort to avoid the formation of a highly centralized, repressive political climate like the one that had developed under Stalin.

Wary of party critics, who opposed collectivization and considered his economic schemes utopian, Mao's invitation "to let a hundred flowers bloom"
was designed to challenge the conformist thinking of party bureaucrats[182] and
expose a new privileged elite with access to special housing, schools, servants,
medical care, and vacations. Mao wanted to encourage critics to speak out
against these abuses.[183] His speech went beyond party issues to include a
twofold message for the members of China's intelligentsia. For example,
while he encouraged scientists to contend for new and different ideas, he
urged writers and artists to experiment with new styles and subject matter but
not with "social and political content."[184] By fostering a more open discussion
of political issues, Mao believed that his speech would win over intellectual
opponents of the regime to the communist cause.[185] Moreover, by inviting
the intellectuals and technicians to participate in the reform process, he
wanted to enlist their knowledge, support, and expertise in remaking Chinese
society and transforming the country's economy. What happened, however,
far exceeded Mao's expectations. Having been invited to participate in the debate, members of the opposition did not stop simply at criticizing excesses
within the system; they went directly to the root of the problem, as they
viewed it, and denounced the very nature and power of the communist
regime and its notion of one-party rule.

When faced with this revolt, Mao quickly changed direction and silenced
the opposition. By Stalinist standards, however, his methods were benign. For
the most part lives were spared, although individuals had to pass through a
"psychologically tortuous ordeal" to make amends for their errors.[186] During
this period Mao also employed "the *hsia-fang* movement," which sent officials
and experts down to the countryside to spend time working with the peasants.[187] The outcome has led some political pundits to persuasively suggest
that Mao had never been interested in this type of reform and had simply designed the post-Stalinist campaign in order to identify the opposition quickly
and dispose of its members. Mao's own words suggest this reading of events:
"We must let the scoundrels appear. . . . Then knock them over the head."[188]
But the intent may not have been that clear. Moreover, the assumption after
the fact that Mao and the party leadership really knew what they intended to
accomplish through this invitation reinforces the image of "an infallible and
unified Leninist party . . . pursuing a well-charted course," which clearly was
not the case.[189]

Characteristic of his inconsistent "zigzag" approach to planning and leadership,[190] Mao's attention now shifted in a totally opposite direction. Rebuffed
by the intellectuals, whose response had been insufficiently red, he turned back
to the peasants and launched the Great Leap Forward in 1958, which in its political, social, and economic consequences was unique even by Chinese standards. Returning to his agrarian roots, Mao rekindled his view of the peasants

as "a clean sheet of paper" upon which one could write a new revolution.[191] Believing in the virtuous nature of China's unlettered rural poor, he celebrated their simplicity and untainted revolutionary potential. When he proudly and defiantly proclaimed that those "with a low level of culture" invariably "triumph" over those "with a high level of culture," he dramatically redefined the nature of their "poor" and "blank" character and their political status as symbols of China's agrarian backwardness.[192]

Turning his back on Soviet-style centralized planning, Mao introduced a "crash program for 'modernization,'"[193] based upon decentralization and a loosely coordinated pattern of economic development.[194] The nucleus of the system was the self-contained people's communes, which he believed could produce all that was necessary for the local community and thereby achieve communism not in some distant future but in the here and now. The communal structure also represented his attempt to reinstill the spirit of voluntarism and his own belief in human determination, "mass action," and "political zeal"[195] as the means for overcoming China's lack of technology and machines and shaping the spiritual transformation of its people.[196]

Although many may have dismissed Mao's excessive emphasis on the role of "human will" and political consciousness as "unscientific,"[197] he believed that what the Chinese lacked in knowledge, skill, and technique they could make up for through "revolutionary enthusiasm and ideological purity."[198] Mao also attacked technical experts, who constituted a "privileged technocratic elite," and called for the creation of individuals who were both "experts and reds" and capable of mastering the technology at the work site while maintaining their political ideals.[199] In keeping with the spirit of Mao's renewed populism, the government also introduced new evening, spare-time, and work-study educational programs in the countryside.[200] In the end, however, for lack of direction, cohesion, and a "detailed socioeconomic blueprint,"[201] the experiment of 1958 and 1959 failed. Moreover, the "haste" surrounding the establishment of the communes had obviously contributed to the creation of an organizational nightmare.[202] It also helped to explain Mao's willingness to assume responsibility—in his own words—"for the chaos . . . on a grand scale."[203] In a smaller yet revealing way, the most notable and humiliating example of the Great Leap Forward's unrealistic expectations was the failure of "backyard furnaces" to increase China's steel production, which generated widespread ridicule in the foreign press and an unusual surge of skepticism within the peasant population.[204]

Disorganized production, floods, pests, and poor agricultural harvests produced a wave of famine and suffering.[205] Western estimates have placed the loss of life as high as 30 million. Confronted with chaos, starvation, the enormous loss of life, and an undercurrent among some party officials, who began to refer to Mao's experiment as the "Great Fall Backward,"[206] Mao retreated to a more orthodox approach based on centralized planning and material incentives. Though far from total, his retreat did place greater reliance on the role of party functionaries, administrators, and technocrats in managing the economy.

In addition to representing a painful personal setback, the debacle also emerged as a monumental political failure for having driven a wedge between the authority of the party and the once solid peasantry.[207]

While Mao's retreat from the vicissitudes of the Great Leap did not deprive him of the title of party chairman, he distanced himself from the day-to-day operations of the party. This admittedly ambiguous position reflected his own personal frustration and momentary "loss of confidence" in the outcome of the revolution.[208] But he hardly remained politically idle. While continuing to lash out at "bureaucratic and technocratic elitism" and the "ideological decay" it bred,[209] he devoted much of his attention to the ideological formation of the army,[210] its role as a "repository of revolutionary values," and the dangers inherent in the growth of a professional officer corps.[211] The message obviously took root, since it was the army, the guardian of Mao's heroic, legendary status, who launched the cult of personality with the initial publication of *Quotations from Chairman Mao Tse-tung* in 1964.[212]

Within the context of the nuclear age, however, Mao's belief in the capacity of the people's will to overcome all physical obstacles generated some rather unorthodox military thinking. For example, the blend of "military romanticism"[213] and revolutionary enthusiasm, which led Mao to extol the heroic virtues of guerrilla warfare and the Long March, also encouraged him to draw the conclusion that wars would not be won "by thermonuclear weapons, but by the courage and perseverance of those who fight them."[214] However, when he pursued this theme in conversations with Khrushchev and suggested that the United States was nothing more than "a paper tiger,"[215] Khrushchev purportedly responded "Yes, but one with nuclear teeth." Fearful of what he viewed as China's maniacal policy on the use of nuclear weapons, Khrushchev announced an end to the exchange of information on nuclear weapons in July 1959.[216] The following June he attacked the Chinese communists as "madmen, who wanted to unleash nuclear war," and announced that the future of international relations would depend upon the Soviet Union and the United States. In July, as the theme of nuclear adventurism and friction between the communist giants mounted, Khrushchev announced "the abrupt withdrawal of Soviet aid," setting the stage for the dramatic Sino–Soviet split, which led to clashes along the Ussuri river in the 1960s over the disputed border between China and the Soviet Union.[217] For Mao, who had always preached the doctrine of "self-reliance," the rupture came as no surprise.[218] Moreover, in Mao's eyes the split divided the revisionist camp of the European West from the revolutionary camp of the Asian East[219] and reinforced his belief that "the East Wind is prevailing over the West Wind."[220]

The reimposition of Chinese rule in Tibet has created a different, but nonetheless significant, domestic and international problem for the Chinese communists. In the fall of 1950, when the communists restored Chinese control over Tibet, the military operation proceeded rather smoothly. But the issue of Tibet's cultural and political independence remained much more difficult to resolve, and it erupted in a Tibetan revolt in 1959, which was smashed by the communist authorities,[221] forcing the Dalai Lama to escape to India.[222] In 1968 the administrative integration of Tibet was intensified by the creation of "revolutionary committees" under the control of the military.[223] Given its record of burning religious books, closing monasteries, and persecuting Buddhist monks and nuns, China's record in Tibet has hardly been exemplary.[224] Moreover, the Dalai Lama remains a troublesome presence on the international scene, as officials in Beijing adamantly insist on Tibet's remaining an integral part of China.

THE GREAT PROLETARIAN CULTURAL REVOLUTION AND BEYOND

Throughout the 1960s Mao fought to perpetuate the "validity" of the revolution and the need to promote revolutionary struggles in Asia, Africa, and Latin America.[225] On the home front, he launched the Great Proletarian Cultural Revolution in 1966 to combat revisionism and reawaken the revolutionary fervor of the people.[226] Unfortunately, "his last revolutionary act" would also prove to be his greatest political failure.[227] As he had in the past, he began by turning to the peasants in the countryside to wage war against a class-conscious urban culture[228] and the suffocating influence of institutional bureaucracies. In his own words, he did not want China to "change color" or alter its revolutionary character. To combat this tendency, he embarked on a campaign to imbue Chinese youth with the heroic sacrifices of the Civil War and secure China's "role as the vanguard of the world revolution."[229] In addition to his desire to perpetuate the original purity and zeal of the revolution, Mao also hoped to build a monument to his own role as the living architect of that revolution.[230]

To accomplish these goals and recapture the original dynamism of the movement, Mao called upon China's youth to lead the revolution and denounce members of the new privileged elite. By closing schools for more than a year and organizing the students into zealous bands of Red Guards, the regime was able to create a new political instrument to mount a postrevolutionary wave of terror. Invoking the "class purity" of the Red Guards, Mao charged them with eliminating all forms of old ideas, culture, customs, and habits as well as demolishing the reactionary values of an antiquated educational system. Much like the army regulars who stormed Tien An-men Square in support of the regime in 1989, the Red Guards were drawn from a similar socioideological matrix whose ranks were made up of workers, peasants, and soldiers in the People's Liberation Army.[231] In 1966, however, the Red Guards relied on the use of large wall posters,[232] personal denunciations, and carefully staged acts of public humiliation to vilify party, government, and educational officials and impose a strict puritanical code of dress, conduct, and political behavior,[233] including prohibitions against wearing makeup, jewelry, sunglasses, and Western-style clothing.[234] Other symbols of counterrevolutionary behavior met a similar fate. Books and religious treasures were destroyed; museums and Buddhist temples ransacked. To signal the revolutionary change in the direction of the revolution, traffic lights were switched so that red meant "go" and green meant "stop."[235]

What resulted, however, was a totalitarian political environment in which degrees of "Redness" were used to discredit the intellectual endeavors and achievements of party members, officials, experts, and technicians.[236] The government also encouraged the Red Guards to stage the public humiliation of their victims in large auditoriums or sports arenas where they were often tortured, beaten, paraded around in dunce caps, and forced to confess their crimes against the revolution.[237] What is particularly significant about these episodes is that they reflect much of Mao's thinking and his willingness to lend the full weight of his personality and authority to the campaign. It is also interesting to note that Mao felt free to call upon his wife, the former actress Chiang Ch'ing, to play a prominent role in directing the Cultural Revolution.[238] After Mao's death, she was convicted for her responsibility in the deaths of thousands of individuals, who perished as a direct result of the movement's fanaticism, and for her role in destroying China's economy as a member of the Gang of Four. Originally sentenced to death, her punishment was later changed to a lengthy prison term. Tenaciously holding to her political convictions, she never recanted, nor did she show any remorse for what she had done. In her own words: "I was Chairman Mao's dog. . . . Whoever he told me to bite, I bit."[239]

Though unified in its message, the movement itself was fraught with political contradictions. For example, while stressing the need to promote spontaneity and grassroots initiative, it lionized Mao's personality and leadership and celebrated his stature as the "Great Helmsman." Featuring enormous public tributes to Mao[240] with masses of people ritualistically singing the "The East Is Red" and reciting sections from the little red book of Chairman Mao's *Quotations*, the staging of huge, monumental gatherings served as powerful testimony to the Chinese people's esteem and devotion to one man and his revolutionary legacy. For some, however, the virtually unlimited power Mao gave to the Red Guards called into question Mao's political maxim that "the party commands the gun, and the gun must never be allowed to command the party."[241]

Unfortunately, Mao's desire to eliminate the influence of a book-learning elite was counterproductive for a society that was in the throes of modernization. By reasserting the popular base of the revolution at the expense of the bureaucrats and technocrats, Mao succeeded in stultifying creative thought, research, and scholarship, skills he himself had identified as critical for China's progress. As Deng Xiaoping, Mao's eventual successor and the author of a more pragmatic approach to Chinese politics and economics, observed: "No one dares to go near the laboratories. . . . Research personnel no longer read books."[242] The same could be said of "artists [who] did not paint and actors and musicians [who] did not perform."[243] Eventually, the chaos and havoc wrought by Mao's desire to smash "the entire party organization"[244] brought the cultural revolution to a halt in 1969 and forced Mao to call in the army to restore order.[245]

Though tainted, Mao's reputation survived the debacle, and the Ninth Congress of the Chinese Communist Party, meeting on April 1, 1969, proclaimed the Thought of Chairman Mao the primary source for revolutionary planning and action.[246] Nonetheless, despite the window dressing, the movement had exposed a pattern of disturbing political and social conflicts within the Chinese communist system. For the most part the Cultural Revolution had been an urban affair with the countryside remaining "politically quiescent."[247] The countryside did, however, benefit from the revolution's decision to expand education into more areas of rural China.[248] In the end, the members of the Gang of Four were tried and held accountable for their crimes and their emphasis on the centralization of political power and the authoritarian role of the state.[249] But the proceedings also served, even if only indirectly, as a means of putting Mao's troubled leadership on trial.[250]

In assessing the meaning and significance of the Cultural Revolution, Robert Jay Lifton emphasizes the importance of "*psychism*" or the power of the will to make things happen, in Mao's thinking.[251] According to Lifton, the entire enterprise was predicated upon Mao's search for "*revolutionary immortality*"[252] as a means of transcending his own death and the spiritual death of the revolution. He believed that the mobilization of "psychic power" to surmount China's material deficiencies could solve all the country's problems, including its lack of advanced technology.[253] When backed by the "coercive power" of the state, Mao's invocation of psychic energy and revolutionary purity and his desire to use the power of the people to transform the revolution into an all-encompassing political movement[254] reflected his belief in "conscious human activity" as the decisive force in history.[255] Earlier, Mao had appealed to the force of will and human labor during the Great Leap Forward as a means of overcoming China's technological insufficiencies. But his attempt during the Cultural Revolution to use the power of human will and labor to avoid "grafting alien Western knowledge and technique onto an immutably Chinese 'essence'" was shortsighted. By ignoring the realities of the immediate environment, he managed inadvertently to transform his most recent monumental undertaking into an exercise in "naive utopianism."[256]

Part of the explanation for the error lay in what Lifton describes as Mao's symbolic attempt to triumph over death and the "law of diminishing conversions" through a massive rebirth and renewal of communist values.[257] Lifton also sees in this particular dynamic of the Cultural Revolution "the psychic contours" of an "*existential absolute*" or an "*all-or-none confrontation with death*"[258] in which Mao wanted to perpetuate his revolutionary achievements and merge eternally with the masses.[259] Lifton also argues that Mao's desire to immortalize his own role as the leader of the revolution prompted him to try to recapture the early enthusiasm of the revolution, attack the claustrophobic views of the bureaucracy, and transcend the intractable layers of social indifference. Moreover, Mao hoped that the convulsive nature of the Cultural Revolution and the injection of a new wave of "revolutionary totalism"[260] would restore "a *sense* of revolutionary power"[261] and enable the true believer "to return to a mythological past."[262] In so doing, Mao also wanted to become the *"eternal survivor,"* secure in the knowledge of the future of his *"revolutionary works."*[263] Since he also feared the possible death of the revolution and the corrosive arguments of intellectuals, who mocked the failure of the Great Leap Forward as a sign of the regime's fallibility, he preferred to attribute the failure to insufficient amounts of *"revolutionary zeal."*[264] But there was also something inherently flawed in what amounted to a form of "national egoism," which led Mao and many of his followers to view the nature and success of the world revolution as contingent upon the outcome of the revolution in China.[265]

Begun under Mao and later successfully implemented by the diminutive, yet remarkably resilient, Deng Xiaoping, the new period of pragmatic alternatives affected China's affairs both at home and abroad. The most dramatic breakthrough occurred in the area of foreign policy, when in the wake of ping-pong diplomacy a sudden and totally unexpected improvement occurred in U.S.–Chinese relations, culminating in President Richard Nixon's visit to China and his meeting with a larger-than-life, though physically debilitated, Chairman Mao in 1972. For China and the United States, the diplomatic rapprochement represented a "tactical accommodation" on both sides to a common Soviet threat.[266] For Mao, however, Nixon's visit must have also represented an outstanding victory for his personal brand of political dialectics—a victory he was undoubtedly able to savor, even if only briefly. With his body ravaged by Parkinson's disease, he largely spent the next four years in seclusion until his death on September 9, 1976.

Under Deng the new pragmatism included initiatives to demystify Mao's historical presence and diminish his political stature as the Great Helmsman. But the assignment was by no means easy, given Mao's popularity, patriotism, and international prestige, as well as his unique standing as "both the Lenin and Stalin of the Chinese Revolution," the architect of a new China, and the heroic bearer of Chinese nationalism.[267] Moreover, the new reformist leadership wanted to proceed cautiously because of Mao's importance in establishing their own political legitimacy and ties to the revolution.[268] With these important political considerations in mind, Deng focused much of his attention on domestic policy issues and the introduction of a more systematic, incremental approach to resolving China's agricultural and manufacturing problems based upon production incentives, while continuing to pursue better diplomatic and commercial relations with the West.

Celebrated at home and abroad as an inspirational revolutionary figure, a heroic military leader, and a utopian visionary, Mao's political stature and historical legacy are clearly enormous. By stressing the need for direct contact between the people and the government, he authored a new people-centered approach to resolving China's problem of agrarian modernization. But unlike Stalin, who abandoned the peasants in favor of rapid industrialization, Mao embraced the peasantry and emphasized the importance of mass psychic involvement in recasting China's economy. His policies did, however, suffer from certain endemic inconsistencies, as he frequently vacillated between the more traditional methods of government experts and the more unorthodox contribution of peasants in the countryside. His approach, however, was truly remarkable in that it enabled the Chinese people to draw upon their own resources and initiative in pursuit of an industrial breakthrough with only minimal help or assistance from the outside world.[269] By placing the peasantry at the center of the revolutionary process and challenging the Leninist persuasion and that of other revolutionary Marxists that the peasants occupied a secondary position to that of the industrial proletariat within the revolution, Mao struck at both the elitist assumptions of Leninism and the bureaucratic arrogance of Stalinism. Coupled with his insistence that the revolution must always combat revisionism and never cut itself off from the masses, these ideological differences defined the fundamental differences separating Maoism and Leninism. The same can be said for differences in military strategy. Mao, for example, allied with the peasants to win over the countryside, encircle the cities, and seize the political victory, while Lenin encouraged the urban industrial proletariat to seize the cities, fashion a revolutionary army, and extend the revolution to the countryside.

In formulating his own political thought, Mao was also able to disseminate a revolutionary political doctrine, which originated from within one of the most backward corners of the world.[270] His role as the architect of a people's war of liberation, which combined social revolution and a prolonged national struggle against foreign oppression, spread throughout Asia, as was graphically demonstrated by the Vietnam War. It is important to note, however, that China later invaded Vietnam when changes in southeast Asia and the bilateral conflict with Moscow altered China's geopolitical interests in the region.[271] But of all his contributions, the one that may persist the longest is his concept of total revolution, of the need to remake the individual as a whole and imbue that individual with a complete, unconditional revolutionary vision, grounded in personal sacrifice and total ideological commitment.

NOTES

1. Stuart Schram, *Mao Tse-tung* (Baltimore, Md.: Penguin, 1967), p. 23.

2. Maurice Meisner, *Mao's China and After: A History of the People's Republic* (New York: Free Press, 1986), pp. 3–4, 10. See also Albert Marrin, *Mao Tse-tung and His China* (New York: Penguin, 1989), pp. 28–29.

3. Meisner, *Mao's China and After,* p. 4.

4. Ibid., pp. 11–14.

5. Ibid., p. 427.

6. Marrin, *Mao Tse-tung and His China,* p. 5.

7. Schram, *Mao Tse-tung,* p. 21.

8. Robert Jay Lifton, *Revolutionary Immortality: Mao Tse-tung and the Chinese Cultural Revolution* (New York: Norton, 1976), p. 85.

9. Ibid., p. 92.

10. Edgar Snow, *Red Star over China* (New York: Random House, 1938 [1961]), pp. 123–31.

11. Ibid., pp. 142–43.

12. Schram, *Mao Tse-tung*, p. 25.

13. Snow, *Red Star over China*, p. 149.

14. Schram, *Mao Tse-tung*, pp. 27, 34.

15. Snow, *Red Star over China*, p. 151.

16. Schram, *Mao Tse-tung*, pp. 36, 44.

17. Snow, *Red Star over China*, p. 146.

18. Schram, *Mao Tse-tung*, pp. 37, 41.

19. Marrin, *Mao Tse-tung and His China*, p. 48.

20. Schram, *Mao Tse-tung*, p. 51.

21. Marrin, *Mao Tse-tung and His China*, p. 44.

22. Schram, *Mao Tse-tung*, p. 47.

23. Ibid., p. 56.

24. *Quotations from Chairman Mao Tse-tung* (Peking: Foreign Languages Press, 1966), p. 23.

25. Schram, *Mao Tse-tung*, p. 49.

26. Marrin, *Mao Tse-tung and His China*, p. 39.

27. *Quotations from Chairman Mao Tse-tung*, p. 9.

28. Snow, *Red Star over China*, p. 118.

29. Schram, *Mao Tse-tung*, p. 60.

30. Snow, *Red Star over China*, pp. 404–6.

31. Schram, *Mao Tse-tung*, p. 67.

32. Ibid., p. 70.

33. See Snow, *Red Star over China*, p. 485.

34. Ibid., p. 410.

35. Ibid., pp. 415–16.

36. Schram, *Mao Tse-tung*, pp. 72–76.

37. Ibid., pp. 81–82.

38. Meisner, *Mao's China and After*, p. 92.

39. *Quotations from Chairman Mao Tse-tung*, p. 285.

40. Ibid., p. 277.

41. Meisner, *Mao's China and After*, pp. 128–29.

42. *Quotations from Chairman Mao Tse-tung*, p. 110.

43. Schram, *Mao Tse-tung*, p. 93.

44. Ibid., pp. 94–95.

45. Ibid., p. 99.

46. Snow, *Red Star over China*, p. 54.

47. Marrin, *Mao Tse-tung and His China*, p. 60.

48. Meisner, *Mao's China and After*, p. 24.

49. Marrin, *Mao Tse-tung and His China*, p. 60.

50. Schram, *Mao Tse-tung*, pp. 99, 103.

51. Snow, *Red Star over China*, p. 170.

52. Ibid., p. 178.

53. Schram, *Mao Tse-tung*, pp. 115, 122.

54. Ibid., p. 126.

55. Ibid., p. 130.

56. Ibid., p. 127.

57. Ibid., p. 107.

58. Snow, *Red Star over China*, p. 283.

59. Ibid., p. 303.

60. Ibid., p. 488.

61. Schram, *Mao Tse-tung*, p. 325.

62. Ibid., p. 135.

63. Meisner, *Mao's China and After*, p. 44.

64. Schram, *Mao Tse-tung*, p. 136.

65. Ibid., pp. 156–58, 164.

66. Marrin, *Mao Tse-tung and His China*, pp. 150–151.

67. *Quotations from Chairman Mao Tse-tung*, p. 58.

68. Ibid., p. 100.

69. Ibid., p. 259.

70. Ibid., pp. 254–55.

71. Jacques Ellul, *Propaganda: The Formation of Men's Attitudes* (New York: Vintage, 1973), p. 307.

72. Snow, *Red Star over China*, pp. 311–12.

73. Ibid., pp. 334–37.

74. *Quotations from Chairman Mao Tse-tung*, p. 157.

75. Snow, *Red Star over China*, pp. 281–83.

76. Ibid., p. 359.

77. Ibid., pp. 102–8, 307.

78. Ibid., pp. 308–9.

79. Schram, *Mao Tse-tung*, p. 143.

80. For a more extensive discussion of the main "principles of operation" of the People's Liberation Army, see *Quotations from Chairman Mao Tse-tung*, pp. 95–98.

81. Snow, *Red Star over China*, p. 177.

82. *Quotations from Chairman Mao Tse-tung*, pp. 256–57.

83. Snow, *Red Star over China*, p. 176.

84. Schram, *Mao Tse-tung*, pp. 152–53.

85. Ibid., p. 151.

86. Ibid., pp. 154–55.

87. Ibid., p. 165.

88. *Quotations from Chairman Mao Tse-tung*, p. 61.

89. Schram, *Mao Tse-tung*, pp. 165–68.

90. Marrin, *Mao Tse-tung and His China*, p. 66.

91. Ibid., p. 211.

92. *Quotations from Chairman Mao Tse-tung*, p. 129.

93. Ibid., p. 125.

94. Ibid., pp. 118–19.

95. Ibid., p. 153.

96. Snow, *Red Star over China*, p. 492.

97. Ibid., p. 195. Altering the focus but not the significance of their action, Albert Marrin provides an alternative interpretation, which suggests that many of the rear guard, who fought bravely to protect the army's escape, survived in large measure due to the help and support of the peasants in the countryside: Marrin, *Mao Tse-tung and His China*, p. 87.

98. Ibid.

99. Ibid., pp. 104, 110.

100. For a superb description and discussion of this important chapter in the history of the Chinese communists, see Snow, *Red Star over China*, pp. 195–218.

101. Marrin, *Mao Tse-tung and His China*, p. 105.

102. Meisner, *Mao's China and After*, pp. 33–35.

103. Schram, *Mao Tse-tung*, pp. 181–82, 192.

104. Snow, *Red Star over China*, p. 222.

105. Schram, *Mao Tse-tung*, pp. 220–21.

106. Meisner, *Mao's China and After*, pp. 35, 49.

107. Snow, *Red Star over China*, p. 273.

108. Ibid., p. 71.

109. Ibid., p. 94.

110. Ibid., pp. 233–36.

111. Ibid., pp. 233–49.

112. Ibid., pp. 233–49.

113. Ibid., pp. 504–5.

114. *Quotations from Chairman Mao Tse-tung*, p. 205.

115. Ibid., p. 312.

116. Schram, *Mao Tse-tung*, p. 216.

117. Ibid., p. 222.

118. Ibid., p. 201.

119. Ibid., p. 196.

120. Ibid., pp. 204–5.

121. Snow, *Red Star over China*, p. 470.

122. Ibid., p. 476.

123. Ibid., p. 457.

124. Marrin, *Mao Tse-tung and His China*, p. 127.

125. Ibid., p. 143.

126. Marrin, *Mao Tse-tung and His China*, p. 124.

127. Schram, *Mao Tse-tung*, pp. 218–19.

128. Marrin, *Mao Tse-tung and His China*, p. 141.

129. Schram, *Mao Tse-tung*, p. 220.

130. Snow, *Red Star over China*, p. 501.

131. Ellul, *Propaganda*, pp. 303–4.

132. Snow, *Red Star over China*, pp. 309–10.

133. Ellul, *Propaganda*, pp. 309–10.

134. *Quotations from Chairman Mao Tse-tung*, p. 150.

135. Ibid., p. 279.

136. Ibid., p. 237.

137. Ibid., p. 279.

138. Ibid., pp. 180, 190.

139. Ibid., p. 162.

140. Ibid., pp. 150–51.

141. Marrin, *Mao Tse-tung and His China*, pp. 160–61.

142. Ibid., pp. 162–64, 175.

143. Snow, *Red Star over China*, pp. 508, 510.

144. Schram, *Mao Tse-tung*, p. 242.

145. Marrin, *Mao Tse-tung and His China*, p. 179.

146. Snow, *Red Star over China*, pp. 304–5.

147. Marrin, *Mao Tse-tung and His China*, pp. 183–86.

148. Ibid., pp. 186–87.

149. Ibid., p. 2.

150. Meisner, *Mao's China and After*, p. 60.

151. Schram, *Mao Tse-tung*, pp. 252–53.

152. Ibid., p. 79.

153. Marrin, *Mao Tse-tung and His China*, p. 190.

154. Ibid., p. 218.

155. Meisner, *Mao's China and After*, pp. 90–91.

156. Ibid., p. 110.

157. Marrin, *Mao Tse-tung and His China*, pp. 192–94.

158. Meisner, *Mao's China and After*, p. 127.

159. For a discussion of the reforms and their implication for the development of a Marxist ideology and the growth of a cult of personality under Mao's leadership, see Marrin, *Mao Tse-tung and His China*, pp. 199–213, 246–47. For a discussion of the use of institutionalized methods of compulsion, see Meisner, *Mao's China and After*, pp. 76–77.

160. Meisner, *Mao's China and After*, p. 117.

161. Ibid., p. 121.

162. Ibid., pp. 153–58.

163. Schram, *Mao Tse-tung*, p. 255.

164. Ibid., p. 254.

165. Ibid., p. 267–68.

166. Marrin, *Mao Tse-tung and His China*, p. 4.

167. Ibid., p. 47.

168. Ibid., p. 19 and p. 21.

169. *Quotations from Chairman Mao Tse-tung*, p. 294.

170. Ibid., p. 297.

171. Marrin, *Mao Tse-tung and His China*, p. 192.

172. *Quotations from Chairman Mao Tse-tung*, p. 298.

173. Schram, *Mao Tse-tung*, pp. 257–61.

174. Marrin, *Mao Tse-tung and His China*, p. 117.

175. Snow, *Red Star over China*, pp. 396–97.

176. Schram, *Mao Tse-tung*, pp. 268–69.

177. Ibid., p. 273.

178. Snow, *Red Star over China*, pp. 255–56.

179. *Quotations from Chairman Mao Tse-tung*, pp. 300–301.

180. Snow, *Red Star over China*, pp. 109–16.

181. Ibid., p. 378.

182. Meisner, *Mao's China and After*, p. 160.

183. Ibid., pp. 188–89.

184. Ibid., p. 178.

185. Schram, *Mao Tse-tung*, p. 289.

186. Meisner, *Mao's China and After*, p. 194.

187. Ibid., p. 200.

188. Marrin, *Mao Tse-tung and His China*, p. 215.

189. Meisner, *Mao's China and After,* p. 196.

190. Schram, *Mao Tse-tung,* p. 283. For a discussion of how Mao developed this tactical flexibility during the years of military struggle see Snow, *Red Star over China,* p. 488.

191. Schram, *Mao Tse-tung,* p. 292.

192. Meisner, *Mao's China and After,* pp. 213–15.

193. Ibid., p. 204.

194. Ibid., p. 222.

195. Schram, *Mao Tse-tung,* pp. 329–30.

196. Meisner, *Mao's China and After,* p. 211.

197. Ibid., p. 479.

198. Schram, *Mao Tse-tung,* pp. 292–95.

199. Meisner, *Mao's China and After,* p. 225.

200. Ibid., pp. 237–38.

201. Ibid., p. 230.

202. Ibid., p. 241.

203. Ibid., p. 245.

204. Ibid., p. 237. See also Marrin, *Mao Tse-tung and His China,* pp. 219, 224.

205. Meisner, *Mao's China and After,* p. 248.

206. Marrin, *Mao Tse-tung and His China,* pp. 222, 225.

207. Meisner, *Mao's China and After,* p. 251.

208. Ibid., p. 267.

209. Meisner, *Mao's China and After,* pp. 282, 286.

210. Ibid., p. 269.

211. Ibid., pp. 293–94.

212. Ibid., pp. 295–97. The publication is frequently referred to as "the little red book."

213. Schram, *Mao Tse-tung,* p. 293.

214. Ibid., p. 296. See also *Quotations from Chairman Mao Tse-tung,* p. 140.

215. Ibid., p. 75.

216. Marrin, *Mao Tse-tung and His China,* 259.

217. Schram, *Mao Tse-tung,* pp. 303–4.

218. *Quotations from Chairman Mao Tse-tung,* p. 194.

219. Schram, *Mao Tse-tung,* p. 308.

220. *Quotations from Chairman Mao Tse-tung,* p. 81.

221. Meisner, *Mao's China and After,* pp. 74–75.

222. Marrin, *Mao Tse-tung and His China,* p. 242.

223. Meisner, *Mao's China and After,* pp. 362–63.

224. Marrin, *Mao Tse-tung and His China,* pp. 242–43.

225. Schram, *Mao Tse-tung,* pp. 311–14.

226. Ibid., p. 320.

227. Meisner, *Mao's China and After,* p. 309.

228. Schram, *Mao Tse-tung,* p. 326.

229. Ibid., p. 321.

230. Ibid., p. 345.

231. Robert J. Lifton, *Revolutionary Immortality: Mao Tse-tung and the Chinese Cultural Revolution* (New York: Norton, 1976), p. 35.

232. Meisner, *Mao's China and After,* p. 333.

233. Schram, *Mao Tse-tung*, p. 341.

234. Marrin, *Mao Tse-tung and His China*, p. 233.

235. Ibid., pp. 236–37.

236. Lifton, *Revolutionary Immortality*, pp. 53, 125.

237. Marrin, *Mao Tse-tung and His China*, p. 239.

238. Lifton, *Revolutionary Immortality*, p. 49.

239. Marrin, *Mao Tse-tung and His China*, p. 268.

240. For a discussion of the "gigantic" rally on August 18, 1966, formalizing the Red Guard movement, see Lifton, *Revolutionary Immortality*, pp. 33, 36.

241. *Quotations from Chairman Mao Tse-tung*, p. 102. For a discussion of this issue, see also Schram, *Mao Tse-tung*, p. 331.

242. Meisner, *Mao's China and After*, p. 387.

243. Ibid., p. 388.

244. Schram, *Mao Tse-tung*, p. 333.

245. Meisner, *Mao's China and After*, p. 357.

246. Ibid., p. 365.

247. Ibid., p. 373.

248. Ibid., p. 381.

249. Ibid., pp. 422–23.

250. Ibid., p. 462.

251. Lifton, *Revolutionary Immortality*, p. 32.

252. Ibid., pp. 81–82.

253. Ibid., p. xvii.

254. Lifton, *Revolutionary Immortality*, p. 51.

255. Meisner, *Mao's China and After*, p. 313.

256. Lifton, *Revolutionary Immortality*, pp. 104–5.

257. Ibid., pp. 31, 129.

258. Ibid., p. 66.

259. Ibid., p. 71.

260. Ibid., p. 72.

261. Ibid., p. 26.

262. Ibid., p. 138.

263. Ibid., p. 15.

264. Ibid., pp. 19, 22–23.

265. Meisner, *Mao's China and After*, p. 398.

266. Ibid., p. 400.

267. Ibid., pp. 458–59.

268. Ibid., pp. 459, 463–65.

269. Ibid., p. 439.

270. Ibid., p. 446.

271. Ibid., p. 455.

Nelson Mandela. Photo by Juda Ngwenya. Reproduced by permission of Reuters/Corbis-Bettmann.

Chapter 3

———— MANDELA ————

AND FREEDOM IN
SOUTH AFRICA

RACE, HISTORY, AND POLITICS

Migrations of African tribes from central and eastern Africa into what is now
South Africa date back as far as the third century A.D. The arrival of white European settlers in this region in 1652 led to the development of a Dutch
Afrikaner culture, rooted in territorial conquest and expansion. When the
British seized control of the Cape Colony in 1806, many of the Afrikaners embarked on the Great Trek inland to preserve their way of life and develop their
system of racial superiority. The discovery of gold and diamonds in the mid-
nineteenth century added greatly to their wealth. To protect their land and
riches, the Afrikaners expanded their area of conquest and imposed strict laws
and regulations over the native African population to ensure their control of
the state and its economy. Though the local tribes mounted a heroic defense
against the onslaught of white settlers, as was the case in the Zulu rebellion of
1906, their resistance proved ineffective against the more advanced and sophisticated forms of European warfare and technology.[1]

The British, who wanted to secure the maritime route to India and acquire
South Africa, began to challenge Dutch control in the nineteenth century. At
the end of the century the British fought a bloody campaign, known as the
Boer War (1899–1902) against the Dutch settlers, which led to a British victory and the signing of the Treaty of Vereeniging in 1902. In effect, the treaty
established a joint British–Afrikaans condominium over South Africa and
"bargained away" the "political rights" of the native peoples.[2] Moreover, in
their desire to reconcile with the Boers, the British passed the Union Act of
1910, which institutionalized white supremacy and the inferior position of
blacks.[3] But while the British tended to adopt a policy of benign neglect,[4] the
inclusion of a highly discriminatory "colour bar clause" in the Union Act
sowed the seeds of black protest, opposition, and revolution.[5] What followed

was blatant discrimination, which included the introduction of blacks-only territorial reserves under the Natives' Land Act of 1913, more stringent enforce-
ment of the pass system to restrict blacks from entering urban areas, and the
disenfranchisement of blacks in the Cape Province in 1936, whose eighty-year-
old right to vote was arbitrarily rescinded. In the words of Cornelis de Kiewiet,
a South African historian: "To destroy the Cape native franchise was to destroy
the most important bridge between the worlds of two races."[6]

Born into the royal house of the Thembu people in the land of Transkei on
July 18, 1918, Nelson Mandela was to emerge as the symbol of popular resistance against European oppression and this century's most heroic voice for
freedom and human dignity. His given name was Rolihala, which he enjoyed
interpreting in the colloquial idiom as "troublemaker." In elementary school
his English-speaking teacher provided him with a proper British name, Nelson, which he believed derived from the celebrated British hero, Lord Nelson.
As the son of a chief, he was groomed from childhood to serve as a leader of
the people of the Xhosa nation. Nestled amidst the lovely hills and fertile val-
leys of the Transkei, the secure surroundings of the village of Qunu provided
Mandela with an idyllic opportunity to play at will, experience the beauty of
nature, herd sheep and cattle, expose himself to the values of tribal culture, and
learn as a boy to respect his opponents and refrain from humiliating them in
defeat. The gentle village setting, made up exclusively of women and children,
also afforded his mother an opportunity to nurture his curiosity and his young,
adventurous spirit.[7]

When Mandela was nine years old his father died and his life suddenly
changed. He left behind his comfortable life among the village huts to live in
the palace of the Chief Jongitaba Dalindyebo, the chief regent of the Thembu
people. Uprooted from his humble origins and thrust into the life of the tribal
court, the chief and his wife raised him as if he were their own son. His presence at the royal court also exposed him to a life of wealth and authority and to
the political culture of the Thembu tribe.[8] As a young man he was able to attend meetings and learn how to give advice and counsel to a king. For example, when comparing the leader's role to that of a shepherd, who directs the
flock from behind, Mandela remarked how the regent protected the right of
everyone to speak and listened carefully to what his people had to say. The
process was open and democratic. No opinions or decisions were forced, nor
was the majority allowed to impose its will upon the minority.[9] As a member
of the royal family, he participated in the ritualistic passage into manhood, including the painful ceremony of circumcision, which he described as "a trial
of bravery and stoicism." But for him and his fellow Xhosas the promise of
manhood was illusory, because they lacked as a "conquered people" the essential condition of "freedom and independence."[10]

As part of his formal training, Mandela was sent to Clarkebury, a Methodist
boarding school, where he followed in the footsteps of the distinguished black
leader and educator, Z. K. Matthews, who believed that education provided the

best means of integrating South African society and achieving the goal of racial peace and harmony.[11] Much like Matthews, who would later serve as Mandela's professor at Fort Hare College, Mandela was captivated by the buildings and grounds of the school, which were even more impressive than those of the regent's palace, and he enthusiastically immersed himself in the tradition of disciplined study, competitive games, and team sports. He was also deeply impressed with the austere yet caring headmaster of the school, Reverend Cecil Harris, who had dedicated his life to the education of young Africans, and to his wife, who introduced Mandela to the pleasures of freshly baked scones, while Mandela worked afternoons in the headmaster's garden. Since many of his peers could also lay claim to their own distinguished lineages, he also discovered that his privileged background was by no means unique.[12]

He eventually left boarding school to attend Healdtown, a Methodist college, whose character and physical presence exceeded Clarkesbury's. The "rigorous" academic and genteel social atmosphere also bred in Mandela and his classmates the same desire Gandhi had experienced in wanting to acquire the respect and status of an educated Englishman. But Mandela's search for his own identity was by no means limited to his quest for the virtues of a British education, as he fully understood the risks of becoming another example in a colonized line of "black Englishmen." By mingling with students from different tribes and backgrounds, he was exposed to new ideas, including intertribal marriage, which, when combined with his strong Xhosa roots, produced a powerful "feeling of kinship with other Africans."[13]

By the time he had arrived at the University College of Fort Hare at the age of twenty, Mandela felt in his own words that "I was being groomed for success in the world." Representing the apex of scholarship and learning for young black Africans, who came from near and distant parts of the continent, Fort Hare bred in its faculty and students a sense of elitism. Mandela was no exception. He too immersed himself in the varied life of a Fort Hare student, participating in cross-country events and testing his mettle as a thespian, when he played in an ironic example of historical symbolism the role of Lincoln's assassin, John Wilkes Booth. Finding himself lacking in certain social graces and sophistication, he decided to take up ballroom dancing and cultivate his own personal manners and impeccable appearance.[14]

While Mandela was at Fort Hare, the Second World War broke out. The conflict, which further politicized many of the students, also led to a discussion over Britain's fortunes in the war and the real meaning of the term "black Englishmen." More militant voices now came forward to argue that the British had oppressed the African people at the same time they were trying to "civilize" them. But as fate in an institution of higher learning would have it, the fortunes of the Great Powers were not the only issue of power at stake at Fort Hare. Student dissatisfaction with the food at the university led members of the student council to resign and call for a boycott of new elections if their demands were not met. As an elected representative to the council, Mandela resigned. When the authorities accepted the resignations and cleverly called for new elections, the climate shifted. As the one remaining dissident voice within the council, Mandela resigned for a second time, because he believed that while the majority of the student body had been present, the majority of those in attendance had not voted. Threatened with expulsion, he was allowed to go home over the summer break and rethink, in his words, the question of "sabotaging [his] academic career over an abstract moral principle that mattered very little." And in what eventually became the hallmark of his political career, he remained true to himself and refused to compromise.[15]

A few weeks after his return home, Mandela faced a new conflict over principle, and in this instance the potential for domestic bliss. The regent confronted him and Justice, the regent's son, with plans for arranged marriages for both the young men. Unequivocally opposed to the thought of such a marriage, Mandela, accompanied by Justice, managed to flee from the prospect. When the regent foiled their attempt to take a train to Johannesburg, they opted for a ride in a car that cost more than a train ticket and left them virtually broke. Still, Johannesburg made a powerful impression on Mandela, who described it as a "vast landscape of electricity, a city of light," which was also known as "eGoli, the city of gold."[16] But for a young man who was impressed by status and authority and membership in the African elite,[17] his fall from grace was "swift." In one fell swoop it seemed as if he had compromised his position at Fort Hare and antagonized his chief benefactor at home.[18]

THE SEARCH FOR HUMAN JUSTICE

But the glitter that was Johannesburg had been built upon the back of black Africans, who were exploited as cheap, "docile" labor in the gold mines of the Witwatersrand.[19] Set against the impoverished conditions of the black township or "Dark City" of Alexandra,[20] the contrast between affluent Johannesburg with its "For Europeans Only" signs and the local poor in the townships was stark and overwhelming.[21] The same could be said of virtually all South Africa's townships, including Orlando and Soweto, where monotonous rows of housing; a lack of stores, bakeries, and pharmacies; and inadequate social services determined the quality of people's lives.[22] Here, amidst a "frontier town" mentality, surrounded by black ghettoes and the attraction of a new bustling city,[23] Mandela met Walter Sisulu, a gentle, highly respected community leader, known for his compassion, generosity, and ability to listen to the concerns of others.[24] Sisulu and his wife Albertina had turned their home into a meeting place and refuge for political dissidents.[25] Sisulu remained Mandela's friend for life and arranged for Mandela to get a job as clerk at his law firm of Witkin, Sidelsky, and Eidelman. There, Mandela's "gadfly" role led him to the world of political activism by associating with members of the African National Congress (ANC), meeting with radical whites, and attending local meetings of the Communist party.[26]

While working at the law firm, Mandela continued his studies through correspondence courses and passed his final examination from the University of South Africa in 1942, enabling him to receive his B.A. and return to Fort Hare for his graduation. He returned, however, a much different man, who had expanded the informal part of his education by participating in a successful boycott against busfare increases. He also realized that his true interests lay not in the pursuit of a comfortable career, but in the more engaging aspects of political activism. To prepare for his entry into South Africa's political life, he became the only black student enrolled in the law faculty at the Afrikaans University of Witwatersrand, where he forged some of his most important lifelong relations with white Marxists, including Joe Slovo and his wife, Ruth First, and the rebellious antiestablishment Afrikaner lawyer, Bram Fischer.[27] As the scion of a wealthy Afrikaner family, Fischer proved to be the "most remarkable communist" of them all. He was also Mandela's first Afrikaner friend,[28] and he ably defended Mandela during the Treason Trial before going underground, where he was captured, convicted, and released from prison only a few weeks before he died from cancer.[29]

Mandela's circle of friendships also extended to Indian students, who along with his white companions enabled Mandela to broaden his political vision and realize that there were people of privilege who were willing "to sacrifice themselves for the cause of the oppressed."[30] Moreover, Mandela discovered that he too had occasionally acquiesced to "paternalistic" British attitudes and the creation of a black elite, which helped to perpetuate British rule by coopting blacks and encouraging them to feel welcome as "cultured," "civilized" members of the colonial system.[31] Although he viewed nationalism as an "unreliable friend and an unsafe historian" in an age in which technology and communication had begun to eradicate the "imaginary differences among people,"[32] he willingly embraced the cause of "militant African nationalism."[33] But he also adopted Gandhi's more global view that "no people in one part of the world could really be free while their brothers in other parts were still under foreign rule."[34]

The vehicle for his protest was the formation of a Youth League within the ANC whose conservative leadership continued to function in keeping with British thinking and manners. In words that mirrored Gandhi's thinking, one critic observed that "by the 1930s the ANC had declined into a virtual talking-shop."[35] As a tall, handsome, authoritative young man[36] with razor-sharp political instincts, Mandela was the quintessential antithesis of ANC's sclerotic image. Having grown impatient with the cautious political style of the old guard, he set out to build the Youth League into an organization that was based upon "grass-roots involvement" in the struggle for black rights and freedom.[37] During this period he also met his first wife, Evelyn Mase.[38] Their marriage, which produced two children, did not survive an elegant Mandela's wandering eye or his consuming commitment to his political work. She in turn became intensely devotional and embraced the Jehovah's Witnesses, which led to a clash over how the children should be raised, she favoring a more spiritual path, while he favored an emphasis on political education. Their irreconcilable values and lifestyles eventually led to their split in 1955 and to their divorce.[39]

The election of 1948 was a major turning point in the history of South Africa and the struggle for black freedom and independence.[40] The surprising triumph of a Nationalist Dutch Afrikaans government under the leadership of Dr. Daniel Malan and the introduction of *apartheid,* which stood for a policy of "complete racial separation,"[41] sent shock waves throughout South Africa. Malan's raising the specter of the "*swart gevaar,* the black peril,"[42] so antagonized blacks that even such a patient, tolerant figure from the old guard as Z. K. Matthews concluded that there was no hope in negotiating with Malan's racist government.[43] In brief, *apartheid,* meaning segregation, was built upon the premise of *baasskap* or "boss-ship" and by way of extension the much larger notion of white supremacy.[44] The formula was simple: "*Eie volk, eie taal, eie land*— Our own people, our own language, our own land," and it obviously echoed in tone and spirit the pernicious words and message of Adolf Hitler's venomous racism.[45] The Dutch Reformed Church also played a prominent role in underwriting the government's racist message, as did a powerful, influential "secret society, the Broederbond," meaning Band of Brothers.[46] What followed was a new wave of racist legislation, including the Prohibition of Mixed Marriages Act; the Immorality Act, outlawing sexual relations between blacks and whites; the Population and Registration Act, which defined groups by race; and the Group Areas Act, which divided living areas within cities on the basis of race.[47]

In response to the government's political offensive, the Youth League urged the ANC leadership to take action and engage the masses through a nonviolent, political campaign. In this particular context, it is important to note that Gandhi's failure to concern himself with African rights[48] did not prevent Mandela from studying Gandhi's campaigns of civil disobedience in South Africa and realizing the symbolic importance of passive resistance and the political meaning of going to jail for violating the law. Dissatisfied with the ANC failure to respond to the call for militant action,[49] the Youth League organized a coup forcing the "autocratic" president-general Dr. A. B. Xuma out of office and replacing him with a more sympathetic Dr. J. S. Moroka.[50] Reflecting the change in emphasis and direction, the New Program of Action called for more militant, less "decorous" forms of protest, including "boycotts, strikes, civil disobedience, and noncooperation." But on May 1, 1950, the call to action came from a different quarter. This time it originated with the Communist party and the Indian Congress, who called for a one-day general strike[51] in the form of a massive, popularly supported "stay-at-home."[52] Though genuinely impressed with the intense commitment of the communists and the Indians to the general strike, the ANC believed that they should concentrate on their own campaign and remained aloof from the political action. The government's response, however, was to crack down on the protesters, which led to the death of eighteen Africans and to the introduction of the Suppression of Commu-

nism Act, outlawing the Communist party,[53] extending the hated banning orders, curtailing freedom of movement and expression,[54] and prohibiting virtually every form of political protest.

The ANC now joined forces with the Indians and the communists in calling
for a National Day of Protest on June 26, 1950, and publicly dedicating themselves to the liberation of South Africa, "black, white, and yellow." In addition
to providing the Indians with much broader support, the new forms of collaboration enabled the ANC to gain valuable "organizational experience" and
"fund-raising" skills from their Indian allies.[55] The success of the protest led to
June 26 being designated Freedom Day within the movement. Mandela, who
now found himself totally consumed by the struggle, also discovered that his
attitudes toward communism were changing.[56] By expanding upon his earlier
exposure to Fabian socialism[57] and reading the works of Marx and Engels,
Lenin, Stalin, Mao, and other Marxist thinkers, he discovered in Marxism the
virtues of a communal life he had already encountered in African culture, the
appeal of an analytical perspective, based upon dialectical materialism with its
emphasis on built-in profit mechanisms within a capitalist economy, and the
desirability of reallocating wealth and resources from the haves to the have-
nots. He also acknowledged the Soviet Union's support for the liberation of
colonial peoples, and while he did not convert to communism, he realized that
he could work with communists.[58]

To counteract the government's campaign of formal, legal segregation, the
ANC with Mandela serving as Youth League president agreed to join with
South African communists and Indians in a Defiance Campaign scheduled for
June 26, 1952, in the spirit of the first Day of National Protest. Admitting to
having some reservations about the newly expanded political alliance, Mandela
nonetheless participated fully in the protest. But he was careful to acknowledge
that his willingness to embrace nonviolent protest based on Gandhi's model of
"passive resistance"[59] was not absolute but conditional, since the government's
overwhelming military and police superiority dictated the choice to be one of
nonviolence as a "practical necessity."[60] He also realized that he had to convey
to his followers that the very nature of nonviolent conflict ultimately required
"more courage and determination" than more violent forms of aggressive political action.[61] In his role as a political strategist, he also maintained that a boycott had to be viewed as a "tactical weapon to be employed if and when
objective conditions permit" and not as an inflexible principle to be applied irrespective of the immediate circumstances.[62] Since Mandela also believed that
the British in India were far "more realistic and farsighted" than the Afrikaners in South Africa,[63] he viewed the boycott more as a question of tactics than
principle, because the approach could readily be changed to accommodate
changes in the political situation.[64]

Responsible for the nationwide effort to recruit volunteers for the Defiance
Campaign, Mandela constituted a "magnificent figure," handsome and "im-
maculately dressed" in his elegantly tailored three-piece suits. Both blacks and

whites found him attractive, including, according to one white observer, "white women, [who] were turning to admire him."[65] It quickly became apparent to friend and foe alike that Mandela "was a born mass leader" who possessed a commanding, magnetic appeal.[66] And while the campaign failed to reverse any of the government's repressive racist legislation, it provided the government with cause for concern about the future of African-Indian cooperation. It also led to the arrest and trial of the campaign's leaders, including Mandela, under the terms of the Suppression of Communism Act. But the campaign had an equally powerful impact within the ANC, which was transformed from an elitist group into "a mass-based organization," where the previous "stigma" of imprisonment now became an emblem of courage. In reviewing his own role in recruiting, organizing, and speaking on behalf of the Defiance Campaign, Mandela recalled how he felt empowered by the events and his ability to "walk upright like a man, and look everyone in the eye with the dignity that comes from not having succumbed to oppression and fear."[67]

That dignity was tested again when Mandela and fifty-one other leaders of the ANC were banned. The detested practice of banning meant that the government could severely restrict the travel of individuals and prevent them from speaking or participating in the activities of named organizations. In Mandela's view banning was a form of "walking imprisonment,"[68] which created a yearning to escape from a form of "psychological claustrophobia."[69] In reflecting upon his own experience as a victim of government banning, Mandela described the treatment he received as an "unconvicted criminal" and how he had been legally transformed into a criminal not for what he "had done, but because of what [he] stood for."[70] The government's smothering tactics also led to a dramatic change in ANC strategy and to Mandela's drafting of the M-Plan, which was named for its author. According to the plan, the ANC would establish an intricate network of underground cells to prepare for the time when the government would outlaw its activities and force its membership to alter the nature of the struggle.[71] Confronted with more intense police surveillance and intimidation in the early 1950s, Mandela envisioned the M-Plan as a means of coordinating the movement's clandestine activity. Unfortunately, its cumbersome structure prevented the plan from living up to Mandela's expectations.[72] While Mandela was setting the M-Plan in motion, he also pursued his other life as a successful lawyer in Johannesburg and opened his own law firm, inviting Oliver Tambo—his friend, ally, and trusted confidante—to join him. They made for an interesting partnership. Unlike Tambo, who was more "reflective" and philosophically inclined, Mandela was a "passionate," "combative" man, who asserted himself whenever the occasion presented itself.[73] He would, for example, intentionally enter court through the whites-only entrance, much to the dismay of court officials.[74] And although practicing law in South Africa was not an easy task for a black man, he somehow managed to draw from the "racial tension in the courtroom"[75] and distinguish himself by his wry wit, defiant manner, and "flamboyant" courtroom style.[76]

Having declared Sophiatown a "black spot" on the South African landscape, the government's decision to move its people and make room for new white neighborhoods fanned the flames of resentment and dissent and presented the ANC with its next real challenge. In the atmosphere of "increasing repressiveness," Mandela emerged as a "rabble-rousing" speaker who ignited the crowds, redefined the movement, and moved in the direction of endorsing violence.[77] In an address known as "The No Easy Walk to Freedom" speech, which borrowed its title from an article by Jawaharlal Nehru, Mandela hailed the Defiance Campaign before members of the Transvaal conference of the ANC as a "battlefield" that unleashed powerful political and social forces among their people. He also took this strategic opportunity to outline his own views on the deteriorating physical and economic situation confronting blacks in South Africa.[78] Blacks, for example, were compelled to comb the countryside for work out of fear of being arrested as a result of their inability to pay the "poll tax." Moreover, those who were arrested often provided cheap labor to sustain the fortunes of white South African businesses and farms.[79] Mandela also endorsed the idea of replacing the "old forms of mass protest" with "new forms of political struggle"[80] and quoted Nehru's belief that "there is no easy walk to freedom anywhere and many of us will have to pass through the valley of the shadow of death again and again before we reach the mountain tops of our desires."[81]

In 1953 the passage of the Bantu Education Act extended the policy of racial subjugation. The new legislation clearly reflected the racist premises of Dr. Hendrik Verwoerd, the Minister of Bantu education, who rigidly believed that "There is no place for the Bantu in the European community above the level of certain forms of labor"[82] and that "natives" needed to "be taught from childhood . . . that equality with Europeans is not for them."[83] Viewing the act as a form of "education for ignorance" in which indoctrination prevailed over free inquiry,"[84] Mandela described the South African system as lifelong submission to menial labor and subordination to white man's rule.[85] Under Verwoerd the state also imposed a more rigorous system of censorship by tightening its grip on the press, literature, and entertainment and gaining control over the media, which became a powerful instrument for promoting anticommunism and rigid social conformity.[86] The information restraints were also accompanied by new, tougher forms of interrogation and torture, which pointed South Africa ever further in the direction of a police state.[87]

In 1955 the ANC was instrumental in coordinating the Congress of the People. A multiracial gathering that included Indians, Coloureds, and whites within a predominantly black audience, the congress was a unique event in South African history.[88] Mandela, who had approved the invitation to the congress, viewed it as a beautifully poetic document that spoke of "the wide lands and the narrow strips on which we toil, . . . of taxes and of cattle and of famine, . . . OF FREEDOM!, . . . OF COAL, GOLD, AND DIAMONDS!, . . . [and] of the dark shafts and the cold compounds,"[89] that undermined the cohesiveness of the family spirit. The congress itself created a "South Africa in microcosm" and openly reflected the socialist orientation of its leadership. Its Freedom Charter called upon all men and women irrespective of color and religion to create a free and democratic state, based upon popular rule with "EQUAL RIGHTS" for "ALL NATIONAL GROUPS," with the ability of all people to "SHARE IN THE COUNTRY'S WEALTH!" and participate in the distribution of the land among "THOSE WHO WORK IT!"[90] By calling for the nationalization of wealth and its distribution among the people, the Charter set forth a revolutionary "programme of action."[91]

Mandela's life as a public advocate for change increasingly thrust him into the political spotlight, and his life as a self-proclaimed "freedom fighter" caused him to reflect upon the need "to remain in touch with his own roots" and guard against the temptations of the "hurly-burly of city life."[92] He also confronted the convoluted nature of his world when he wanted to give money to a white woman begging on the street, only to realize that in South Africa "to be poor and black was normal, to be poor and white was a tragedy."[93] When the government announced its plan to create "bantustans" or homelands on marginal land with poor soil and inhospitable living conditions as separate territories of development for the black people of South Africa, the intention was clear.[94] The Nationalist government had decided to turn South Africa into a patchwork of "ethnic enclaves" or "Reserves" in "poverty-stricken areas" in violation of the principles of "*democracy*," "*sovereignty*," and "self-determination."[95] Supported by the tribal chiefs, who viewed their authority as hereditary and not elective,[96] the government exploited the divisions within the African community and pursued a policy of *apartheid* on a grand scale[97] by relegating 70 percent of the population to live on only 13 percent of the land.[98]

Confronted with this challenge, Mandela turned to the pen and published a series of articles in the left-leaning journal *Liberation* from June 1953 to May 1959,[99] outlining his political views. He cataloged the widespread human suffering brought about by inadequate food, disease, poor medical care, and people's hunger for land. He also condemned the abusive labor policy, which contributed to the cycle of misery and frustration among South Africa's blacks.[100] He openly criticized the government's desire to create a pool of migrant laborers, separated from their families and forced to live in hostels as a means of undermining the emergence of a powerful African labor movement. And he condemned the "forcible detention of Africans . . . for spurious statutory offenses" as a means of creating a "vast market of cheap labor"[101] to feed South Africa's economic expansion. He and his colleagues also exposed white reluctance to advocate the "democratic principle [of]' one adult, one vote'" and labeled the Liberal Party's "high-sounding principles" of economic growth and expansion reactionary, because they perpetuated the *de facto* existence of the underclass.[102] Moreover, he openly accused the white Liberal government, despite its denials of being inspired by any of Hitler's ideas,[103] of being a "fascist regime" and of raising the "specter of Belsen and Buchenwald" in South Africa.[104]

On December 5, 1956, Mandela and other members of the ANC leadership were arrested for high treason and sent to jail. Mandela would later admit that his own "foolhardy behavior" and inattention to detail had contributed to his arrest.[105] When the accused appeared for their trial, their vans were greeted with a triumphant salute from ANC supporters. In court they were forced to sit inside a cage hemmed in "like wild beasts," until the court acceded to the protests of the defense to have the cage removed. In presenting the charges, the prosecution cited the Freedom Charter as evidence of communist intent and of a desire to overthrow the state.[106] Faced with the charge of violent revolution and aware that the scales of justice were tilted against them in a predominantly Afrikaner court, the defendants chose to turn their trial into a countertrial and indict the government, its unjust racial policies, and the tyrannical domination of 13 million blacks by 3 million whites.

During a recess in the preparatory phases of the trial, Mandela happened to spot a beautiful young woman, Winnie Nomzano, on the streets of Johannesburg, only to see her again in his office a few weeks later. What followed was a whirlwind romance in which Mandela by his own admission both courted Winnie Nomzano and politicized her.[107] In love and in awe of a man who was able to inspire such "confidence, faith, and courage," she simultaneously entered his life and the political world of the ANC.[108] He in turn found new hope in their relationship and marriage, at a time when women had become openly active in the freedom struggle and had begun to contribute new strength to the movement.[109] He believed, however, that despite an upsurge in political activism Winnie found it difficult to fashion "her own identity in my shadow."[110] Their union produced three children, who possessed their father's warmth and magnanimity, despite his reputation as a stern authority figure and disciplinarian,[111] and the crusading, restless spirit of their mother.

Although the outcome of the Treason Trial, as it came to be known, hinged on the government's ability to prove its case that the ANC had in fact "plotted violence,"[112] the future of the trial was also influenced by developments and events outside the courtroom. One such development was a defection by "exclusivists," who, under the influence of Marcus Garvey's doctrines of "Africa for the Africans" and "Hurl the Whiteman into the sea," broke from the ANC and in 1959 formed the Pan Africanist Congress (PAC) led by Robert Sobukwe.[113] But while Mandela also emphasized the importance of maintaining African leadership and control of the movement, he preferred to alter the tone of Garvey's message to read as follows: "While I was not prepared to hurl the white man into the sea, I would have been perfectly happy if he had climbed aboard his steamships and left the continent of his own volition."[114]

From the very beginning, the relations between the two organizations were, in Mandela's words, "more competitive than cooperative."[115] Opposed to collaboration with whites, Indians, and communists, the PAC insisted on a black movement for black people only and accused the ANC of "selling out" to foreign interests.[116] It is interesting to note that although PAC's conduct hardly made them the darlings of the South African government, Mandela believed that their avowed anticommunism made them "the darlings of the Western press and the American State Department."[117] In March 1960 PAC announced its own pass campaign, calling upon blacks to leave their passes at home and surrender peacefully to government authorities.[118] What followed was a cycle of protest, repression, and the imposition of martial law, following the eruption of the Sharpeville massacre. Of the sixty-nine Africans dead, most had been shot in the back while trying to flee the confrontation. According to Mary Benson, Mandela's biographer, "the people went berserk . . . as riots swept the country." News of the bloody event penetrated the courtroom and reverberated around the world, prompting the international community to follow events in South Africa more closely and the UN Security Council to pass a resolution holding the South African government responsible for the shootings.[119]

Meanwhile, Mandela was arrested at home as part of the official crackdown and placed in a cell where the stench, cockroaches, and vomit-soiled blankets served as a rude introduction to a new political reality. In keeping with the *apartheid* spirit, food was rationed, with blacks getting smaller proportions than Coloureds or Indians. Blacks were also denied bread on the assumption the blacks did not like bread, because it represented a "more sophisticated . . . 'Western' taste." Sharpeville also provoked a government crackdown, including the decision to outlaw both the ANC and PAC under the Suppression of Communism Act.[120]

The Sharpeville massacre also marked a turning point for the opposition, as younger, more radical black political leaders advocated going underground and adopting more violent guerrilla tactics.[121] It also had an impact on the significance of the Treason Trial,[122] which now became, in Mandela's words, "a test of the power of a moral idea versus an immoral one."[123] He, in fact, used the trial as a platform to denounce imperialism, lecture on commercial exploitation, and expose the fallacy of foreign investment as a means of raising people's standard of living by citing "low wages, . . . poverty, . . . misery, . . . illiteracy," and the rise in "squalid tenements" as proof to the contrary.[124] When the government, basing sections of their case on Mandela's writings and speeches,[125] tried to portray him as a communist, he took the opportunity to thank the communists in his testimony for the support the ANC had received, while scrupulously making the point that he was not a communist. He also warned of a new, different type of foreign intervention in which Europeans would pay greater attention to the ANC's economic pressure in South Africa.[126] When the court finally rendered its verdict and declared the accused not guilty, it did so on the grounds that the government had failed to prove that the ANC had "acquired or adopted a policy to overthrow the state by violence," irrespective of all its inflammatory rhetoric. The victory, however, was bittersweet because Mandela and his colleagues realized that in future proceedings the government would make sure that the courts would return a guilty verdict.[127]

Following the Treason Trial, Mandela made an electrifying appearance[128] at the All-In African Conference, which served as a "unity forum" for a loosely knit alliance of opposition groups. Made up primarily of blacks, but including some white representatives, the conference called upon the government to convene a "national convention." If the government refused to comply, the participants set in motion plans for a three-day stay-at-home to begin on May 29, 1961.[129] As the secretary of the national action committee, Mandela was responsible for drafting the letter to the government and coordinating the stay-at-home. When the protest drew less support than had been expected, Mandela decided to call it off in its second day, despite what he described as a show of "solid and massive support throughout the country,"[130] which included enthusiastic university students, "Coloured People," and the "entire Indian community," who participated in the action.[131] He did, however, single out the "treacherous" press for its biased reporting and the malevolent police for its "fraudulent" announcement of the stay-at-home's collapse.[132] He also began to question whether it was "politically correct to continue preaching peace and non-violence when dealing with a Government whose barbaric practices have brought so much suffering and misery to Africans."[133] On behalf of the people, who produce the mass of wealth of the country, he argued that militant "non-collaboration is the weapon we must use to bring down the government."[134] Moreover, he also came to the conclusion that since he had been forcibly "denied the right to live a normal life," he had no choice but to go underground, "live the life of an outlaw,"[135] organize a guerrilla campaign, and embrace the use of violence as a political weapon.

For Mandela "living underground require[d] a seismic psychological lift," which turned him into a "creature of the night." As South Africa's "Black Pimpernel," an obvious adaptation of the fictional Scarlet Pimpernel of the French Revolution, he surreptitiously made his way through the country in an assortment of motley disguises. With all his energy now focused on making the case for revolution in the immediate political environment, he believed, as had Fidel Castro, that the movement should not rigorously follow "textbook conditions" or slavishly adhere to the Marxist concept of inherent contradictions in the social structure to justify the use and timing of violent political action. What was most important was to lead the people and not allow them to move ahead of the revolutionary leadership.[136] It is interesting to note that in his reading of Edgar Snow's *Red Star over China* Mandela believed that "it was Mao's determination and nontraditional thinking that led him to victory."[137] To achieve its goal, the ANC decided to form a new organization, *Umkhonto we Sizwe* (the Spear of the Nation), also known as MK, which was to remain separate from the ANC and organize the underground struggle against South Africa's racist regime through the use of violent means, including explosives. In June 1961 Mandela released a letter in which he spoke with conviction, passion, and the charismatic voice of an inspirational leader, quoting Abraham Lincoln to support the creation in South Africa of "a democratic government of the people, by the people, and for the people." In his letter he also announced his refusal to submit to arrest and declared his commitment to fight the government because "The struggle is my life. I will continue fighting for freedom until the end of my days."[138]

Mandela found temporary "sanctuary" in the LiliesleafFarm located in Rivonia, a northern suburb of Johannesburg, which provided a temporary safe haven for MK's guerrillas within the confines of what he described as an "idyllic bubble." The decision to pursue sabotage as the primary form of violence reflected the movement's desire to inflict as little harm as possible on individuals and to focus its attack on military targets, communications, and transportation as a means of frightening away foreign capital and investments and calling attention to the plight of South Africa's black community. MK chose December 16, the day Afrikaners traditionally celebrated their victory over the Zulus in 1838, to stage its attack. In this instance the explosions hardly constituted a celebration for whites, although they did serve as a signal to both blacks and whites that a "powerful spear" was now aimed at the "heart of white power."[139] Once again, the movement insisted that it had been forced to resort to violence because the government "had interpreted the peacefulness of the movement as weakness."[140]

In February 1962 Mandela led the ANC delegation to the Pan African Freedom Movement conference in Addis Ababa. The trip, which was designed to search for outside support, funds, and opportunities for military training, provided Mandela with an opportunity to see more of the world, experience the absence of color bars in public places, observe a black man doing a "white man's job" flying an airplane, and luxuriate in the thrill of feeling like "a free man . . . for the first time in my life." In words that recalled the legacy of Martin Luther King, Jr., he described the feeling of "being judged . . . not by the color of my skin but by the measure of my mind and character." In Ethiopia he was deeply moved by the presence of Haile Selassie and the sight of black generals commanding black soldiers honoring black leaders in the presence of a black head of state.[141] In Addis Ababa he delivered a passionate speech, identified by the phrase, "A Land Ruled by the Gun," in which he attributed the shift "away from the path of peace and non-violence" to the minority government's willful determination to maintain "its authority over the majority by force and violence."[142] To reinforce the sense of dedication among his own people to the goals of national liberation, he stressed his unwavering commitment to popular self-reliance and his faith in the people of South Africa to combine their efforts and engage in "united action" to achieve their freedom.[143]

In Egypt Mandela learned more about ancient African art and architecture and contemplated the impact Gamal Abdel Nasser's socialist reforms would have on the people of South Africa. But it was in Algeria that he encountered the model of a struggle by an indigenous people against colonial rule imposed from abroad that most closely corresponded to the situation at home. The underground freedom fighter then made his way across Europe to visit England, where his candid anglophile assessment praised the style and manners of the British, the quality of British officials he met, and the majesty of Westminster Abbey, the tower of Big Ben, and the houses of Parliament. On his way home he stopped in Ethiopia for military training and affirmed his belief that military training must be combined with appropriate forms of political training "to create a just and fair society."[144]

THE PRISON YEARS

Mandela's brief freedom ended abruptly on August 5, 1962, after his return to South Africa. Charged with having left the country illegally and having incited workers to strike, Mandela decided to represent himself in court to accentuate the symbolic plight of a "black man in a white man's court."[145] When he entered the same Old Synagogue that had served as the site of the Treason Trial in a resplendent Xhosa leopard-skin *kaross,* the gallery in the courtroom shouted "*Amandla!*" "Power!" and "*Ngawethu,*" "The power is ours!"[146] He then questioned the legitimacy of laws made in a Parliament in which he and his people had no representation and attacked the white magistrate and white prosecutor as a part of a system that denied his people the right to vote and prevented him from obtaining a trial "by his own kith and kin, by his own flesh and blood." He argued that "equality before the law . . . is meaningless and misleading"[147] and called attention to the plight of black Africans who had to settle for morsels of food that fell from the "tables of men with White skin"[148] or, in the words of Dr. Xuma, who had lobbied the UN on behalf of starving Africans: "When we ask for bread, we get lead."[149] Mandela later accused the government of launching "savage attacks on the rights and living conditions of the African people"[150] and of failing to live up to the standards of the "civilized world."[151]

By comparison, he recalled the peaceful democratic rule of his youth, where there were no classes and the land belonged to all the people. He made clear that in a matter involving a conflict between conscience and law, he could do only one thing and stand by his conscience. He again accused the government of having "provoked violence by employing violence to meet our nonviolent demands"[152] and warned that government "violence can only . . . breed counterviolence" and lead to a settling of the "dispute between the government and my people" through force and violence.[153] He concluded by condemning "race discrimination" and "racial arrogance"[154] and declaring that he would remain steadfast in his struggle to eradicate all forms of social injustice.[155] The five-year sentence he received might have led some to question his resolve, particularly when confronted with the deplorable conditions in South African jails, the brutal isolation in which "every hour seemed like a year," and the suffocating stagnancy of prison life, which "robs you of your freedom . . . and . . . identity." In Mandela's own words: "Nothing is more dehumanizing than the absence of human companionship."[156] But while the trial deprived him of his freedom, it

also marked the beginning of his international reputation.[157] The dehumanization process, which forced Mandela as "a life-loving man to live like a monk,"[158]
continued when he was transferred from Johannesburg to the prison at Robben
Island off the Cape of Good Hope, and he and his fellow prisoners suffered the
indignity of having to use a "sanitary bucket" while "shackled together" in a
moving vehicle. When they arrived at the island, the guards urinated on them
from above and attempted to intimidate them verbally and physically, which
prompted Mandela to respond with "bravado" to counteract his fear, by threatening to take one of his warders to court.[159]

In the summer of 1963 Mandela learned that government authorities had
discovered Rivonia, the small farm outside Johannesburg that had served as a
safe haven for the ANC leadership. Mandela also learned that he and his colleagues had been charged with sabotage and that they now faced the death
penalty. The evidence included the plans for guerrilla warfare, known as Operation Mayibuye, and documents in Mandela's own handwriting. The virtual
lack of security at the farm and the "careless" way the conspirators conducted
themselves underscored their amateurish behavior and provided the prosecution with powerful evidence for their case.[160] This time the proceedings,
known as the Rivonia Trial, attracted cheering, supportive crowds and journalists and government representatives from around the world. When the new
charges were read, they clearly bore the ideological stamp of the 1960s, with
references to guerrilla warfare, foreign influence, and plots to stage a violent
communist revolution.[161] Eager to whip up a public mood of fear and hysteria,[162] the government made it seem as if the red menace had captured the heart
and soul of the revolution.

When it came time for the accused to enter a plea, they all pleaded "not
guilty" and intimated that it was the government's behavior that was criminal.[163] They also decided to use the trial as a "platform to highlight [their]
grievances"[164] and to continue the struggle by different means. When Mandela
rose to make his case before the court, he firmly denied that South Africa had
fallen under the influence of foreigners and communists. He did, however,
admit to having "planned sabotage" and defended his action as the best means
"to defend ourselves against force." He then elaborated on the ANC's views on
African nationalism and its inclusive character, which was in direct opposition
to Marcus Garvey's less tolerant call to oust the white man from Africa. He also
returned to the topic of communism; acknowledged cooperation between the
two groups, who shared a common goal to put an end to "white supremacy";
and observed that the communists "were the only political group in South
Africa . . . to treat Africans as human beings."[165] But he was also careful to draw
an important distinction between the communists, who "sought to emphasize
class distinctions," and the ANC, which sought "to harmonize them."[166] When
he addressed the topic of having cooperated with the communists, he insisted
that cooperation in pursuit of a common goal did not constitute "proof of a
complete community of interests."[167] And as a high-profile example of such co-

operation, he cited the political alliance linking Winston Churchill, Franklin D. Roosevelt, and Joseph Stalin during World War II. Still, while he acknowledged the influence of Marxist thought on his political ideas, he disagreed with communists, who dismissed the Western traditions of representative government as "undemocratic and reactionary." He also acknowledged that he admired the parliamentary institutions of the West with their commitment to constitutional rights and judicial integrity[168] and insisted in marvelously synthetic fashion that he remained free "to borrow the best from the West and from the East."[169]

On the thorny question of violence and plans for sabotage, Mandela emphasized that once the government denied the black community an avenue of "peaceful protest," the movement decided to undertake "violent forms of political struggle and . . . form Umkhonto we Sizwe."[170] And while he acknowledged that in the face of government oppression individuals often found themselves involved in the activities of both the ANC and *Umkhonto,* he drew a firm distinction between ANC as a nonviolent mass political organization and *Umkhonto,* which as a "small organization" was committed to sabotage and responsible for recruiting its own members.[171] He also managed to contextualize the source of black unrest when he spoke of poverty, malnutrition, disease, unequal education, the lack of a "living wage," and job practices that separated workers from their families and the implacable perpetuation of the hated pass laws,[172] all of which contributed to the degradation of human values and the deterioration of individual and collective morality. Moreover, the blind pursuit of these benighted policies resulted in the institutionalization of black inferiority and a growing fear of democracy among the white minority population. After four hours of presenting his views and extolling the virtues of a free and democratic society, he finished by proclaiming in an extraordinary act of political eloquence that it was an "ideal for which I am prepared to die."[173] Given the issues at stake and the nature of the proceedings, the trial captured worldwide attention. The UN Security Council, minus the abstentions of Britain and the United States, voted to urge South Africa to put an end to the trial and grant amnesty to the accused and those imprisoned for crimes under *apartheid.* At the University of London, students elected Mandela president of the Union, while others joined a sympathetic vigil at Saint Paul's Cathedral.[174]

During the course of the proceedings it became clear that the defense had failed to prove that a definite date had been set for initiating guerrilla warfare and that the two organizations remained separate. As the world watched, Judge Quartus de Wet rendered his verdict and pronounced all of the defendants guilty on all counts. The next day the defendants appeared before the judge for sentencing. When he declared that this was not a case of "high treason" and sentenced them to life in prison, the men, who had just looked death directly in the face, were jubilant. As representatives of a noble cause, they had won support from common people and powerful figures throughout the world, including trade unions and dockworkers; members of the British Parliament and the U.S.

Congress, who marched and protested; Soviet president Leonid Brezhnev, who pleaded for leniency; and Adlai Stevenson, U.S. ambassador to the United Nations, who wrote in opposition to the death sentence.[175]

Upon his return to Robben Island, Mandela continued to confront the layers of institutional racism and the degrading nature of prison life. Deprived of hot showers and sharing his cell with a lightbulb that burned both day and night, Mandela confronted the inhumane conditions, psychological abuse, and "corrupt and demeaning" classification system, which placed black political prisoners at the bottom of the prison hierarchy[176] and required blacks to wear short trousers to remind them that they were "boys." The damp cold, pervasive isolation, and grim reality of having to spend the entire day seated in the prison courtyard crushing stones with a hammer were constant reminders of the hostile environment.[177] Cut off from the outside world and allowed to write only one letter of 500 words to his family every six months, Mandela and his fellow prisoners waged their own internal war against routine, repression, and despair.[178]

"Noncontact visits" by family members, lasting only thirty minutes and carefully monitored by prison guards, severely restricted the level of emotional exchange and topics of conversation. The visits passed so quickly that they acquired enormous emotional significance, since it would often be years before the authorities would approve another visit.[179] Other vicissitudes of life continued to penetrate Mandela's existence, including the death of his mother and the death of his son Madiba after an automobile accident. Both losses occasioned deep feelings of guilt for having put the people's welfare before that of his own family. When he asked if he could attend his mother's funeral and that of his son, he received the same insensitive, implacable response: "Permission . . . denied."[180]

The inmates' leperlike existence continued when they were sent to work in the glare of a lime quarry without sunglasses, until they were granted permission to purchase their own. As conditions slowly improved over the years, it was Mandela who emerged as the natural spokesman for the group, and his persistent demands to the prison administration gained valuable privileges for the inmates, including the right to enroll in correspondence courses and study for degrees. In Mandela's words: "At night, our cell block seemed more like a study hall than a prison." In time the prisoners received stand-up desks, which were eventually lowered, and stools to improve the quality of their study time.[181] They even established a system in which inmates taught courses to one another and established their own university. Mandela, for example, taught a course in political economy, which reflected his progressive political views and socialist perspective.[182]

As the insatiable search for information about the outside world increased, newspapers rapidly became a precious commodity. Whenever possible, the prisoners would search the trash, steal copies from warders, and arrange for a network of minuscule copies, carefully copied by hand, to circulate among the inmates. They also devised ingenious means of communications to coordinate their protests and air their complaints, including the use of false bottoms in matchboxes to relay messages, the placing of messages wrapped in plastic tape under the lip of toilet bowls, and the use of milk to write invisible messages in a "tiny, coded script." They even established a "clandestine communications committee," which enabled them to share information through the assistance of some sympathetic warders. One of their protests, a food strike, triggered a totally unexpected result, when the prisoners learned that warders had engaged in their own food strike, not out of sympathy for the prisoners, but out of their own desire for better food.[183] As an advocate of prisoners' rights, Mandela drew upon one of his favorite strategies, dating back to his early law office experience, when he learned to pepper authorities with so many requests and interrogatories that a hostile accusation would be dropped or a basic need would be met.[184] But his forceful personality and unforgiving candor also revealed the "dogmatic," "overbearing" side of his personality, which he frequently visited upon his colleagues when they engaged in fierce political discussions and debate.[185]

But more than anything else, it was solitary confinement that enabled relentless time to play tricks on the mind. The strict regimen and seclusion of being cut off from one's circle of friends, coupled with meager portions of food limited to servings of rice water three times a day, taxed both mind and body. But amidst the seclusion and deprivation, Mandela refused to give in, insisting that "your spirit can be full even when your stomach is empty."[186] Moreover, when he and his friends were allowed to return, they were able to draw upon each other's solace, support, and courage and the strength of their individual and collective determination "to stand firm."[187]

The rigors of prison life also greatly depended on one's warder. Mandela, for example, was blessed during many, but not all, of his prison years, one of the decent men being James Gregory, with whom he established a close personal relationship based on mutual respect and admiration.[188] In a true gesture of human understanding and reconciliation, Mandela even invited three of his former warders to attend his inauguration as president of South Africa in 1994.[189] But not all warders could claim to be as humane. Mandela's description of Van Rensburg, a crude, sadistic Afrikaner, who sported a swastika tattoo on his wrist, was particularly chilling. As a model of gross behavior and as an expression of utter contempt for black prisoners, Van Rensburg would regularly make it a practice to urinate beside them when they were about to eat lunch at the quarry.[190] Relief, however, periodically arrived in the form of visits by members of Parliament or foreign delegations. In one such case, Mandela registered his disapproval of Van Rensburg's behavior in his presence, which resulted in the warder's being transferred back to the mainland, making the inmates' lives more tolerable.[191] On another occasion Mandela convinced a group of visiting judges to recommend the removal of an equally despicable commanding officer, Colonel Piet Badenhorst, who threatened Mandela in front of the judges. Mandela's penetrating observation, "If he can threaten me here, in your presence, you can imagine what he does when you are not here," sealed Badenhorst's fate. Later on, Mandela would argue that it was not Badenhorst's inhumanity that was at fault but an "inhuman system," which "rewarded . . . brutish behavior."[192]

As the prison regime began to relax, Mandela was able to rekindle his interest in drama, dating back to his portrayal of John Wilkes Booth at Fort Hare. In his new role he emerged as Creon in Sophocles' *Antigone,* a character Mandela interpreted as both wise and "patriotic" and willing to put the greater good of society above the bonds of individual loyalty. He also hailed Antigone as "a freedom fighter, for she defied the law on the grounds that it was unjust."[193] When the prisoners suddenly were moved from the lime quarry to comb seaweed from the beach, Mandela and his comrades enjoyed a new sense of freedom and an opportunity to dine daily on salt water delicacies, including Mandela's favorite, abalone.[194] But the sea was a fickle mistress, and it continued to serve as the "uncrossable moat" surrounding Robben Island."[195] In an attempt to straddle that barrier and provide people with a record of the struggle, Mandela began work on his memoirs, only to have a buried draft accidentally discovered by prison officials, which led to the suspension of his study privileges for no less than four years.[196]

In the wake of the brutal suppression of the Soweto uprisings in 1976, Mandela also received his first look at some of the young militants who made up the Black Consciousness Movement of the 1960s. Stephen Biko, who led the BCM, managed to fill the vacuum created by the imprisonment of the ANC leadership[197] by appealing directly to the concept of "black assertiveness,"[198] based on the inner dynamics of the individual and not on loyalty to an organization. As the head of SASO, the black South African Student Organization, Biko's movement indicted white racism on its own terms and castigated black liberals for believing in the efficacy of a "gradualist approach to integration." By appealing to the culture of alienation surrounding young South African blacks and addressing the need for blacks to overcome their "inferiority complex," Biko invoked the credo of self-reliance and called upon militant blacks to "overthrow the present pigmentocracy" and rally around the slogan "Black Man You Are on Your Own."[199] Beginning as a "cultural awakening process" designed to provide blacks with hope for the future, the movement soon became overtly political and challenged the government's authority.[200] The violent circumstances surrounding Biko's death[201] in the custody of police officials only served to antagonize and radicalize Biko's followers. The rise of the Black Consciousness movement, however, created a generation gap between the ANC and Biko's followers.[202] Mandela, for example, remained uncomfortable with the attitudes, tactics, and style of this new breed of black revolutionary. In his words: "these angry and audacious young people were [the] progeny" of Bantu Education, who "had come back to haunt its creators." Rejecting their "exclusionary . . . philosophy," he continued to mediate amongst the various prison factions and stress to the newcomers the importance of taking a more inclusive approach.[203]

As the political climate continued to change within South Africa and foreign pressure began to bear down on the plight of the victims of *apartheid*, physical labor suddenly came to a halt. The effect was "liberating." With time to spare, Mandela was now able to cultivate his own garden, enjoy playing tennis on the newly painted Wimbledon that appeared upon the cement of the prison court-yard, and sustain his exercise program and disciplined regime of running in place. He nourished his soul on the works of Nadine Gordimer, John Stein-beck, and Leo Tolstoy. Information of the outside world also trickled in via carefully censored news broadcasts across the prison's intercom. The inmates were able to see films, including *The King and I*, highlighting the cultural dif-ferences between East and West; *Cleopatra,* which raised the issue of Western propaganda's unwillingness to portray her as an African woman; and the stormiest of all, *Hell's Angels,* after which Black Consciousness members de-fended the bikers' rebellious actions against authority despite their "unsavory" ways, while the older prisoners felt uncomfortable with what they perceived as the film's amorality. The film obviously had a powerful impact on Mandela, who recalled wondering if he "would appear to be a political fossil," when he finally emerged from the confines of his prison existence. As the entertainment improved, so too did the food. There was more meat and vegetables.[204] Sports began to flourish within the walls and provided the prisoners with an outlet for their tension, boredom, and frustration. A soccer league was formed, rugby matches organized, and even cricket was awarded its appointed time,[205] as were volleyball and table tennis. Prisoners formed their own band; choral singing was encouraged. And Christmas became, in Mandela's words, the "one day of the year, . . . when the prison authorities showed any goodwill towards men."[206]

Important mental nutrition also arrived in the form of newspapers, which Mandela once described as the "most precious contraband on Robben Is-land."[207] Although newspapers had been banned from printing Mandela's pic-ture or any words he had ever said or written, when the prisoners were able to buy newspapers in 1980, they spotted the headline FREE MANDELA! and a peti-tion for his release and that of other political prisoners. He was even nomi-nated to the ceremonial position of Chancellor of the University of London and finished second to another royal, who happened to be the daughter of the Queen of England.[208]

The physical beginning of Mandela's deliverance began in 1982, when he unexpectedly left his craggy island home of eighteen years and was transferred to the Pollsmoor Prison in Cape Town on the South African mainland.[209] Compared to the prison at Robben Island, Pollsmoor was a "five star hotel" with "palatial" accommodations.[210] The conditions surrounding Mandela's ex-istence improved in every respect, including the beginning of "contact visits," which enabled him after years of separation to touch Winnie's hand.[211] These gestures of goodwill eventually extended to drives through the city of Cape Town, when Mandela, who "felt like a curious tourist in a strange land,"[212] suddenly confronted himself alone and "unguarded . . . for the first time in twenty-two years."[213] In 1984 the new minister of justice, Kobie Coetsee, whom Mandela both liked and admired, began testing the waters by allowing Mandela to visit with prominent foreign political and legal officials.[214]

But despite the changed mood and circumstances, Mandela still waged the political struggle. For example, in an interview with journalists from the conservative *Washington Times,* Mandela had to defend himself against claims that he was a communist and point out the difference between Martin Luther King's ability to work within a democratic system, which affirmed constitutional rights and upheld "nonviolent protest," and the nature of the South African "police state with a constitution that enshrined inequality." When faced with a government offer of freedom in return for his unconditional rejection of "violence as a political instrument," Mandela declined. He insisted, as he would throughout the entire process leading up to his release, that it was the government that had initiated the violence and that the ANC had been forced to reply in kind. Moreover, given the genesis of the problem, he believed that the government should be the first to give guarantees that it would refrain from violence. He also insisted that the existing process of discussions was fatally compromised, since "only free men can negotiate."[215] Mandela's attitude did not mean, however, that he was reluctant to act independently from the members of his group. When he wrote that "there are times when a leader must move out ahead of the flock, go off in a new direction, confident that he is leading his people the right way," he clearly staked out his position.[216] Part of Mandela's political genius also lay in his ability to "revert to a more moderate position"[217] and seek out "unifying points among people of differing views," a gift that mirrored his tolerance and ability to listen.[218] And it was the combination of his "diplomatic strength and refusal to accept a conditional release," coupled with de Klerk's open style and risk-taking leadership, that initiated the historic change in South African politics.[219]

International concern over Mandela's status and the future of *apartheid* led the British Commonwealth of Nations to send an Eminent Persons Group to visit Mandela in prison. Neatly attired in a shirt and tie and a newly tailored pinstriped suit, Mandela was greeted by the somewhat prophetic remark from the prison commander: "Mandela, you look like a prime minister now, not a prisoner." In his meeting with the group, Mandela spoke to the root causes of violence and reassured the delegation that he was a "South African nationalist, not a Communist," that he opposed a violent solution to the racial problem, and that he was committed to a multiracial solution[220] and a more "accommodating" multiracial perspective[221] in the form of what he later described as a "non-racial democracy."[222]

As his relationship with Coetsee continued to grow, Mandela became more convinced of the government's goodwill and his own independent role in achieving a solution and having to present his colleagues with a "fait accompli."[223] In subsequent discussions with government authorities, Mandela continued to argue that when confronted with government violence, the ANC had resorted to violence in "self-defense." Nor would he take orders from the government and dissociate with the communists, who had supported the ANC. And he cleverly asked what would make him take orders from the communists, if the present government was unable to change his views. He also reassured his interlocutors that their fear of majority rule was misplaced and stated that in a multiracial state, belonging to both white and black South Africans: "We do not want to drive you into the sea."[224]

In 1988 as sanctions against South Africa mounted in Europe and the United States and foreign investors became wary of conditions in South Africa, Mandela was transferred to a lovely cottage, which he aptly described as a "halfway house between prison and freedom," that came equipped with its own cook, modern appliances, and a swimming pool.[225] In the summer of 1989 Mandela had a meeting with South African president P. W. Botha, who was widely known for his stiff-necked and irascible nature. With Mandela, however, he was thoroughly gracious, even "deferential," as he politely served tea to his celebrity guest.[226] But it was left to Nobel Peace laureate Archbishop Desmond Tutu, to capture the real irony of the moment, when he puckishly observed: "You could say it is the outgoing president meeting someone who is going to succeed him."[227]

When Mandela tried to establish some common ground by drawing an analogy between the struggle of blacks in South Africa and the Boer rebellion against the British, Botha demurred, maintaining that their "rebellion had been a quarrel among brothers, whereas [Mandela's] struggle was a revolutionary one." Though the talks remained inconclusive, Mandela walked away believing that they had, in fact, in Botha's words, crossed the Rubicon and there could be "no turning back."[228] A month later, however, Botha resigned as president, and F. W. de Klerk succeeded him. De Klerk quickly sent out signals that the future was now. He opened South African beaches to blacks and put an end to segregated parks, restaurants, theaters, and government facilities. De Klerk also decided to give Mandela his freedom, although he wanted to extract a commitment from him on suppressing violence and his acceptance of a formula on group rights as a means of preserving white minority rights. But Mandela refused to accept de Klerk's terms. Even the last-minute wrangling over the details of Mandela's release could not divert the outcome. The die was clearly cast; and Mandela's trial by imprisonment was about to come to an end.[229]

"FREE AT LAST"

On February 11, 1990, Mandela walked through the gates of Pollsmoor Prison with a clenched fist victory salute from his right hand and Winnie's hand in his left. After twenty-seven years in prison he was greeted by a swarm of international media and an audience of exuberant supporters, who saw "their hour of deliverance in his face."[230] Once again, his charismatic presence exuded hope and self-confidence. To cite the words of Archbishop Tutu, Mandela had what black South Africans called "shadow," "substance," or "presence," which contributed to his "regal" stature and demeanor.[231] In an emotional speech to his followers, he thanked them for the sacrifices they had made to obtain his release and placed himself in their hands for the rest of his life. In his press conference he spoke of the need to secure political rights for blacks and reminded his international audience that although he was "out of jail," he "was not yet free."[232] His dignified bearing and human compassion also revealed the heart and soul of a man who could "walk with kings and . . . walk with beggars."[233] The next morning he spoke before a crowd of more than 100,000 people in a soccer stadium in Soweto. By no means a great orator, he addressed the yearnings of the gathered throng in disciplined, schoolmasterly tones.[234] He articulated their dissatisfaction with inadequate housing, inferior schools, crime, and unemployment, reassuring them that at the age of seventy-one he too had little time to waste.[235] He did, however, face a new and different enemy among suspicious blacks, who viewed his elegant suits, cultivated tastes, and enthusiastic receptions abroad as a sign that he had compromised with the white establishment.[236] By focusing his criticism on the *apartheid* system and not on the "white community,"[237] his message of peace, reconciliation, and forgiveness caught many of his supporters off guard. But it also reinforced his moral stature at home and his reputation abroad.

Two other prominent figures in South African politics were to play an important role in the transition from a white supremacist state to a multiracial one. The first, obviously, was President de Klerk; the second, Chief Mangosuthu Buthelezi. Initially, Mandela praised de Klerk as "a man of integrity."[238] But his description of de Klerk's character would later come back "to haunt" him and raise questions about the quality of Mandela's leadership.[239] And it was de Klerk's cautious, gradualist approach, his attempt to override majority rule with "group rights,"[240] and his unwillingness to curb white right-wing violence, that ultimately undermined the relationship between the two men.[241] Moreover, Mandela realized that the real threat came from the Afrikaner Volksfront (AVF), a right-wing "umbrella group" committed to the creation of an Afrikaner homeland or *volkstaat*. Unlike many of de Klerk's associates, who were more concerned about their positions, pensions, bank accounts, and investments, the genuine concern of the AVF's leader, General Constand Viljoen, about preserving Afrikaner culture impressed Mandela and helped them to establish a healthy rapport in sorting out some of South Africa's problems.[242]

Buthelezi's case was quite different. He appealed directly to "Zulu pride and [its] martial tradition"[243] and called upon Zulu warriors to appear menacingly in public, brandishing their traditional *assegais* or short spears, wooden clubs, and cowhide shields.[244] He also insisted on a prominent position for himself and his Inkhata Freedom Party in the new government. But his insistence on "maximum devolution" through a highly decentralized form of government[245] and his demand for formal recognition of Zulu independence threatened the cohesiveness of the new state and perpetuated the strategy of dividing one black tribe from another. In more specific terms, his demands meant pitting Zulus against Xhosas, which eventually led to the eruption of deadly, widespread black-on-black violence between Inkhata and the ANC.[246] The situation further deteriorated when a clandestine "mysterious 'Third Force,'"[247] composed of the police, government security forces, and most notably the Department of Military Intelligence, favored the Zulus over their Xhosa rivals.[248] De Klerk's attempt to attribute these actions to a "few rogue" elements;[249] his dilatory approach to investigating the charges, including police funding of Inkhata; and his reluctance to act on the evidence raised the specter of his favoring the Zulus and provoking a collapse over the discussions for a new constitution.[250]

Mandela also had to deal with fractious internal issues dividing different generations of leadership within the ANC. By exercising his legendary "authoritarian streak"[251] and invoking the power of his moral standing, he managed to allay the fears of radicals and conservatives within his own party as well as those of extremists within the white political community. Within the Communist party, a more activist group, known as the "insurrectionists," wanted to bring down the government by pursuing the "Leipzig option" modeled after East European protesters, who had successfully taken to the streets in 1989.[252] Mandela also emerged as a national leader, following the assassination of Chris Hani, whom Mandela greatly admired and who served as a "legendary . . . hero to millions of black youths." At a time when de Klerk's government seemed to disappear into the political shadows, it was Mandela who emerged as a model of statesmanship and restraint. When many clamored for revenge, he called for calm and peace in the streets as the best means of expressing one's honor to Hani's memory.[253] The theme was not new to Mandela. On many occasions, when faced with an angry crowd boiling over with frustration, he would advocate a similar approach, maintaining that "the solution *is* peace; it *is* reconciliation; it *is* political tolerance."[254] Only two weeks later the news of the death of his dear friend, Oliver Tambo, forced Mandela to withdraw momentarily and contemplate his fate as the "loneliest man in the world."[255]

Despite the clearly less than euphoric mood within the country, the tortuous process of negotiations between the ANC and white South African parties began on December 20, 1991, under the auspices of CODESA, the Convention for a Democratic South Africa. Neither the Inkhata Freedom Party nor the PAC chose to attend. When de Klerk asked to change the order and speak after Mandela at the final session, he publicly unloaded a political bombshell by accusing the ANC of failing to honor its commitment to turn in its weapons. Mandela then rose to the occasion to dispute de Klerk's accusations, castigating his "illegitimate, discredited minority regime" and raising the awkward question of the government's failure to address the role of a third force in the spread of mass killings.[256] Although their political relationship would never again be the same, Mandela did pay tribute to de Klerk's "courage" and "foresight" in recognizing the importance of a new future for all the people of South Africa during their awkward appearance as corecipients of the Nobel Peace Prize in 1993.[257] Yet despite the increasingly bitter deterioration of their relationship, Mandela realized, as *Time* magazine noted, when it named them both "Men of the Year" in 1993, the importance of de Klerk's role in reaching a political settlement for South Africa. In Mandela's words: "My worst nightmare is that I wake up and de Klerk isn't there. . . . I need him. Whether I like him or not is irrelevant. I need him."[258]

Mandela also faced problems at home. His marriage with Winnie was but an empty envelope. It lacked any passion and intimacy. Her willful, "impetuous" nature and political naïveté had made her an easy target for the police[259] and led to her being banned and imprisoned for her political activism. But it was her dealings with political thugs and her involvement in the brutal deaths of young black Africans that obviously strained their tenuous relationship. Her higher profile-activities were also associated with a rising tide of political unrest and violence in South Africa. Broadcast around the world, the sight of "the necklace," a tire placed around the victim's neck, filled with gasoline, and lit on fire as a means to kill blacks who were suspected of collaborating with the enemy,[260] shocked an international audience. Her role in mothering the Mandela United Football Club in Soweto turned into an "evil mess." Young teenage boys, who lived in her house, constituted themselves into a ring of terror and unleashed a wave of self-appointed reprisals in the form of abductions, beatings, and murders of blacks who were suspected of betraying the cause and serving as police informers. Though indirectly implicated in the circumstances surrounding the mysterious disappearance and brutal murder of a fourteen-year-old boy, Stompie Moeketsi, whom she allegedly accused of being a "sellout," Winnie managed to weather the storm.[261] Moreover, her "increasingly imperious" behavior, political ambitions,[262] and extravagant lifestyle[263] aggravated the problem. It seemed as if she viewed herself as the first lady of the movement, which fueled her political aspirations as the self-designated "Mother of the Nation" and the "champion of the poor and dispossessed." Although Mandela always maintained that he believed in her innocence, he finally accepted the reality of a public divorce, which was for him yet another painfully humiliating event.[264]

Personal loss and disappointments notwithstanding, Mandela pursued his idea of a transitional government in order, in his words, to "level the playing field."[265] Inkhata's dissident role during the CODESA 1 meetings, de Klerk's truculent assault on the ANC at the end of the meetings, and Mandela's public denunciation of de Klerk's behavior[266] hardly augured well for the political future. Pressure from within the black community to solve the problem by force and not by talk also contributed to Mandela's decision to strengthen his hand after the CODESA 2 talks deadlocked in May 1992. He did so by focusing attention on de Klerk's obstinacy and calling upon the ANC and its supporters to mount a mass action campaign in the summer, which would culminate in a general strike on August 3. The stratagem worked, forcing de Klerk to sign a Record of Understanding, which, although it supported "power-sharing," excluded a "minority veto" and provided for a democratically elected constitutional assembly and the formation of a transitional government of national unity.[267] Inkhata, however, refused to participate in the election, until Mandela and de Klerk agreed to a mutually acceptable "constitutional role for the Zulu monarchy."[268] With an agreement in place, South Africa was ready to plan for its first free, open, and truly democratic election on April 27, 1994. As a candidate, Mandela emphasized a new political realism, telling crowds not "to expect to be driving a Mercedes the day after the election or swimming in your own backyard pool." But he also focused upon the thrill of enjoying a new sense of "self-esteem" and earnestly urged whites not "to leave the country."[269]

Going to the polls for the first time was obviously a liberating experience for blacks. As one black woman, who waited in line for eight hours to vote, put it: "I've been waiting for 46 years. I don't mind waiting a little longer."[270] The experience was also an act of liberation for "a new generation of white South Africans," many of whom faithfully stood in line alongside blacks, because they resented the racist legacy of the past and disliked being viewed as international "pariahs" in the eyes of the world.[271] For Mandela election day was also a sentimental day, as he recalled old friends like Tambo and Fischer and poignantly remarked that he "did not go into the voting station alone," but cast his vote "with all of them."[272] The results of the elections contained hardly any surprises. The ANC won a resounding victory, and de Klerk was gracious in defeat. Mandela in turn thanked the members of the ANC for their hard work and dedication and congratulated de Klerk for his strong showing. A particularly poignant moment occurred when, with Coretta Scott King on the podium, Mandela looked over and invoked the inspirational words of her slain husband: "Free at last! Free at last!" At his presidential inauguration in Pretoria on May 10, Mandela expressed how privileged he and others felt as former "outlaws" to "host . . . the nations of the world on our own soil" and celebrate "a common victory for justice, . . . peace, [and] human dignity"[273] and South Africa's future as a "rainbow nation at peace with itself and the world."[274] And he concluded his address with the following stirring remarks: "Let freedom reign. God Bless Africa."[275] Perhaps no single event marked the symbolic transition from outlaw to president than the sight of people singing two different anthems, one for whites, another for blacks, as jets flew overhead with the colors of the new South African flag streaming from their wings in salute to the new head of state.[276] In the words of Martin Meredith: "Many who witnessed that moment of national catharsis were moved to tears."[277]

Once he had secured a "negotiated revolution" and led his country in jubilant celebration, Mandela faced the daunting task of having "to reinvent the South Africa." The economic chasm between whites and blacks was enormous, the disparity in incomes overwhelming, with whites earning eight times as much as blacks. While wealthy whites lived in the affluent suburbs and middle-class whites lived in clean, well-serviced residential communities, a large number of blacks inhabited meager shacks without clean water, sanitation, or electricity and faced a diet of unemployment, lawlessness, and violent crime.[278] As he had during the campaign, Mandela cautioned his followers not to expect a quick, effortless trip to a land of milk, honey, and luxury cars. But he now went one step further, urging his followers to "shed their bad habits" and raise themselves from poverty by working hard, learning how to cook a decent meal and polish floors, as he did.[279] But the "lack of urgency" within Mandela's government to address the fundamental economic causes of the problem bred a new wave of disillusionment. Faced with the enormous, seemingly insurmountable obstacles at hand, Mandela preferred to turn to personal diplomacy and make "national reconciliation [a] personal crusade." In a symbolic effort to heal a wounded nation, he invited wives and widows of former *apartheid* leaders and black activists to "a reconciliation lunch." He later extended a similar invitation to Percy Yutar, the former prosecutor in the Rivonia Trial, who was deeply moved by Mandela's gesture and by what Yutar described as the "great humility of this saintly man."[280] But one gesture more than any other stood out as a mark of Mandela's inspirational leadership. Making it a practice of adopting national sports teams, Mandela extended the same support to the national rugby team during the Rugby world cup held in Cape Town in 1995, when he openly proclaimed how "proud" he was of "our boys." Since rugby had always been viewed as a "Boer game," symbolizing "white supremacy," Mandela's appearance in the stadium, sporting a green rugger's cap and the number 6 jersey of the team captain, François Pineaar, electrified the white crowd, who shouted in response "Nel-son! Nel-son!" Contributing mightily to the legend of "Madiba magic," his actions also inspired members of an all-white team, with the exception of a single black player, to win the championship. When Mandela congratulated Pineaar for "what you have done for South Africa," the team captain eloquently replied, "Thanks for what *you* have done to South Africa."[281]

Of course, not everything in South Africa was blessed with such a storybook ending, and Mandela did make his share of mistakes. None was so great as the appointment of Winnie to his cabinet as deputy minister of arts. It was a decision he quickly regretted, as he was forced to threaten her with dismissal because of her questionable financial dealings, association with disreputable figures, and disruptive conduct. When she attempted to defend herself in public by criticizing the government for trying "to appease" white interests and failing to correct the abuses of *apartheid*, "Mandela ordered her to retract her remarks or face dismissal." When she later protested that she had been forced to sign a letter of apology "under duress" and that she no longer had "the right of free speech," the conflict hardened. When new charges of personally abusing her office through kickbacks and the misappropriation of funds surfaced, Mandela had no choice but to overcome his obdurate personal loyalty to her and dismiss her from office. What followed was divorce, and Mandela's insistence that although Winnie "had suffered gross persecution and brutal treatment" under the previous government, "she was not alone. . . . She was no exception."[282]

Mandela exhibited a similar loyalty to many of his friends and associates, who occupied prominent positions in his government and who benefited financially from their offices and access to influence and power. The situation became so fractious that it actually led to a public row between Mandela and Tutu, who accused the president of behaving "like an ordinary politician" and "impugning my integrity" for having called attention to these important matters.[283] Controversy also swirled around the establishment of a truth and reconciliation commission empowered by the government to subpoena witnesses and grant amnesties. White politicians, led by de Klerk, labeled the process "a witch-hunt,"[284] while ANC leaders suddenly faced accusations of "human rights abuses" they allegedly had committed during the struggle against *apartheid*.[285]

To see Mandela in his eighties, however, one would think that, despite his less than nimble pace and his long history of personal suffering, he had led a charmed, privileged existence. He was in his ascendancy the world's most respected living monument to resilience, human courage, and the strength of individual conscience. His personal life shines in the company of Gracha Machel, the widow of the former president of Mozambique, whom Mandela married on his eightieth birthday. Machel, who is no stranger to adversity, also possesses her own impressive "revolutionary credentials."[286] As a testament to Mandela's standing in the eyes of the South African people, his eightieth birthday became a symbol of national unity and cause for celebration amidst chronic social and economic hardship.[287] Yet, despite the waves of public adulation, Mandela still remained the same enigmatic, "intensely private," and austere individual he was during the decades of resistance, and his punctilious manners and courteous behavior continue to frame his personality.[288] "While public concern about a future without him" as the "founding father of democracy" remained high, he dismissed the notion of "an octogenarian" running for a second term as president in 1999 and leading South Africa into the next millennium. In his own candid, self-effacing manner, he has also observed that the thing he missed most about prison was the opportunity "to sit down and think." He also admitted that he now viewed himself as less of "an asset" and more of "a decoration" in the day-to-day operations of South Africa's government.[289] On the diplomatic front it also came as no surprise that his distinctively maverick approach to politics extended equally to matters of foreign policy. For example, he would later stir the diplomatic pot by acknowledging

the support of Libya and Cuba for the black liberation movement. And he refused to disavow Moammar Khadafi's and Castro's leadership,[290] because he
refused to compromise his principles and jettison those who had rendered assistance while others had barely lifted a finger to advance the black cause in
South Africa.

As a leader in our time, Mandela has truly been without peer, because no
contemporary political figure possessed the distinctive character trait that
made Mandela truly exceptional, namely his moral authority. Moreover, his
generous spirit, tenacious personality, and passion for tolerance have enabled
him to transform the racial politics of South Africa and bequeath to his country a rare legacy of political compassion and new hope for racial harmony.[291]
Out of his own deep suffering and that of his people, Mandela constructed his
own political statement, grounded in the virtues of "humanity" and "solidarity."[292] It is one that builds character from the "depth of oppression" and de-
fines courage not in the "absence of fear" but in the ability to triumph over fear.
What is more, Mandela sees in "goodness . . . a flame that can be hidden but
never extinguished," a flame that generates power in times of adversity, a flame
that ensures victory over oppression and frees both the oppressed and the op-
pressor.[293]

NOTES

1. Tim J. Juckes, *Opposition in South Africa: The Leadership of Z. K. Matthews, Nelson Mandela, and Stephen Biko* (Westport, Conn.: Praeger, 1995), pp. 13–18.

2. Ibid., pp. 18–24.

3. Ibid., p. 24.

4. Martin Meredith, *Nelson Mandela: A Biography* (New York: St. Martin's Press,
1998), p. 43.

5. Juckes, *Opposition in South Africa,* p. 24.

6. Meredith, *Nelson Mandela,* pp. 44–46.

7. Nelson Mandela, *Long Walk to Freedom* (Boston: Little, Brown, 1994), pp.
1–9.

8. Ibid., pp. 12–16.

9. Ibid., pp. 18–19.

10. Ibid., pp. 22–26.

11. Juckes, *Opposition in South Africa,* pp. 26, 29, 30, 35.

12. Mandela, *Long Walk To Freedom,* pp. 27–31.

13. Ibid., pp. 42, 31–37.

14. Ibid., pp. 37–41.

15. Ibid., pp. 42–45.

16. Ibid., pp. 46–51.

17. Meredith, *Nelson Mandela,* p. 3.

18. Ibid., p. 26.

19. Nelson Mandela, *No Easy Walk to Freedom* (London: Heinemann, 1989), pp.
43–45.

20. Mandela, *Long Walk to Freedom,* pp. 63–66.

21. Meredith, *Nelson Mandela,* pp. 29–30.

22. Ibid., p. 325.

23. Mandela, *Long Walk to Freedom,* p. 59.

24. Meredith, *Nelson Mandela,* p. 32.

25. Ibid., p. 50.

26. Ibid., p. 70.

27. Mandela, *Long Walk to Freedom,* pp. 74–80.

28. Meredith, *Nelson Mandela,* p. 89.

29. Mandela, *Long Walk to Freedom,* pp. 410–11.

30. Ibid., pp. 79–80.

31. Ibid., p. 85.

32. Mary Benson, *Nelson Mandela: The Man and the Movement* (New York: W.W. Norton, 1994), p. 216.

33. Mandela, *Long Walk to Freedom,* p. 85.

34. Benson, *Nelson Mandela,* p. 216.

35. Ibid., p. 26.

36. Ibid., p. 22.

37. Juckes, *Opposition in South Africa,* pp. 50–51.

38. Mandela, *Long Walk to Freedom,* p. 88.

39. Ibid., pp. 178–81.

40. Juckes, *Opposition in South Africa,* p. 64.

41. Ibid., p. 69.

42. Meredith, *Nelson Mandela,* p. 76.

43. Juckes, *Opposition in South Africa,* pp. 67–68, 61.

44. Mandela, *Long Walk to Freedom,* p. 97. See also Mandela, *No Easy Walk to Freedom,* p. 48.

45. Mandela, *Long Walk to Freedom,* p. 97.

46. Benson, *Nelson Mandela,* p. 35.

47. Mandela, *Long Walk to Freedom,* pp. 98–99.

48. Meredith, *Nelson Mandela,* pp. 56–57.

49. Benson, *Nelson Mandela,* pp. 37–38.

50. Juckes, *Opposition in South Africa,* pp. 72–73.

51. Mandela, *Long Walk to Freedom,* pp. 100–101.

52. Juckes, *Opposition in South Africa,* p. 74.

53. Mandela, *Long Walk to Freedom,* pp. 101–2.

54. Benson, *Nelson Mandela,* p. 52.

55. Ibid., pp. 40–41.

56. Mandela, *Long Walk to Freedom,* pp. 104–5.

57. Benson, *Nelson Mandela,* p. 31.

58. Mandela, *Long Walk to Freedom,* pp. 104–5.

59. Juckes, *Opposition in South Africa,* p. 75.

60. Mandela, *Long Walk to Freedom,* pp. 110–11.

61. Benson, *Nelson Mandela,* p. 43.

62. Mandela, *No Easy Walk to Freedom,* p. 64.

63. Mandela, *Long Walk to Freedom,* p. 137.

64. Ibid., p. 111.

65. Benson, *Nelson Mandela,* pp. 44, 46.

66. Ibid., p. 51.

67. Mandela, *Long Walk to Freedom,* pp. 110–22.
68. Ibid., p. 118.
69. Ibid., p. 126.
70. Benson, *Nelson Mandela,* p. 63.
71. Mandela, *Long Walk to Freedom,* pp. 126–27.
72. Meredith, *Nelson Mandela,* pp. 111–12.
73. Benson, *Nelson Mandela,* p. 55. See also Meredith, *Nelson Mandela,* p. 100.
74. Meredith, *Nelson Mandela,* pp. 100–101.
75. Ibid., p. 104.
76. Mandela, *Long Walk to Freedom,* pp. 128–33.
77. Ibid., p. 136.
78. Mandela, *No Easy Walk to Freedom,* pp. 21–26.
79. Ibid., p. 45.
80. Mandela, *Long Walk to Freedom,* p. 141.
81. Mandela, *No Easy Walk to Freedom,* p. 31.
82. Mandela, *Long Walk to Freedom,* p. 145.
83. Meredith, *Nelson Mandela,* p. 123.
84. Mandela, *No Easy Walk to Freedom,* pp. 47–50.
85. Mandela, *Long Walk to Freedom,* p. 145.
86. Meredith, *Nelson Mandela,* p. 232.
87. Ibid., pp. 235–36.
88. Ibid., p. 135.
89. Benson, *Nelson Mandela,* pp. 65–66.
90. Mandela, *Long Walk to Freedom,* pp. 148–53.
91. Mandela, *No Easy Walk to Freedom,* p. 56.
92. Mandela, *Long Walk to Freedom,* p. 158.
93. Ibid., p. 163.
94. Ibid., p. 165.
95. Mandela, *No Easy Walk to Freedom,* pp. 71–75.
96. Ibid., p. 71.
97. Mandela, *Long Walk to Freedom,* p. 165.
98. Ibid., p. 200.
99. Benson, *Nelson Mandela,* p. 59.
100. Ibid., p. 60.
101. Mandela, *No Easy Walk to Freedom,* p. 41.
102. Ibid., pp. 32–35.
103. Ibid., p. 47.
104. Ibid., p. 42.
105. Meredith, *Nelson Mandela,* p. 221.
106. Mandela, *Long Walk to Freedom,* pp. 174–78.
107. Ibid., pp. 185–87.
108. Benson, *Nelson Mandela,* p. 75.
109. Mandela, *Long Walk to Freedom,* pp. 188, 191–94.
110. Ibid., p. 197.
111. Meredith, *Nelson Mandela,* p. 148.
112. Mandela, *Long Walk to Freedom,* p. 203.
113. Juckes, *Opposition in South Africa,* p. 59. See also Meredith, *Nelson Mandela,* p. 69.

114. Meredith, *Nelson Mandela,* pp. 66–67.

115. Mandela, *Long Walk to Freedom,* p. 384.

116. Juckes, *Opposition in South Africa,* p. 90.

117. Mandela, *Long Walk to Freedom,* pp. 197–99.

118. Juckes, *Opposition in South Africa,* p. 95.

119. Benson, *Nelson Mandela,* pp. 84–85.

120. Mandela, *Long Walk to Freedom,* pp. 206–12.

121. Juckes, *Opposition in South Africa,* p. 96.

122. Meredith, *Nelson Mandela,* p. 178.

123. Mandela, *Long Walk to Freedom,* p. 218.

124. Benson, *Nelson Mandela,* p. 80.

125. Ibid., p. 72.

126. Mandela, *Long Walk to Freedom,* pp. 218–20.

127. Ibid., pp. 225–27.

128. Mandela, *No Easy Walk to Freedom,* p. 90.

129. Juckes, *Opposition in South Africa,* pp. 99–100.

130. Mandela, *No Easy Walk to Freedom,* p. 94.

131. Ibid., pp. 102–3.

132. Ibid., p. 97.

133. Juckes, *Opposition in South Africa,* p. 101.

134. Mandela, *No Easy Walk to Freedom,* p. 106.

135. Benson, *Nelson Mandela,* p. 97.

136. Mandela, *Long Walk to Freedom,* pp. 231–37.

137. Ibid., pp. 239–40.

138. Mandela, *No Easy Walk to Freedom,* pp. 108–9.

139. Ibid., pp. 243–49.

140. Benson, *Nelson Mandela,* p. 111.

141. Mandela, *Long Walk to Freedom,* pp. 250–56.

142. Juckes, *Opposition in South Africa,* p. 104.

143. Mandela, *No Easy Walk to Freedom,* pp. 116, 118.

144. Mandela, *Long Walk to Freedom,* pp. 258–67.

145. Ibid., pp. 282–84.

146. Ibid., pp. 271–77.

147. Mandela, *No Easy Walk to Freedom,* p. 127.

148. Ibid., p. 130.

149. Benson, *Nelson Mandela,* p. 34.

150. Mandela, *No Easy Walk to Freedom,* p. 132.

151. Ibid., p. 152.

152. Mandela, *Long Walk to Freedom,* pp. 287–89.

153. Juckes, *Opposition in South Africa,* p. 105.

154. Mandela, *No Easy Walk to Freedom,* pp. 159–60.

155. Mandela, *Long Walk to Freedom,* p. 290.

156. Ibid., pp. 290–92.

157. Meredith, *Nelson Mandela,* p. 229.

158. Mandela, *Long Walk to Freedom,* p. 544.

159. Ibid., pp. 296–98.

160. Meredith, *Nelson Mandela,* pp. 240, 247.

161. Mandela, *Long Walk to Freedom,* pp. 304–9.

162. Meredith, *Nelson Mandela,* p. 248.

163. Mandela, *Long Walk to Freedom,* p. 310.

164. Ibid., pp. 314–15.

165. Ibid., pp. 316–20.

166. Benson, *Nelson Mandela,* p. 151.

167. Mandela, *No Easy Walk to Freedom,* p. 179.

168. Mandela, *Long Walk to Freedom,* pp. 320–21, and Benson, *Nelson Mandela,* p. 154.

169. Mandela, *No Easy Walk to Freedom,* p. 183.

170. Ibid., p. 169.

171. Meredith, *Nelson Mandela,* p. 266.

172. Mandela, *No Easy Walk to Freedom,* pp. 185–88.

173. Mandela, *Long Walk to Freedom,* pp. 321–22.

174. Meredith, *Nelson Mandela,* p. 271.

175. Mandela, *Long Walk to Freedom,* pp. 324–29.

176. Ibid., pp. 342–48.

177. Ibid., pp. 333–39.

178. Ibid., pp. 339–42.

179. Ibid., pp. 350–52.

180. Ibid., pp. 387–90.

181. Ibid., pp. 352–61.

182. Ibid., pp. 406–8.

183. Ibid., pp. 361–69.

184. Ibid., pp. 372–73.

185. Meredith, *Nelson Mandela,* p. 294.

186. Mandela, *Long Walk to Freedom,* p. 363.

187. Meredith, *Nelson Mandela,* p. 286.

188. Mandela, *Long Walk to Freedom,* pp. 449–50, 490. See also Benson, *Nelson Mandela,* p. 246.

189. Meredith, *Nelson Mandela,* p. 520.

190. Mandela, *Long Walk to Freedom,* pp. 377–79.

191. Ibid., pp 381–82.

192. Ibid., pp. 398–403.

193. Ibid., p. 397.

194. Ibid., pp. 405–6.

195. Ibid., p. 413.

196. Ibid., pp. 415–18.

197. Juckes, *Opposition in South Africa,* p. 111.

198. Ibid., p. 11.

199. Ibid., pp. 130–35.

200. Ibid., pp. 141–43.

201. For a discussion of the significance and the circumstances surrounding Biko's death, see Juckes, *Opposition in South Africa,* pp. 151–55.

202. Meredith, *Nelson Mandela,* p. 330.

203. Mandela, *Long Walk to Freedom,* pp. 420–24.

204. Ibid., pp. 425–28, 434–37.

205. Meredith, *Nelson Mandela,* pp. 303–4.

206. Ibid., p. 314.

207. Ibid., p. 301.
208. Mandela, *Long Walk to Freedom,* pp. 439–40.
209. Ibid., pp. 443–44.
210. Ibid., pp. 447, 457.
211. Ibid., pp. 450–51.
212. Meredith, *Nelson Mandela,* p. 369.
213. Mandela, *Long Walk to Freedom,* p. 463.
214. Ibid., p. 452.
215. Ibid., pp. 453–56.
216. Ibid., pp. 458–59.
217. Juckes, *Opposition in South Africa,* p. 109.
218. Benson, *Nelson Mandela,* p. 205.
219. Juckes, *Opposition in South Africa,* p. 158.
220. Mandela, *Long Walk to Freedom,* pp. 459–62.
221. Juckes, *Opposition in South Africa,* pp. 164–68.
222. Mandela, *No Easy Walk to Freedom,* p. 168.
223. Mandela, *Long Walk to Freedom,* pp. 459–62. See also Meredith, *Nelson Mandela,* pp. 371–72.
224. Mandela, *Long Walk to Freedom,* pp. 468–69.
225. Ibid., p. 473.
226. Ibid., p. 479. See also Meredith, *Nelson Mandela,* pp. 391–92.
227. Benson, *Nelson Mandela,* p. 250.
228. Mandela, *Long Walk to Freedom,* pp. 479–80.
229. Ibid., pp. 481–86.
230. Juckes, *Opposition in South Africa,* p. 172.
231. Benson, *Nelson Mandela,* p. 7.
232. Mandela, *Long Walk to Freedom,* pp. 489–96.
233. Benson, *Nelson Mandela,* p. 13.
234. Ibid., p. 256.
235. Mandela, *Long Walk to Freedom,* pp. 496–98.
236. Ibid., pp. 498–500, 507–9.
237. Meredith, *Nelson Mandela,* p. 408.
238. Mandela, *Long Walk to Freedom,* p. 494.
239. Meredith, *Nelson Mandela,* p. 405.
240. Mandela, *Long Walk to Freedom,* pp. 502–5.
241. Meredith, *Nelson Mandela,* pp. 431–32.
242. Ibid., pp. 492–94.
243. Ibid., p. 421.
244. Ibid., p. 513. See also Mandela, *Long Walk to Freedom,* p. 513.
245. Meredith, *Nelson Mandela,* p. 494.
246. Mandela, *Long Walk to Freedom,* pp. 501–2.
247. Ibid., p. 511.
248. Meredith, *Nelson Mandela,* p. 469.
249. Ibid., p. 480.
250. Mandela, *Long Walk to Freedom,* pp. 511–13.
251. Meredith, *Nelson Mandela,* pp. 412–13.
252. Ibid., p. 466.
253. Ibid., pp. 482–84. See also Benson, *Nelson Mandela,* p. 267.

254. Meredith, *Nelson Mandela,* p. 495.

255. Ibid., pp. 485–87.

256. Mandela, *Long Walk to Freedom,* pp. 517–21.

257. Ibid., pp. 532–33.

258. Meredith, *Nelson Mandela,* p. 499.

259. Ibid., p. 290.

260. Ibid., p. 354.

261. Ibid., pp. 375–87, 435.

262. Ibid., p. 343.

263. Ibid., p. 481.

264. Mandela, *Long Walk to Freedom,* pp. 522–23. See also Meredith, *Nelson Mandela,* pp. 438, 463.

265. Mandela, *Long Walk to Freedom,* p. 524.

266. Meredith, *Nelson Mandela,* pp. 449–52.

267. Mandela, *Long Walk to Freedom,* pp. 525–29.

268. Ibid., pp. 535–37.

269. Ibid. p. 535.

270. Benson, *Nelson Mandela,* p. 271.

271. Meredith, *Nelson Mandela,* p. 398.

272. Ibid., p. 516.

273. Mandela, *Long Walk to Freedom,* pp. 539–41.

274. Meredith, *Nelson Mandela,* p. 521.

275. Mandela, *Long Walk to Freedom,* p. 541.

276. Meredith, *Nelson Mandela,* pp. 519–21.

277. Ibid., p. 521.

278. Ibid., pp. 522–25.

279. Ibid., pp. 503, 525–26.

280. Ibid., pp. 526–29.

281. Ibid., pp. 2, 529–31.

282. Ibid., pp. 531–39, 442.

283. Ibid., pp. 541–42.

284. Ibid., p. 547.

285. *Boston Globe,* May 9, 1998, p. A2.

286. Meredith, *Nelson Mandela,* p. 3.

287. *Washington Post,* July 18, 1998, p. A13.

288. Meredith, *Nelson Mandela,* pp. 1–4.

289. Ibid., pp. 551–54.

290. Ibid., p. 414.

291. Ibid., pp. 555–56.

292. Benson, *Nelson Mandela,* p. 217.

293. Mandela, *Long Walk to Freedom,* pp. 542–44.

Chapter 4

GORBACHEV

AND THE COLLAPSE OF
THE SOVIET UNION

LEADERSHIP, CHARISMA, AND IDEOLOGICAL REFORM

Throughout the course of Mikhail Gorbachev's meteoric career, it always seemed that there was something larger at stake than the simple pursuit of a political agenda or the formation of a new political coalition. But alongside those remarkable flashes of political exuberance, a painful feeling frequently resurfaces when recalling Gorbachev's dramatic initiatives and wondering again what might have been had he not failed. At the center of this phenomenon stood the combination of Gorbachev's personality, the news media, and the power of the television screen. No less a pivotal figure in Soviet politics than Andrei Sakharov remarked, when he first saw Gorbachev on television, that "It looks as if our country's lucky. We've got an intelligent leader."[1]

The reciprocal relationship between Gorbachev's dynamic personality and the West's fascination with the prospect of change within the Soviet Union also enhanced his status abroad as a symbol for change. Gorbachev was good press, and the Western press knew it.[2] It would be misleading, however, to suggest that Gorbachev acquired his favorable image abroad solely because of his gregarious manner or some chance coincidence of favorable political circumstances. In fact, his early success in the West can be traced back to his campaign to forge a new Soviet identity by invoking "Kennedyesque" themes that championed the cause of humanity and world peace, while warning against the danger of a nuclear holocaust.[3] Gorbachev's arrival on the scene had also altered the international political calculus. Whether one used the term *propaganda* or the one preferred by the Soviets—"public diplomacy"[4]— it clearly appeared at the outset that Gorbachev intended to write a new chapter in the familiar book of how to make friends and influence people both at home and abroad.

Mikhail Gorbachev. Photo by Luc Novovitch. Reproduced by permission of Reuters/Corbis-Bettmann.

Unlike his predecessors, Gorbachev assiduously cultivated a more cosmopolitan worldview. In his desire "to shape a better future he came across as an incorrigible optimist" with a broad international perspective.[5] Moreover, his boundless energy, urbane, reformist image, and commanding political presence—when combined with his quasi-legendary verbal agility, sharp, penetrating wit, animated gestures and facial expressions—laid the foundation for his early success in political communication. He was also a gifted speaker, whose fondness for language and uncanny talent for improvisation became indispensable tools of persuasion, as he grew more and more to rely "on words as his main political weapon."[6]

Gorbachev's affinity for motivational speeches reflected his belief that he could will a peaceful revolution into existence through words, scoldings, encomia, and exhortations that would generate enthusiastic popular support and "somehow . . . make . . . his reforms . . . real."[7] His charismatic appeal, his subtle, almost intuitive feel for the political issues, his visionary qualities, and his ability to reach his audience without creating the impression of speaking to them "from Olympian heights,"[8] explain why he was "the first Soviet leader to [become] an instant television personality"[9] and employ his sense of urgency[10] to breathe new life into the public debate. As a consequence of the nuclear environment and geopolitical necessity, Gorbachev's political gaze tilted almost automatically toward the West. And in his willingness to reach out to the Western press he also skillfully influenced the shaping of his stature and his image as an international statesman.

Of course, when Mikhail Sergeyevich Gorbachev rose to the pinnacle of Soviet power on March 11, 1985, no one could have anticipated the magnitude of his impact or his ability, in the words of Robert Kaiser, to orchestrate "the most dramatic display of political leadership . . . in the second half of the twentieth century."[11] His humble family origins in the village of Privolnoe, in the Stavropol region of southern Russia, where he was born on March 2, 1931, hardly prepared him or the world for what was to come. It was against this bucolic background that young Mikhail distinguished himself as a model student.[12] Others who knew him, however, recalled how his mercurial behavior, proclivity for the speaker's podium, and love for the theater combined to form a more complex character and nurture his ambitions for "the world stage."[13]

Fortunately for Gorbachev, his native Privolnoe was spared the brutal consequences of the Second World War and German occupation, and he was able to follow in his father's footsteps, working long hours in the blistering sun perched atop his tractor. His exceptional effort earned for him the prestigious Red Banner of Labor in 1949. The award, which was an unusual achievement for such a young man, helped pave the way for his admission to Moscow State University.[14] When contrasted with the rubble that littered the Russian countryside, the "politically sophisticated" atmosphere of Moscow, as the center of Soviet power, must have made a deep impression on the young man from Privolnoe.[15]

But while Gorbachev used his university experience to prepare for political leadership, his decision to study law is much more difficult to contextualize. In addition to establishing a symbolic link with Lenin, who had also studied law,[16] Gorbachev's interest in history and political thought enabled him to use the law school curriculum to analyze the philosophical and political works of Plato and Aristotle[17] and the western political ideas of Jean-Jacques Rousseau, Georg W.F. Hegel, Niccolò Machiavelli, and John Stuart Mill.[18] Law school also provided him with an opportunity to develop his skills as a speaker. When combined with his natural theatrical flair and his love of the stage, his oratorical training in public discourse, courtroom rhetoric, and argumentation[19] accentuated the dynamic aspects of his political personality. His ability to deliver a forceful speech and move quickly from verbal combat to the art of persuasion became one of the signature characteristics of his political style, leading Medvedev eventually to designate Gorbachev as "probably the best speaker there has been in top party echelons since Trotsky."[20]

In addition to books, ideas, and the companionship of his academic colleagues, Gorbachev's education included falling in love with Raisa Maximova, a sociology student at the university. Though from different social backgrounds and different regions of the Soviet Union, they discovered that they shared a youthful reformist spirit and a thirst for Moscow's stimulating cultural and intellectual environment. In many respects Raisa served as Gorbachev's guide to the arts and cultural treasures of the Soviet capital. But their interests extended beyond the arts to political issues and socioeconomic developments within the Soviet Union.

As unlikely as it may have seemed at the time, the Gorbachevs discovered that their road to success and their return to Moscow lay through Gorbachev's native Stavropol, where he embarked on a career as a party official, and she as an instructor in philosophy and sociology in 1955. For the most part the years spent in Stavropol seem to have been pleasant. Gorbachev set about his business with the same persistence he had exhibited as a law student and began his steady rise through the ranks by diligently discharging his responsibilities within the propaganda department of the city's Komsomol organization.[21] Of course, Gorbachev did not singlehandedly engineer his climb to the top of the Stavropol ladder. Things simply did not work that way in the Soviet Union, and like many young and ambitious Soviet officials, Gorbachev understood the importance of having a mentor. The first in what would become a distinguished list of politically prominent patrons was Fyodor Kulakov, who was impressed with Gorbachev's work in the Komsomol organization. When Kulakov returned to Moscow as party secretary for agriculture and became a member of the Politburo, he arranged for Gorbachev to succeed him as secretary of the Stavropol region in 1970.[22] Under painful circumstances, Gorbachev would again succeed Kulakov, this time as secretary of agriculture upon Kulakov's death in the fall of 1978.

Once again it seemed that Gorbachev had benefited from being in the right place at the right time. Moreover, despite its reputed isolation, Stavropol had served Gorbachev well. Its location had provided him with opportunities to make contacts with prominent members of the party elite, such as Leonid Brezhnev, Yuri Andropov, Konstantin Chernenko, and Kulakov, who regularly passed through the resort towns of the south.[23] By the time he returned to Moscow, Gorbachev had matured politically and positioned himself well for his next move up the bureaucratic ladder. He was no longer the wide-eyed transplant from the south who was awed by the power and energy of the capital. Now that he understood the system, he quickly became well versed in the inner workings of Kremlin politics. His rise through the ranks was meteoric.[24] Within a year he was appointed an alternate member of the Politburo, and the next year, in 1980, at the tender Soviet political age of forty-nine, he became a full, and the youngest, member of the Politburo. The climb was not without its anxious moments, as failures in Soviet agriculture and Gorbachev's inability to leave a "real mark on agricultural policy"[25] could have endangered his political career. But his diligent work ethic and his determination to see things improve served him well and earned him a reputation as "a quick study,"[26] who was "eager to make his mark"[27] and sustain his standing within the upper levels of the party's power and authority.

But Gorbachev's "penchant for changing things" also threatened the conservative nature of the Soviet system[28] and fostered the notion of his role as a radical reformer and a political crusader. Hedrick Smith acknowledged that once Gorbachev came to power, his considerable political skills and gifts as a communicator enabled him "to proclaim the Grand Reformation of the Soviet system"[29] and challenge the status quo. When Andrei Gromyko, the Kremlin's elder statesman, nominated Gorbachev as Chernenko's successor to the post of General Secretary he praised Gorbachev's "brilliant" analytical skills and his ability to "grasp . . . changes . . . on the international stage."[30] Beyond the walls of the party conclave, people greeted the news of Gorbachev's election with cheers of joy and celebration, since it seemed that, after a procession of stonefaced Kremlin figures and a grim sequence of burials that marked the passing of Brezhnev, Andropov, and Chernenko, the new Soviet leader was "strong and healthy." Others believed that his "accession symbolized" the orderly transfer of power from one generation to another.[31] His youth and energy also figured prominently into an actuarial analysis of Gorbachev's political longevity, which suggested that he would be in power well into the twenty-first century to assess the outcome of his reforms.[32] Of course, the actual scenario turned out to be something quite different. But in 1985 hardly anyone could have imagined the improbable sequence of events that led to Gorbachev's fall from power in 1991, including members of the Western media who rushed to invest Gorbachev with "the status of a superman, . . . who [would] stand up to Reagan and . . . push and pull the Soviet Union fully into the modern era."[33]

At the outset, the prospects for reform were indeed promising. But Gorbachev's flexibility and penchant for change also revealed the less flattering inconsistent and unpredictable side of his political behavior. In fact, "many Russians [began to] speak of 'two Gorbachevs,' the *apparatchik* and the reformer, who often struggle with one another."[34] Yet despite his complicated personal makeup, Gorbachev realized that the Soviet Union needed "something more than a mere facelift"[35] or cosmetic reforms[36] and that in order to communicate his message of reform, he needed to capitalize on the certainty and vigor that peppered his early speeches. In support of this effort, Gorbachev broke new ground by establishing the first Public Opinion Institute in the Soviet Union to measure popular moods and attitudes and assess the impact of his message.[37]

Although Gorbachev liked to cast himself as a "visionary leader" who understood that "politics is the art of the possible,"[38] he remained forever self-conscious about his public image. He realized that in his new role as political impresario he had to refrain from announcing bold new policy initiatives or radical reforms until he felt secure enough to press his own agenda. When he began to outline his plan during the February 1986 Party Congress, he introduced *perestroika* or "restructuring" as a means of dealing with the institutional lassitude that afflicted nearly every level of Soviet society. Sensing that he had further solidified his political position, he later upped the political ante and condemned with the zeal of a public prosecutor Brezhnev's legacy of political decay that bred "Parasitism," a "decline in moral values," and most significantly the period of "stagnation (*zastoi*)."[39] In order to redirect the energy of the Soviet people, he even introduced the much-maligned term, psychology, when he told factory workers that it "was necessary to change . . . 'our attitudes and psychology,'" and our "style and method of work."[40]

While Gorbachev's desire to reform the Soviet Union was never really in doubt, his frustration in trying to transform the Soviet system and overcome its intractable resistance to change often caused him to dismiss the criticism of political figures, pundits, and members of the press as unwarranted challenges to him personally or to the Soviet Union politically. Robert Kaiser believes that Gorbachev's erratic behavior, oscillating as it did between periods of "intense, creative activity" and "longer phases of relative calm and apparent withdrawal," revealed a "somewhat manic-depressive" side to his personality.[41] Although the clinical accuracy of this observation remains untested, it does provide insight into the "mood swings" that triggered the "dizzying" cycle of "sudden ups and downs."[42] Kaiser also likens the thin-skinned, peevish side of Gorbachev's personality to that of a "reformer czar [who] found it difficult," when challenged, "to give up the czar's prerogatives."[43] Gorbachev's contentious behavior and caustic remarks were by no means limited to the home audience, as evidenced in his jousting in London with a Tory member of Parliament over the issue of human rights in the Soviet Union and Northern Ireland.[44] At times, when thrust into combative situations, his behavior revealed a self-confidence bordering on vanity and arrogance and a need to demonstrate his intellectual superiority at home and impress his international audience abroad. But he also enjoyed the give and take that came with his celebrity status and the opportunity to use his bully pulpit to preach the gospel of reform.

When necessary, Gorbachev's finely tuned political instincts, ruthless pragmatism, and mercurial nature enabled him to shift allegiances virtually overnight, as demonstrated most vividly in his dramatic political reversals during the months of political uncertainty leading up to the August coup. This aspect of his behavior led others to detect a certain "quicksilver" quality to his personality that enabled him to adjust almost effortlessly "his personal chemistry" to suit the needs of those around him.[45] By the time of Gorbachev's trip to Washington in 1990, one Soviet journalist who had staunchly supported Gorbachev during the early years of reform remarked how much the Soviet leader had given in to "narcissistic tendencies."[46] Even Michel Tatu, one of Gorbachev's early supporters and most influential European advisers, felt compelled to revise his earlier assessment of Gorbachev's role as an agent for change and comment on his indecisiveness, authoritarian tendencies, "taste for the trappings of power," and difficulty with criticism that made him quick to take offense.[47] These criticisms notwithstanding, as late as 1990 Gorbachev the reformer continued for the most part to be portrayed in the Western press "as the tsar liberator" and "the Copernicus, Darwin and Freud of communism all wrapped in one." Nor, for that matter, was there any suggestion in the press that the "political magician" might some time in the future run out of tricks.[48]

It would be a mistake to suggest that there was something camera-ready in Gorbachev's personality, since, despite his Rolex watch and preference for tailored Italian and British suits,[49] he worked hard both on and off camera to shape his populist image, as he and Raisa had done during their visit to Leningrad in May of 1985. News telecasts, featuring Gorbachev mixing with the people and soliciting their opinions on political issues,[50] showcased his animated personality and created a fever of public interest. For example, when "a woman . . . yelled 'You should be closer to the people,'" he "replied: 'How can I be any closer?'" In that impromptu exchange the contrast between Gorbachev's youthful spontaneity and the decrepit old men of the past[51] could not have been more vivid. Gorbachev would later recall how important he viewed his contact with the "the *narod* or masses," because "there are no hints, recommendations, and warnings that are more valuable than those you get straight from" the people. And though these engagements were, strictly speaking, far from spontaneous, everything suggests that Gorbachev drew great "sustenance from these encounters" and that he genuinely desired to discover things firsthand.[52]

As part of his attempt to combine culture with his high-profile populist style, he and Raisa made it a point, when they went to the theater in Moscow, to sit in the more plebeian orchestra stalls rather than avail themselves of a special government box.[53] Early on, Muscovites even referred to him as "*skromny* (modest)" on account of his choice of "only one Zil limousine and one Volga sedan [for] security." By 1988, however, his motorized entourage had swelled to "a phalanx of four Zils" with lights flashing and sirens blazing, as they sped along the Chaika Lane that was reserved for high-ranking government offi-cials.[54] But it would be a mistake to underestimate the sincerity of Gorbachev's early attempts to transform the symbolic trappings of office, because he sin-cerely believed that redefining the presentational components of power could help bridge the gap between the Soviet people and their government. While his early attempts to impose a more understated, less pompous style in public were designed to broaden the base of his popular appeal, his openness and re-liance on newspaper and television discussions of political issues also served as a public relations model for other party officials.[55]

At home Gorbachev used his communication skills to reinforce his political position. In a May 1985 speech at the Smolny Institute in Leningrad, which had served as Lenin's headquarters during the heroic days of the Bolshevik Revolution, Gorbachev laid claim to Lenin's legacy and made it clear to party regulars that "adjustments . . . would have to be made" and that "those who do not intend to adjust . . . must simply get out of the way."[56] While party regulars did not for obvious reasons take kindly to the content of Gorbachev's remarks, he welcomed the public's positive response, since he knew that he would need their backing as a political lever in dealing with the congenitally recalcitrant members of the party and state apparatus. At the outset, when he began to ad-dress the semantic ambiguities of reform, he relied more and more on "rhetoric . . . to dramatize the need for change and . . . create a climate con-ducive" to reform.[57] Moreover, in his new role as a beacon of change, it ap-peared "that, for first time since Lenin," the Soviets had a leader who was willing to "rely more on the force of his ideas and program than on the power of an *apparat*" to communicate his message of social and political renewal.[58] Given the dimensions of the task and the nature of the opposition, Gorbachev was fortunate at least at the outset to have the support of responsible reform-minded advisers such as Eduard Shervardnadze, who served as a voice for "New Thinking" in Soviet foreign policy, as well as Alexander Yakovlev, the Westernized diplomat and political theoretician who returned from Canada to formulate the broader intellectual framework for *perestroika*. The same can be said of Tatyana Zaslavskaya, who shared Gorbachev's "historic vision" and pos-sessed the "will and courage to see perestroika through to the end."[59] The en-dorsements also extended beyond Gorbachev's inner circle to an array of distinguished cultural figures and media personalities such as Elem Klimov, the newly elected first secretary of the Filmmakers' Union, who was inspired by Gorbachev's efforts to encourage "Russia's best people . . . to start a new life."[60]

Gorbachev treasured the support of prominent members of the *intelligentsia* because he valued their acceptance and approval and wanted to use their influ-ence to move beyond the arid, scholastic conventions of Soviet Marxism to make possible "learning . . . a new language" in "internal politics."[61] Given the nature of the challenges he faced, Gorbachev played the game masterfully.[62]

He began by invoking "Leninism as the ideological basis of his policies"[63] and eagerly appropriated Lenin's mantle as teacher and guide "to impress upon the people that democratization involved taking personal responsibility."[64] He even challenged the party leadership to represent "Lenin's ideal of a revolutionary Bolshevik" and reject "officialdom, red tape, patronizing attitudes and careerism."[65] But he quickly discovered that appealing to historical ideals and dealing with contemporary political reality are two different things, particularly since his reformer's message clashed with the vested interests of the *nomenklatura*, the party aristocracy that Stalin once described as an "Order of Sword Bearers," shrouded in "mystique [and an impenetrable] aura of secrecy."[66] Membership was based upon a carefully constructed, hierarchical table of ranks, titles, positions, and privileges that were carefully protected by rigorous bureaucratic procedures and political conventions.[67] Of course, members of the *apparat* viewed these ranks and privileges as entitlements and stubbornly opposed measures that would threaten their power and influence.[68]

Others, however, observed something ironic in Gorbachev's role as the *apparatchik* turned reformer, given his elevated position within the system and his own share of responsibility for the country's poor economic condition.[69] The sheer magnitude of the problems that the Soviet Union faced meant that Gorbachev's range as a leading man and his skills as a producer and director would be seriously tested, as would his political flexibility, in a performance that required rapid and numerous costume changes and role reversals. But his shift in political direction also meant that Gorbachev was willing to expand his ideological lens and acknowledge changes in the "global process," the evolution of Marxism, and the lessons of European social democracy.[70]

To overcome this myriad of obstacles, Gorbachev turned to the communication media to make sure that his speeches and pronouncements received "wide publicity." His words appeared regularly on the front page of *Pravda*, and Soviet television regularly showcased his high-profile foreign policy initiatives, summits, and the diplomatic receptions that reflected his international prominence.[71] He also did not refrain from taking up the verbal cudgel. During the February 1986 Twenty-seventh Party Congress, he chided his audience for delaying progress on reform: "Stop for an instant, as they say, and you fall behind a mile." By Soviet standards, the risks Gorbachev was willing to take were enormous. But he also realized that to be effective his reforms would have to provide a fresh "psychological insight" that radically altered "the way Russians live and think."[72]

On another level, Gorbachev understood that if he hoped to succeed, he would have to confront the enormous weight of the Soviet Union's past and provide a compelling ideological alternative for the future. The issues of allegiance and morale were particularly important, given the formative, cohesive role ideology had played in the Soviet past, as compared to the present, when government surveys indicated that people were more concerned about economic issues and creature comforts than ideology.[73] Understanding the full significance of this dilemma, Gorbachev set out with his customary dispatch to

fill the void. At the outset, his new style of political discourse constituted an in-
vigorating metaphor for change. People liked what they saw, and they liked
both the message and the messenger. As for Karl Marx, who was the font of all
socialist wisdom, his reputation had suffered, since none of his prognoses had
come to fruition concerning the inevitable collapse of capitalism and the advent of revolution in the more advanced, industrialized states of the West.[74]
Within the Soviet Union, the fact that Marxism had also failed to live up to the
scientific claims of historical materialism, including the construction of a communist society and the eventual "withering away of the state" presented Gorbachev with the difficult challenge of having to redirect the ideological focus,
once the prophecy had failed.[75]

In his book, *Perestroika: New Thinking for Our Country and the World*, Gorbachev described the restructuring process as a renewal of life that "*unites socialism with democracy* and revives the Leninist concept of socialist construction both
in theory and practice."[76] In keeping with Gorbachev's quest for an updated version of Marxism-Leninism, Gorbachev attempted to recapture the inspirational
qualities of Lenin. But given his position, he had neither the time nor the luxury
to engage in a lengthy philosophical disquisition on the contemporary merits of
Marxism. Instead, he needed to engage quickly in a bold act of political leadership. He needed to use his considerable political skills and the means of communication at his disposal to speak, write, threaten, and cajole into existence a
movement that would transform the Soviet state from within and create for the
Soviet people a more dynamic political culture and future.

PERESTROIKA AND GLASNOST

In his desire to revitalize Soviet society, Gorbachev realized that he needed a
political program he could present to the Soviet people with confidence and
conviction. But given the ambiguity that surrounded the terms *perestroika* (restructuring) and *glasnost* (openness), many, including some of his supporters,
feared that his program might prove to be "all ideas and no substance."[77] To set
his reforms in motion, Gorbachev decided to shed the misleading stereotypes
of the past and employ the tools of the social sciences to reshape public opinion.[78] To do so he embraced Tatyana Zaslavskaya's reformist views concerning
"the human capital thesis" and the need to "activate . . . the human factor"[79]
and courted members of the *intelligentsia*,[80] who constituted Russia's unofficial
opposition.

Having set the reform process in motion, Gorbachev knew he would have
to sustain his high-wire act and the political momentum of the reform program. During the January 1987 Central Committee Plenum, he introduced
the concept of *demokratizatsiya* (democratization)[81] and broke with tradition
to allow his speech to be broadcast on television. His decision to "appropriate
the electronic press as a pulpit for *perestroika*"[82] and rely on his celebrated skills
as a communicator reflected his belief that he could disseminate his message of

change without undermining, at least consciously, the party's authority and integrity. Here, his facility with language and his command of a rich store of political metaphors served him well, as he delivered an executive analysis that was part theory, part exegesis, and part political revivalism.

For Gorbachev, restructuring meant having to go beyond theoretical issues and administrative reforms to the formation of a new Soviet political culture and a complete de-Stalinization of the Soviet system.[83] But the problem of systemic inertia extended well beyond the issue of "the bureaucratic rust of Stalinism"[84] and embraced the popular demands for individual and constitutional rights as redress against the unlimited authority of the state.[85] In the words of Anatolii Sobchak, Leningrad's youthful and dynamic reformist mayor, who had also been educated as a lawyer: "It's hard to be a lawyer in a lawless state!"[86] Gorbachev, as a lawyer, supported the creation of "a socialist *pravovoe gosudartsvo*," meaning a state based on the rule of law[87] in keeping with the principles of a *Rechtstaat*: "Everything that is not forbidden by law is permitted,"[88] he declared. As a reflection of the change in official attitudes, the government stressed the importance of *zakonnost*, or legality or lawfulness, as the fundamental principle of the legal system.[89] The Soviets even formed their own public commission to monitor the observance of human rights in accordance with the Helsinki accords. Soviet authorities also began to exhibit more tolerance toward environmentalists and Jews, Armenians, and other national groups who protested in public. In keeping with the spirit of *glasnost*, the Soviets even allowed a team of U.S. psychiatrists to inspect mental hospitals reputed to torture political dissidents.[90]

Among the many challenges Gorbachev faced, none was as important as the state of the Soviet economy. His skills in communicating a political message and his administrative-technocratic approach to solving problems combined to reinforce in the public's eye his image as a manager's manager and a bureaucrat's bureaucrat, thereby lending greater credibility to his leadership. The need to reformulate and communicate a new political reality also meant "re-imaging . . . the past" by rendering justice to history's victims and searching for models of reform in the Soviet past[91] such as Lenin's New Economic Policy (NEP).[92]

Since the tsarist notion of "reform from above" and the Soviet institutional emphasis on "revolution from above"[93] recalled the autocratic traditions of the past, Gorbachev attempted to place *perestroika* within a more contemporary context by emphasizing its simultaneous nature as "revolution 'from above' and 'from below.'"[94] In more concrete terms, this meant placing greater emphasis on introducing market principles, promoting private property, and implementing the transition from within a political economy.[95] Of course, reform also meant westernization. But westernization was an eclectic process, and it raised the question of which West the Soviet Union should emulate. Was it the West of the revolutions of 1789, 1848, or even 1968 or the West of mass consumption, rock music, or a popular culture defined by uninspired television programming, advertising, and commercials?[96]

For these reasons substantial reform could not be a litany of words, slogans, or public statements of encouragement, although Gorbachev continued to labor under the misconception that it was in part possible, given the right amount of political skill and energy, to make a revolution or speak it into existence through words and determination. The problem, however, went beyond an analysis of verbal discourse and inherited political structures to the party's inability to create a new set of social images and symbols to replace the bureaucratic codes and language of the past.[97] In this regard Gorbachev was more than marginally successful, since he did deliver the Soviet people from "fear of thought and speech,"[98] enrich the quality of Soviet political discourse, and promote the concept of "*political pluralism*."[99]

As one attempts to analyze the bifurcated nature of Gorbachev's legacy and move beyond his Olympian rhetoric, one feels constrained to ask: While Gorbachev talked the good talk, had he walked the good walk? A brief look at some of his early speeches suggests that he succeeded in the former, but failed in the latter. In his February 1986 address to the Twenty-seventh Party Congress, he called for improving social relations, framing a new mentality, and forging a new psychology.[100] But he revealed his penchant for grandiosity when he challenged the Togliatti auto workers in April 1986 to step up and become the fashion leader in the world automobile industry.[101] Yeltsin later described the "shame and horror" felt among the engineers and technicians at such a charge, which may have revealed more about Gorbachev's political misperceptions than it did about his political exuberance.[102] Still, although Gorbachev's optimism would frequently soar, it by no means went unchecked. And he also discovered early on that instead of swimming swiftly downstream, he was often struggling to make his way in the opposite direction.

These moments of candid public reflection, though significant and revealing, did not prevent Gorbachev from remaining on message. On the occasion of his February 1987 speech to the Trade Unions Congress, entitled "Restructuring—A Vital Concern of the People," he proudly cited the Soviet Union's "unprecedented advance from the wooden plough and the primitive lamp to space flights." The metaphorical allusion to a transition from rural Russia to a new space age technology also set the stage for his sermon on productivity and efficiency, emphasizing labor ethics and the need for more pride and responsibility in the workplace. He then summoned the members of his audience to combat the "inertia" and the "stagnation and dormancy" that were sapping Soviet society of its energy, and he denounced sluggishness, corruption, greed, and the abuse of public funds.[103] Given the symbolic role of a workers' audience in a socialist state, the approach was vintage Gorbachev, as he had gone on site and directly challenged the Soviet workforce to increase productivity and support the call for change through restructuring.

On a much larger scale, however, the bitterness and criticism that accompanied *perestroika*[104] also revealed Gorbachev's lack of a plan for comprehensive political and economic reform, as well as the absence of any quick fix that could miraculously dispose of the command-administrative model. Moreover, his inability to find a way to transform a centrally planned economy into "a market-oriented decentralized" consumer economy cost him politically, as he switched back and forth from one counterproductive policy to another.[105] Moreover, by "going directly to the people" and encouraging citizens to vent their frustrations publicly,[106] he not only changed the style of political discourse and raised popular expectations, he also fueled the "combustible combination of perestroika and glasnost"[107] that transformed the political process from within and eventually provoked the system's demise. Thus, despite all his enthusiasm and energy, Gorbachev's initial approach was doomed to failure,[108] and instead of triumphing as the bold new leader with a new vision of the future, he found himself cast in the role of the man in the middle who was unable, despite all his vigorous leadership, to transform centuries of behavior and a Potemkin village mentality[109] into a city of political accountability.

Nowhere was Gorbachev's political myopia more apparent than in his inability to comprehend the disruptive dynamics of the nationalities question within the Soviet Union. Of course, Gorbachev deserved much of the credit and the blame for the "explosive" nature of the nationalities problem,[110] since he had underestimated the destabilizing impact of his reforms and overestimated his ability as the author of *glasnost*, to "unleash a 'search for truth' and control it or stop it" whenever he pleased.[111] In *Perestroika*, Gorbachev began his discussion of the nationalities question with an obligatory invocation of the Soviet Union's diversity as a sign of its "might" not of its "weakness." But political shortsightedness led him to chastise those experiencing a reawakening of national self-consciousness for descending to the level of nationalism.[112] His efforts to present "*Soviet* patriotism" as a medley of nationalities living in freedom and in religious and ethnic harmony as proud members of a great Eurasian power[113] further exposed his naïveté and often exacerbated existing conflicts and frustrations, as did his assertion that Russian served a natural role as "a common means of communication" within "our vast multi-ethnic country."[114] In fact, the resistance among many non-Russian peoples to Soviet domination and "cultural assimilation" and the failure of government officials living in the provinces to learn the local languages[115] put the lie to the multicultural premise.

For millions of Soviet citizens, the desire to conjure up the Stalinist past was a difficult and risky proposition. And Gorbachev's willingness to rehabilitate many of Stalin's victims[116] provided a new stimulus to end the "Great Silence."[117] Simply put, the question was whether one could balance the rapid and massive industrialization of the Stalin era and the emergence of the Soviet Union as a superpower against the personality cult and the millions who died as a result of collectivization, the purges, and the Soviet Union's inadequate preparation for the Nazi invasion in 1941. The process of judicial revision and historical rehabilitation was fraught with problems. Since Soviet historians were by nature and profession timid, conservative, and circumspect in their political thinking, they were reluctant to participate in "disinterring the truth"[118] and acknowledging Soviet "culpability" for specific crimes such as the Katyn massacre of Polish officers during World War II[119] or the massive reign of terror that had gripped the Soviet Union under Stalin's rule. The task of this critique fell to playwrights, filmmakers, novelists, and journalists such as Mikhail Shatrov, Tengiz Abuladze, and Anatoli Rybakov, whose artistic forays into the sacred preserve of Soviet history provoked a saber-rattling confrontation with historians. And while many of the Soviet Union's leading historians distanced themselves from the debate, mavericks like Yuri Afnasyev, the newly appointed director of the Institute of World History, called for the Soviet Union to overcome its "historical amnesia" and confront its Stalinist past.[120] In a similar vein, the Memorial Society, originally formed to erect a monument to Stalin's victims, had rapidly developed into a nationwide organization advocating a radical de-Stalinization of the Soviet system.[121] As a thriving network of information, it labored "to restore" a nation's memory and expose the terror of the *gulag*[122] by flooding the public consciousness with new revelations concerning the horrible events of the Stalinist past.[123]

As the scales fell from Soviet eyes and the public's vision began to improve, the style of combat began to intensify, as evidenced in the publication of Nina Andreyeva's March 13, 1988, letter, "Polemics: I Cannot Forego My Principles," in *Sovetskaya Rossiya*. The letter took the form of a militant "manifesto against *glasnost*" and served as a template of conservative reaction to *perestroika*.[124] As an indictment of *perestroika*, it also conferred upon the author newfound status as a standard bearer for the political right. A dedicated chemistry teacher with a perfect proletarian pedigree, Andreyeva quickly established her political credibility and her ability "to write a complex article" that reflected "the voice of 'the people.'" The fact that her parents were workers in the Putilov factory in Leningrad, the birthplace of the revolution, and "that a member of her family [had been] 'repressed' under Stalin and posthumously rehabilitated in 1953" provided additional weight and passion to her political broadside.[125] "Packed with anti-Semitism, patriotic xenophobia and nostalgia for Stalinism,"[126] the letter arrived as an unexpected ideological thunderbolt, castigating the Soviet leadership for losing its "political bearings" and creating "ideological confusion" among Soviet youth.[127] Andreyeva also attacked cosmopolitans and refuseniks and condemned their tendency to characterize "Great Russian national pride as . . . great power . . . chauvinism."[128] She took aim at prominent members of the Soviet cultural elite, including the distinguished playwright Mikhail Shatrov, for distorting the historical significance of Lenin's role in the revolution. She also chided the controversial novelist, Anatoli Rybakov, for borrowing "from emigre publications" in his *Children of the Arbat*[129] and alluded to Tengiz Abuladze's disturbingly evocative film, *Repentance,* as an illustration that "attempts to place historical nihilism on a pedestal do not always work."[130] An enthusiastic champion of the crusade against cultural nihilism and moral degeneracy, Andreyeva defended traditionalist thinkers in their struggle against mass culture and registered her dismay at student remarks that conveyed the idea "that the class struggle is supposedly an obsolete term, just like the leading role of the proletariat."[131]

It is easy to see why the letter "burst," in T.S. Bialer's words, "like a bombshell on the Moscow political scene."[132] The day after it was published, party officials held a special session on Leningrad television to discuss the letter's meaning and significance.[133] Within the Politburo, Gorbachev made Yakovlev responsible for coordinating the party's reply to Andreyeva's letter, which appeared as "Principles of *Perestroika*: The Revolutionary Nature of Thinking and Acting" in *Pravda* on April 5, 1988. In the reply, Yakovlev acknowledged "Stalin's indisputable contribution to the struggle for socialism," but he also criticized Stalin "for the mass repressions and lawlessness" that had occurred during his "arbitrary rule." In response to Andreyeva's comments on the lessons of history and the morale of Soviet youth, he critiqued the need to "pursue nostalgia for the past" and attributed the nihilism and rebelliousness among Soviet youth to a "disease . . . rooted in the past," not in some notions of a new permissiveness that had led Soviet society astray. He praised the *intelligentsia* for preparing the public to understand the need for profound changes and defended the critical voice of the press against those who accused the media of undermining popular confidence in Soviet institutions and traditions.[134] While the response may not have had the same jarring impact as Andreyeva's letter, it did send a clear signal from the top. The public's reaction was one of relief. The jubilation of the intellectuals was mirrored in a "Moscow Spring" of 1988 and the birth, almost overnight, of a new argumentative political culture that suddenly transformed Pushkin Square into Moscow's Hyde Park Corner.[135]

In the complex world of Soviet politics, where symbolism and institutional transformation were closely intertwined, Gorbachev's decision to free Andrei Sakharov was perhaps the most significant public-relations gesture of the *glasnost* era and was as much the act of a practical politician as it was a humanitarian gesture.[136] But despite the enormous symbolic significance of Gorbachev's act, the respectful, often formal nature of the Gorbachev–Sakharov relationship could not mask what constituted an historically odd political couple. Theirs "was a fascinating partnership . . . very much a Russian affair,"[137] as each sought through his association with the other to advance his political vision of the future. After their initial encounter in January 1988, Sakharov came away with the impression that Gorbachev was intelligent, self-possessed, quickwitted, and consistently liberal in his outlook.[138] On the eve of the Congress of People's Deputies in the spring of 1989, however, Sakharov tempered his enthusiasm, warning of Gorbachev's "desire to obtain unlimited personal power"[139] that could lead to a "personal dictatorship."[140] Nonetheless, Sakharov did not withhold his support of Gorbachev, since he saw no alternative to Gorbachev at this critical juncture, and he acknowledged Gorbachev's catalytic role in having altered the psychology of the country and its people.[141]

The election of representatives to the Congress of People's Deputies in the spring of 1989 was the first real test of political strength for the reformist cause[142] and the first opportunity for the media to cover events and provide the candidates with a forum to air their views in public.[143] For Gorbachev the election results provided a major victory, which garnered another feather in his reformer's cap for having "orchestrated the first real elections in the history of the Soviet Union."[144] As had been the case during the Nineteenth Party Conference, Gorbachev insisted that the sessions be televised in full. And the congress turned into "such a hot running political soap opera,"[145] that "almost no one in the Soviet Union was doing his or her regular job—nearly everybody was glued to a television set."[146] Sakharov maintained that "some took vacations so they could watch all day."[147] Boris Yeltsin, who was fully aware of the transformational aspects of the congress and the number of people who were riveted to their television sets, neatly summed up the situation: "On the day the Congress opened, they were one sort of people; on the day that it closed, they were different people."[148]

The real threat to Gorbachev's authority surfaced when the audience heard delegates, emboldened by their public mandate to debate Gorbachev's election as chairman of the Supreme Soviet, say things "that they had never dreamed might be broadcast on Soviet television." A truck driver named L. I. Sukhov attacked Gorbachev by comparing him to Napoleon, who had turned "a republic [into] an empire"; Sukhov berated Gorbachev for succumbing to the "adulation and influence of . . . yes-men" and "your wife."[149] When asked about the less-than-veiled reference to being portrayed as Gorbachev's Josephine, Raisa, who was present at the congress, replied that it was "No big deal," since "everyone speaks as he perceives the world."[150] One delegate insisted on knowing whether a dacha had been built for Gorbachev in the Crimea, while another criticized Gorbachev's recent speeches for lacking "clarity and boldness" and chided him for failing to achieve the same "brilliant successes" at home that he had achieved in the international arena.[151] The most controversial and potentially explosive issue before the congress was the question of Gorbachev's political legitimacy and the call for a president to be elected directly by all the people.[152] With his persuasive powers seemingly still intact, he managed to elude the unknown consequences of a direct popular election and secure a victory as the new chairman of the Supreme Soviet by a margin of 2,123 votes in favor and 87 opposed. Having won the election, he returned to the task of presiding over the congress.[153] The image "of Gorbachev with his headphones, his arms waving, his quick flashes of temper, or his gestures of conciliation" reinforced the perception of his importance to the process, the party, and the government as a whole.[154]

In addition to generating electricity and excitement,[155] Gorbachev's proposals for reform also produced heated exchanges, flashes of personality conflict, and political theater of the highest order. At the center of the controversy stood the two leading protagonists—with Gorbachev occupying the middle ground and Yeltsin pushing the pace of reform from within. Unlike Gorbachev, who was able to combine his roles as choirmaster, choreographer, and impresario into one grand, virtuoso performance, Yeltsin was brusque, temperamental, erratic, and lacking in both political sophistication and a sense of public decorum. Given the deadly political rivalry that eventually developed between the two men, it is ironic that Gorbachev at first enthusiastically advanced Yeltsin's career by appointing him Communist party secretary for Moscow in December 1985 and naming him to the Politburo a year later. Yet, despite a common reformist outlook, the two moved in different political directions, as Yeltsin assumed the populist role of Slavophile to Gorbachev's Westernizer and earned the distinction of being the "most colorful political figure of the Gorbachev era."[156] Yeltsin's strong-willed, authoritarian personality and his irrepressible, flamboyant style contributed to his profile as an energetic political crusader. But Yeltsin's rebel image also set him on a collision course with Gorbachev. And when Yeltsin publicly confronted conservative party ideologue Yegor Ligachev over the issue of party privileges and the future of reform, the party machinery was quickly set in motion. As might be expected, Gorbachev managed to position himself as the indispensable man in the middle and remained above the fray, providing leadership and direction.

At the November 11 meeting of the Moscow City Party Committee, the Yeltsin issue came to a head. Gorbachev phoned Yeltsin and summoned him from his hospital bed in the Kremlin to attend the special meeting. Despite Yeltsin's protests, Gorbachev reassured Yeltsin, who was recovering from nervous exhaustion and under heavy medication, that the doctors would help him get out of bed and attend the meeting.[157] At the meeting Gorbachev presided over a raft of speeches denouncing Yeltsin, even joining in the attack to excoriate Yeltsin for his excessive "vanity" and putting his ambitions above "the interests of the Party."[158] Savaged by the attack,[159] Yeltsin relinquished his responsibilities as an alternate member of the Politburo and head of the Moscow City Party Organization and acknowledged his errors.[160] Yeltsin would later condemn Gorbachev's "cruelty"[161] and refer to his attackers as "a pack of hounds," who "flung themselves on me at the bidding of the chief huntsman."[162]

By the time of the opening of the Nineteenth Party Conference in June 1988, Gorbachev was less concerned about Yeltsin than he was about the future of *perestroika*. The conference itself was a watershed in Soviet history. The "first modern gathering of the Communist Party . . . not fully scripted from first to last,"[163] it provided Gorbachev with a political platform to perform at his theatrical best. For those participating and those watching his management of the proceedings, his dexterity[164] and rhetorical flourishes contributed to his image as a responsive and capable leader. By allowing the sessions to be broadcast on television, he once again succeeded in capturing the imagination of the Soviet people and transforming the proceedings into a showcase of *glasnost* at work.[165]

Yeltsin's presence, though diminished, remained a political thorn in Gorbachev's side. Gorbachev had handled "the Yeltsin affair" badly. Instead of strengthening his hand, it had actually damaged his authority[166] and cast him in the role of "a bully."[167] As a high-profile test case for *glasnost,* Yeltsin's ouster and the imposing on him of an "official silence" constituted a disaster that could hardly be considered "a shining example of increased 'transparency.'"[168] In fact, the confrontation transformed Yeltsin into "a folk hero" in the eyes of the people.[169] Although he quickly dismissed these views as delusionary, even Gorbachev felt constrained to admit that "many intellectuals, especially young people" viewed Yeltsin's departure "as a blow to *perestroika.*"[170]

As the feud intensified, Yeltsin remained undaunted in his search for personal vindication, viewing those responsible for his political crucifixion as having bestowed upon him a "martyr's halo."[171] His appropriately titled *Against the Grain,* published in 1990, was part of that effort. It reads as its author speaks. It is blunt, candid, controversial, and frequently self-referential. It also provides valuable insights into what Yeltsin describes as Gorbachev's "indecisiveness,"[172] "inconsistency and timidity,"[173] and the personalities, events, and issues that contributed to the Gorbachev–Yeltsin split and the restless mood of the people when confronted with "the party's go-slow attitude to *perestroika.*"[174] Yeltsin's criticisms cut deeply into Gorbachev's credibility, because they questioned Gorbachev's populist credentials and accused him of behaving like a "czar."[175] Yeltsin cited flaws in Gorbachev's character and his desire, shared with Raisa, "to live well, in comfort and luxury." Yeltsin also undermined Gorbachev's value as an international spokesman for the Soviet Union when he conceded that although the Gorbachevs appeared natural and normal in the prosperous West their behavior was inappropriate for the Soviet Union.[176] And while Yeltsin acknowledged that Gorbachev's significance would "go down in the history of mankind," he warned that Gorbachev had set out to blaze a new trail and climb a new mountain in which the Soviet people would either scale the heights of Everest or "be swept away by an avalanche."[177]

Yeltsin's tenacity notwithstanding, it still appeared that Gorbachev, who was more polished and more urbane than his rough-and-tumble, given-to-excess opponent, had secured an insurmountable advantage over his opponent, because he exuded a brilliance and charm that made him more attractive. Yet despite Gorbachev's early media edge, what developed between the two men was a tale of two audiences, as Russians and Muscovites in particular responded enthusiastically to Yeltsin's message, while the party hierarchy and foreign governments tended to underestimate his appeal. Foreign governments, for their part, wanted Gorbachev to succeed because of their interest in his peace and disarmament agenda. Because they felt uncomfortable with Yeltsin's impulsive, impetuous style, they were more willing to invest their own political hopes and aspirations in Gorbachev, who corresponded more closely to their preconceived notion of what an international statesman should be. Gorbachev's telegenic personality and his desire to focus on the new communication technologies as an essential component of the reform effort revealed his awareness of the dynamic properties of the media and his belief that a well-orchestrated message could serve as a powerful tool to involve the Soviet people in the reform process. Technological innovations such as television and the advent of communication satellites promised to shrink the enormous expanses of the Soviet Union, eliminate pockets of isolation, and shape a broad popular consensus.[178] Ironically, however, Gorbachev's frequent appearances on foreign television also earned for him the dubious distinction of being "the first Soviet leader to be a cult figure in the West . . . as he became a fallen icon at home."[179] The actual transformation of the political consciousness of the Soviet people, however, involved an enormous effort in behavior modification, which is why Gorbachev turned to the newer instruments of mass persuasion, and television in particular, to deliver his message.[180] But Gorbachev's attempt to restructure the psyche of the nation[181] through mass social therapy and "moral purification"[182] rested precariously upon his own flawed assumptions about the media's persuasive powers and its capacity to transcend bureaucratic opposition.[183] But engineering a major shift in popular attitudes[184] would require more than simply liberating the international airwaves for *glasnost*: new attitudes also had to take root within the body politic.

Since *glasnost* stood for more open, self-critical forms of communication and the desire to create greater "transparency" within Soviet society,[185] it made available to the public information that had been "previously concealed."[186] But the term did not mean freedom of the press.[187] Nor did it "mean freedom of speech"[188] or the right to speak out against *perestroika*.[189] In Soviet parlance, the term dates back to Lenin's use of "*glasnost* . . . as a tool for the mobilization and education of the toiling masses."[190] In its updated version under Gorbachev, *glasnost* signified a means of engaging the Soviet people in public discourse and using the "Leninist principles of transparency" to restructure governmental attitudes and policies[191] and ensure the irreversibility of the reform process. The commitment to transparency, however, rarely translated into practice. And the Soviet government's closed attitudes had long been a staple of Soviet behavior, and they extended beyond military secrecy to domestic affairs, where the government feared that admissions of failure would undermine public support for the regime. To combat these tendencies, Gorbachev offered *glasnost* as an instrument to restore people's faith in government. Although Gorbachev highlighted the importance of "straight talk"[192] in government, he carefully stressed that criticism did "not mean torpedoing socialism and its values."[193]

Of the many areas touched by Gorbachev's reforms, *glasnost* had its most powerful impact on the relationship between politics and culture. Much of the new cultural vitality came from members of the *intelligentsia*, their cultural prestige contributed to the perception of *glasnost* as a "thinking man's revolution." Gorbachev, of course, eagerly welcomed the *intelligentsia*'s support and did everything he could to encourage them to come in from the cold of the Brezhnev years. Despite the excitement surrounding the new openness, con-

servatives had a powerful case in believing that too much criticism could po-
larize the people and breed pessimism among the masses.[194]

This hostile, conservative climate saw the emergence of *Pamyat* (Memory),
a "reactionary, nationalistic, . . . rabidly anti-Semitic"[195] society that was the
most visible manifestation of Russia's new ultranationalism. In their anti-
Semitic zeal, members of the right never failed to stress that Marx was a Jew
and made outlandish claims that Stalin had fallen under the influence of Leon
Trotsky and Lazar Kaganovich, who were also Jewish. Given Trotsky's execution at Stalin's behest, it is hard to imagine a more preposterous charge than
that of Stalin's having succumbed to Trotsky's influence. The right even
claimed that Lenin had a Jewish grandfather and kept three copies of the *Protocols of the Elders of Zion* in his library.[196]

Given Gorbachev's desire to turn the media into a "tool for 'psychological
reconstruction,' "[197] his attempts to transform the propaganda function of the
press into a vehicle for providing information on changes within the Soviet
Union were more than cosmetic.[198] He even believed that the media would
have to assume greater responsibility in combating inefficiency, corruption,[199]
favoritism,[200] and the "sclerotic" opposition to reform within the party hierarchy.[201] In keeping with these pronouncements, the February 13, 1986, issue
of *Pravda* printed a scathing indictment charging that party members had
"stopped being Communists long ago" and called for a purge of the *apparat*
and an end to the abuses and privileges that created inequalities within the
system.[202] The advent of *glasnost*, however, also raised a number of questions
concerning the Soviet Union's ability to withstand the effects of the new
transparency. One area of immediate concern was the leadership's ability to
manage changes in the state's communication and information network in a
way that would prevent the party's losing its authority.[203] The fundamental
problem involved the free flow of information and the role of the press in
public edification. The arrival of more information from abroad via the new
communications technologies also made it increasingly difficult for the state
to seal off frontiers and isolate communities from outside influences.[204]

In *Perestroika*, Gorbachev praised the Soviet press for its incisiveness and
willingness to engage in polemical issues concerning the progress of restructuring.[205] He also repeated his famous dictum—"We need *glasnost* as we need
the air"—and reinforced the importance of the media's role in "enhancing the
political maturity of the people."[206] The relaxation of rigid controls over the
press also opened fresh journalistic windows on the West, as enterprising edi-
tors and pro-*glasnost* party officials provided Soviet readers with greater access
to foreign news and commentary. For the first time, newspapers such as the
Guardian, Financial Times, and *International Herald Tribune* were available to
readers in the Soviet Union. What came as a real surprise, however, was
Pravda's emergence as a primary source of information. Its decision to include
unedited commentary from U.S. Senate president Robert Dole and prominent
American Sovietologists and historians such as Zbigniew Brzezinski and

Richard Pipes on political issues was clearly in keeping with the new spirit of openness.[207] The dramatic changes in political outlook, however, hardly provided a windfall for *Pravda* and *Izvestia*, as Soviet citizens eagerly subscribed to *Moscow News* and *Ogonyok*, while the circulation of *Pravda* and *Izvestia* "plummeted."[208]

Additional access to information from the West also created a greater thirst for international news[209] and a greater awareness among Soviet authorities of the risks involved in relinquishing control over "agenda-setting" in the face of the public's desire for greater information from a wide variety of sources. But the "galloping tempo of the information revolution" abroad and the emergence of a "much more complex audience . . . at home" put pressure on Soviet officials to revise their policies in favor of a more open approach to the presentation of news and information.[210] The new openness was reflected in the decision to lift the ban on the BBC's Russian broadcasts and later the Voice of America, although the Soviets still viewed Radio Liberty in Munich as the "Number One Enemy" and continued to jam its transmissions.[211]

Even more than the role of Soviet and Western newspapers and access to foreign radio broadcasts, it was television's coverage of Gorbachev as a political figure and a reformer that was primarily responsible for redefining the new Soviet political idiom. Gorbachev's ability to personalize politics and his legendary charisma enabled him to shape public opinion[212] and capitalize on his high-profile visits to Western capitals to reinforce his image as a world statesman who was respected and admired both at home and abroad.[213] To be sure, the favorable treatment Gorbachev received in the media did not mean that the press was simply a pliant tool for Gorbachev's public relations. For example, he was often furious with the press for its coverage of the nationalities question, especially for inflammatory pieces in the media appearing at these tense moments when he was trying to tone down the rebellious mood in the Baltic states.[214]

With the advent of new information technologies that made it possible to reach across frontiers to promote peace and international understanding, Soviet reformers turned to satellite hookups to connect viewers with foreign audiences around the world.[215] The Soviets revealed an almost innocent belief in the power of the new communications technologies to change the world. But the information revolution posed a different, and in some ways a more powerful, challenge in a critical area where the Soviets were lagging behind the United States—computer technology. For the KGB and members of the Politburo, however, the fascination with the tools of international communication and the desire to provide greater access to information through a network of personal computers and home modems posed a dangerous threat to the system's survival.[216] But the countervailing danger of what might happen to the Soviet Union's technological and economic aspirations,[217] if it failed to integrate the computer as "the basic tool of the new technological age,"[218] could not be ignored. The leadership approved a transitional process they believed would guarantee government security and enable the party to manage the flow of information and maintain its "claim to power."[219]

Of the many problems that plagued Soviet information policy and the use of communication technologies, Chernobyl provided the most vivid example of the government's inability to manage the flow of information during a crisis. The sudden and unexpected explosion of the nuclear power plant at Chernobyl, a prized piece of Soviet technology,[220] on the morning of April 26, 1986, revealed the Janus-like personality of Soviet science and engineering. The government's initial imposition of a news blackout[221] accompanied by a wave of bureaucratic confusion made it difficult to detail the scope of the emergency, treat the injured, evacuate the victims, and assess the threat posed by radiation. From all indications, it appears that Gorbachev was kept informed of developments, although he preferred to remain silent and follow "the Kremlin routine."[222] When initial news of the accident came from Sweden (which experienced nuclear fallout from the explosion) and not from the Soviet Union,[223] the decision to withhold important information only made matters worse. To say the least, Chernobyl was not Gorbachev's "finest . . . hour."[224]

When Gorbachev finally appeared on Soviet television and broke the public silence, he attributed the delays in providing information to the need to obtain an accurate scientific evaluation of the situation. He dismissed the invention of a "'lack' of information . . . campaign" as pernicious[225] and accused the West of waging an "unrestrained anti-Soviet campaign." He also condemned Western governments and the media for spreading the "most brazen and malicious lies" about what had happened at Chernobyl.[226] But his emphasis on criticizing the West rather than discussing the consequences of the catastrophe[227] failed to reassure viewers either at home or abroad. His errors of omission passed over the damage caused by radiation, health hazards, and the ill-considered siting of nuclear power plants.[228] In nearly every respect he failed to achieve the high standards he had set for himself as a leader[229] and the goals he had set for *glasnost*.[230] Ironically, the government's secretive and dilatory behavior transformed the Chernobyl disaster into a devastating failure for *glasnost*[231] and the corollary concept of *operativnost*, which referred to the timely provision of information to the public.[232] Gorbachev's less-than-forthright behavior and delay in addressing the issue hardly burnished "his reputation for decisiveness and openness"[233] and raised the crucial question: "What did Gorbachev know about Chernobyl, and when did he know it?"[234] Writing later of Chernobyl in *Perestroika*, Gorbachev tried to set a less strident, more conciliatory tone, as he acknowledged the need for "full and unbiased information" and cited the absence of any "vested interests that would compel us to conceal the truth."[235] But the damage had already been done, and while the tone was willing, his message was weak.

For Gorbachev *glasnost* also meant reviving the Soviet *intelligentsia* "from their slumber by liberating" their artistic creativity[236] and enlisting their political support. With his support *glasnost* also managed to prevail over the objections of party conservatives. Works by Russian authors that had been previously published abroad, including Alexander Solzhenitsyn's *Gulag Archipelago,* Boris Pasternak's *Doctor Zhivago,* and Vladimir Nabokov's *Lolita,* now appeared in the Soviet Union,[237] as did works by foreign authors such as Franz Kafka's *The Castle,* Aldous Huxley's *Brave New World,* James Joyce's *Ulysses,* George Orwell's *Animal Farm,* Arthur Koestler's *Darkness at Noon,* Umberto Eco's *Name of the Rose,* and even Ken Kesey's *One Flew over the Cuckoo's Nest.*[238] But the most important publication of the period came not from the émigré literature but from within the Soviet Union, with the spring 1987 appearance of Anatoli Rybakov's *Children of the Arbat.* In much the same way that Tengiz Abuladze's film *Repentance* became the cinematic focus of the period in exposing Stalin's cruelty, Rybakov's novel served as the main literary weapon in the assault on Stalin's tyranny. In Gorbachev's words, Rybakov's work "helped to conquer the fear that many people still had of the consequences of unmasking totalitarianism."[239]

In his novel, Rybakov attempted "to reconstruct the psychological world of" Stalin's organized madness[240] by casting him as "The Supreme Power [who] was ALL-KNOWING, ALL-WISE, ALL-POWERFUL."[241] What dominates the work is a ubiquitous sense of fear and foreboding within a regime permeated by implacable ruthlessness, a regime in which the hopes, dreams, and plans of all the characters—except one, Stalin—are subject to sudden and capricious reversal.[242] Rybakov's remarkable ability to recreate the power, detachment, and terror in Stalin's mind through the fictional reconstruction of his own words and internal monologues is particularly chilling.

Rybakov chooses the theme of crime and punishment and structures his narrative in the form of a journey of personal awareness. The hero, Sasha Pankratov, a naïve and trusting young man in his early twenties who belongs to Moscow's young urban elite, finds himself summarily banished to the outer limits of the Soviet penal system in Siberia for having been found guilty of nothing more than the innocent insertion of some political doggerel into a student wall bulletin. But the journey is not his alone to make. It is also a powerful metaphor for a similar journey undertaken by the Soviet people as a whole. Sasha's mother, appropriately named Sofya, though simple in her ways, is both wise and resourceful. She is a symbol of mother Russia, who provides strength and stability to nurture the dreams and the love between Sasha and Varya, the romantic and equally courageous young woman in his life, who shares the pain of their separation across the vast reaches of the Soviet landscape. The book was a huge success within the Soviet Union as well as in the West. No one could deny its penetrating insights into that gruesome period of Stalin's terror. Emphasizing the need to rehabilitate "the Stalin-damaged psyche of the entire community,"[243] Rybakov viewed his work as part of an ongoing cultural process to awaken people's initiative and transform "the psychology of every man and woman" through novels, film, theater, and television.[244]

Like books, films also played a prominent role in upsetting the pre-*perestroika* consensus. In film, the artistic revolution began in May 1986 with the election of Elem Klimov as president of the Filmmakers' Union, an event Klimov wryly described as "historic . . ., though some . . . prefer to call it hysteric."[245] As a committed social reformer, Klimov believed that it was necessary to engage in "a real moral cleansing and a public condemnation" of those who "refuse to repent" for their past actions. As a conscientious artist, he assigned direct responsibility for the sorry state of contemporary affairs to the impoverished condition of mass culture and the mass media in the Soviet Union.[246] In true visionary fashion, he also held out the hope that a new wave of independence in the film industry and "a new pluralistic" outlook in film criticism[247] could "improve the moral and spiritual atmosphere around the world" and create a new interconnectedness among peoples and nations by addressing issues of real political and social significance.[248]

The documentary film provided Soviet filmmakers with an important vehicle to vent their political views. Documentaries such as *Pain* and *Homecoming* spotlighted the brutality, aimlessness, anger, and bitterness associated with the war in Afghanistan. Juris Podnieks's *Is It Easy to Be Young?,* which Gorbachev himself proclaimed "one of the first birds of *glasnost,*" explored the world of the physically and emotionally maimed veterans of the Afghan conflict; the alarming level of violence and drug abuse in Soviet society;[249] and the iconoclastic attitudes and tortured lifestyles among Soviet youth. Podnieks applied the same kind of social criticism in his treatment of alienation and social unrest in his feature film *Little Vera,* which included shocking portrayals of nudity, drug abuse, and explicit sex. The film was also politically and ideologically controversial because of its "candid portrayal of the caldron of frustration and rage among Soviet workers."[250]

When it premiered in 1986, Tengiz Abuladze's film, *Pokanie* (*Repentance*), triumphed as a powerful beacon of cinematic political expression. Laden with futuristic imagery, the film's rich visual texture and composition artfully blend images of flowers and funerals with music and speeches to evoke the beauty of life and the ritualistic, often painful aspects of human existence. One of the most compelling scenes in the film depicts characters encased in a new, depersonalized structure resembling an enormous elevated hothouse, while guards, hovering ominously above, make their rounds peering down through the glass on the prisoners within. Another disturbing scene involves a Dali-like presentation of police dressed as medieval soldiers inexorably pursuing their prey through the streets of the city and into the countryside, where no one can escape the grasp of Varlam, the film's ubiquitous and menacing presence.

Varlam, whose name means No One, is a dictator whose style and sinister behavior recall the manner of an Oriental despot.[251] Through Varlam the film resurrects the paranoid, institutionalized fear of the Stalinist past, as underlings vie for Varlam's favor while he poses on his balcony like Mussolini to observe the citizens of his city pass in review. He is both malevolent and charming, predatory and genteel, as demonstrated by his visit to the home of the artist Sandro, who represents human dignity and a belief in spiritual, artistic values. Varlam arrives drunk and exposes the sinister side of his nature through his cunning, sadistic demeanor and sudden and capricious outbursts of rage and anger. What renders Varlam truly frightening, however, is that he is both crafty and culturally literate, which he demonstrates first by performing as an operatic singer and then reciting Shakespeare's sonnet 66 on disillusionment. Yet, despite these poetic and musical interludes, the pervasive moral depravity of the novel resurfaces when soldiers enter the room of Sandro's wife Nino, issuing the hollow blessing, "Peace unto your house," before they arrest her. The symbolism of the film is further developed during the burial of Sandro, who metaphorically emerges as a vessel for the universal creative spirit. The rituals surrounding Sandro's death and burial are accompanied with passages from Schiller's *Ode to Joy,* as rendered in Beethoven's *Ninth Symphony.* As his body passes through water to recall his baptism, death, cleansing, and redemption, the music pays homage to his soul. Then the church that he had labored so strenuously to preserve suddenly blows up.

The theme of rising from the dead resurfaces, albeit in a different form, when Varlam dies but refuses to remain in his grave. In cartoonlike fashion he randomly reappears after every interment to strut about as his former imperious self. Sandro's daughter Keti wants Varlam's family to exhume Varlam's body so that he and his crimes will not be forgotten. When Tornike, Varlam's grandson, finds out about Varlam's crimes, he confronts his father Abel with the truth of Varlam's deeds. Abel offers his son a traditional explanation based upon political necessity and a public servant's need to forego private concerns. But it is only after listening to the popular western song "Sunny" that young Tornike decides to confront his parents. Failing to obtain a satisfactory explanation, he commits suicide by shooting himself in the head with a revolver. In Tornike's collapsed body lies the image of yet another generation of Soviet youth, lacking direction, at a loss for fixed social, cultural, and political values, confused about the present, anxious about the future, and haunted by the specter of individual and collective self-destruction that had become part of the new Soviet reality.

Tornike's suicide shocks Abel and forces him to confront his past. He turns to God in search of moral principles, to the power of the Georgian Church, to the symbolic values represented in a fish's skeleton, to his reflection in a mirror, to an encounter with the devil, and even to solving the riddle of Rubik's cube. In the end Abel discovers that he must act: He exhumes his father's corpse and throws it over the edge of a cliff overlooking a new, modern city. In that act, he frees himself and his family not only of his father's corpse but of Stalin's corpse as well. In the final scene of the movie an old woman stops at Keti's window to ask her where she can find the church. Keti tells her it is not there. And when the woman inquires as to the name of the street, Keti tells her it is Varlam street, prompting the old woman to reply in a marvelously synoptic comment on the Stalinist past: "What good is it, if it doesn't lead to a church?"

Under *glasnost* the search for institutional meaning and inspiration also produced dramatic changes in the previously monolithic character of Soviet theater. Gorbachev's desire to court the *intelligentsia* and recast the state's relationship with the theater began to bear fruit when the distinguished playwright Mikhail Shatrov and the renowned Soviet actor Mikhail Ulyanov combined their political zeal and artistic passion to speak out in support of reform. As had been the case with Rybakov's novel *Children of the Arbat* and Abuladze's film *Repentance,* Shatrov's plays provided new insights into the controversial debate over reinterpreting the Soviet past, depicting in *That's How We'll Win!* a "painfully isolated" Lenin, assessing his incomplete mission and the future course of the revolution.[252] In *The Dictatorship of Conscience* Shatrov raises the crucial question of Lenin's responsibility for paving the way for Stalin and the imposition of the Stalinist system,[253] only to have Lenin declare in *Onward, Onward, Onward!*: "I want everyone to know that I entirely accept the guilt and moral responsibility for what happened."[254] But of all Shatrov's plays the one that created the greatest public controversy was *The Brest Peace,* in which Lenin's sacrilegious "genuflection . . . to Trotsky," imploring Trotsky to sign the Treaty of Brest-Litovsk, enraged party conservatives and the cultural custodians of political orthodoxy.[255]

If Shatrov was *glasnost*'s playwright and political conscience, then Mikhail Ulyanov was its leading man. Ulyanov's political persona was as intriguing as his stage presence. Like Klimov and Shatrov, Ulyanov was no newcomer to the Soviet political scene, and he emerged under *glasnost* as a major spokesman for cultural freedom and political reform as the elected leader of the new Russian Theater Workers' Union.[256] As an activist, he enthusiastically embraced the political role of the Soviet theater[257] and celebrated his commitment "to make the theater a force for political culture and democratization."[258] In his "raging passion for perestroika,"[259] Ulyanov depicted Stalinism as "a plague on our country"[260] and praised Gorbachev's leadership and willingness to pass the torch to the artistic *intelligentsia.*

Compared to the dramatic changes in the Filmmakers' Union, conservative members of the old guard within the Composers' Union insisted on chastising Soviet youth for their indifference to "high culture" and Russia's classical musical tradition and their fascination with rock music and the "bad taste," "lack of ideals,"[261] and "cult of mindless entertainment" it represented.[262] Soviet youth, of course, viewed the matter differently. And their defiant behavior, blue jeans culture, and commercialism had clearly transformed the youth movement into a political battleground, where conservatives blamed the corrupting influence of the West for the rise in juvenile delinquency, drug abuse, and sexual excess[263] and launched a puritanical attack on eroticism and permissiveness for undermining the Soviet Union's morality.

Glasnost also produced lively disputes in the visual arts over what constituted contemporary art and which avant-gardists and cosmopolitans from the artistically degenerate past should be rehabilitated. The publicity surrounding a

Marc Chagall exhibit in 1989 stirred the greatest controversy and provoked the ire of conservatives, who in typical Soviet fashion needed a statement by the minister of culture to conclude that "the avant garde was also a fact."[264] But the new attitudes also reawakened pride in famous Russian-born émigré artists such as Kandinsky and Malevich and a new interest in foreign painters such as Salvador Dali, whose surrealist works were officially exhibited in Moscow for the first time in the spring of 1988.[265] It would be a mistake, however, to measure the artistic ferment under *glasnost* by referring exclusively to changes within the official arts organizations and government-sponsored activities, since the more unorthodox manifestations of "unofficial pop" in the form of innovative theater groups, street art, and the ecology movement also reflected a new spirit of independence and freedom of expression.[266]

"NEW THINKING"

Gorbachev's "New Thinking" represented a radical break with the past[267] and the adoption of a more open foreign policy to reflect how sophisticated and up to date Soviet society had become. Gorbachev was, by temper, predisposition, and ability, obviously well suited to a new approach to international relations emphasizing a new cosmopolitan outlook, the art of public diplomacy, and the importance of political persuasion.[268] In an effort to transform the conventions of public diplomacy, Gorbachev took the world by surprise with the fall 1987 publication of *Perestroika: New Thinking for Our Country and the World*. As a foreign policy manifesto, the book was part publicrelations folder, part self-promotion, and part challenge for the international future. By treating *perestroika* as *"An Urgent Necessity"*[269] Gorbachev raised the possibility of a genuine relaxation in international tensions and of greater cooperation between the world's two superpowers.

In tone and presentation the book also marked a new chapter in the ideological conflict between East and West by recalling the new diplomacy of Lenin and Wilson at the beginning of the twentieth century. Like Lenin, Gorbachev emphasized the importance of "public opinion" and "citizen diplomacy." He forthrightly acknowledged that "in this age of mass information and mass interest in international problems," political communication had to be "accompanied by propaganda," because ideas "must 'impress.'"[270] But he also reinforced the urgency of his message by appealing to the notion of a single global community, faced with the threat of nuclear war and destruction[271] and to the need for a new internationalism and "universal human values"[272] to take precedence over revolutionary class conflict.[273]

Though generous in his worldview, Gorbachev was unrelenting in his criticism of government officials and members of the Western press for wanting the Soviet reform effort to fail. And he was most deeply offended by the "uncivilized attitudes"[274] of American officials, who portrayed "the October Revolution [as] a blunder in history" and the Soviet Union as an "evil empire."[275]

These new reservations notwithstanding, Gorbachev used *Perestroika* to campaign for "a nuclear-weapon-free and nonviolent world,"[276] and he targeted the arms race and the threat of nuclear war as part of his campaign to call into question the West's "moral superiority."[277] He expressed his dismay over how the Stars Wars program, for example, could "be classified as peaceful aspirations," and he challenged his American audience to "get in our shoes and see how you would react."[278] Given his views on the suicidal and unwinnable nature of nuclear war, he set out in earnest to transform the nature of the superpower rivalry between the United States and the Soviet Union and translate his new political outlook into a global structure for peace.[279]

Gorbachev realized, however, that if the transformational process were to be successful, the Soviets would have "to get over [their] inferiority complex" in order for both countries to overcome the wall of "suspicion" that divided the two states.[280] Pending an ideological ceasefire, however, Gorbachev continued to challenge America's self-perception as virtuous with its "almost missionary passion for preaching about human rights and liberties," while refusing to ensure "those same elementary rights" to its own citizens. Gorbachev showed that he too was capable of applying rhetorical stereotypes by challenging the validity of America's image "as a 'shining city atop a hill,'" since the United States still had to cope with urban crime and widespread poverty despite its "enormous material wealth."[281]

Gorbachev also felt constrained to address the insecurity implied by "strategic parity" in nuclear weapons. And to reach a point of nuclear stability, he believed that the West would have to give up "the illusory hope" of using the arms race to provoke the political disintegration and/or economic collapse of the Soviet Union.[282] He also summarily dismissed Reagan's claims "about the defensive character" of SDI as "fairy tales for naive people."[283] Of course, the root cause of the U.S.–Soviet rivalry lay not in the nuclear calculus or even in the technological dynamics of the arms race, but in the political and military origins of the Cold War that had given birth to the deadly military competition. And the Soviets placed the burden for starting the Cold War squarely on the U.S. decision to drop the nuclear bomb on Hiroshima and Nagasaki.[284] But Soviet attitudes were also beginning to change under *glasnost*, as the Soviets began to acknowledge their role in the Cold War and Stalin's imposition of control in Eastern Europe through fear and power politics.

In his desire to break the political stalemate between the United States and the Soviet Union, Gorbachev set out promote the cause of world peace and avert another costly round in the arms race. Gorbachev's new style of diplomacy also made an excellent impression in Europe,[285] since he appealed to a shared political tradition, a common cultural heritage, and the concept of Europe as "Our Common Home,"[286] which gave birth to a new political phenomenon known as "Gorbymania."[287]

Gorbachev's view of the external threat to Europe originating from within the United States, however, extended well beyond the issues of war and militarization. The threat also included "an onslaught of 'mass culture' from across the Atlantic."[288] In an obvious attempt to court Western Europeans, Gorbachev condemned the exportation of American violence and pornography,[289] while extolling Europe's common cultural heritage and its enormous economic, scientific, and technical potential. In retrospect, as the Soviet Union's primary ambassador of goodwill and "New Thinking," Gorbachev sometimes seemed best suited to a role as mayor of Europe, who could draw from a rich collection of metaphors to illustrate his political positions and regional thinking. For example, in a speech he delivered in Murmansk in October 1987, he described the Arctic and North Atlantic as a "weather kitchen" where "one can feel . . . the freezing breath" of the Pentagon's nuclear arsenal of ships and submarines and the need to create a "zone of peace" nurtured "by the warm Gulfstream of the European processes" and sheltered from "the Polar chill" of suspicion and prejudice.[290]

Although Gorbachev's peace offensive and dramatic proposals for arms control and reductions had elicited an enthusiastic public response in the West, his attempts at the "'decoupling of Europe' from America" did not sit well with Western European governments and many foreign policy experts,[291] who viewed Gorbachev's "idea of a Common European Home" as an attempt to weaken the Atlantic Alliance[292] and "drive a wedge between Western leaders and their publics."[293] Even Margaret Thatcher, who admired Gorbachev as a political figure, expressed concern over a strategy that was designed to divide the Western alliance and create a split between Europe and the United States[294] and assumed a combative pose when she clashed with Gorbachev over the denuclearization of Europe.[295]

Of course, the situation in Eastern Europe was completely different, since the region had served as the Soviet Union's front line of defense against an attack from the West since the end of World War II. But Gorbachev's flexibility as a member of the new generation of Soviet leaders also suggested that he might challenge the conventional wisdom concerning Soviet domination in Eastern Europe.[296] Expectations of such a shift were manifested by the crowds in Eastern Europe who hailed him as "Mikhail the Liberator."[297] Gorbachev was shrewd enough to use this infectious wave of "Gorby fever" to counter the endemic postwar resentment of the Soviets. During his April 1987 visit to Prague, Gorbachev made his way through the crowds "jubilantly pressing the flesh," while "the normally Russophobic residents" of the city greeted him with "shouts of '*Druzhba! Druzhba!*,' the Russian word for friendship."[298] When asked during a press conference to comment on "the difference between the program of the ousted reformer Alexander Dubček and Gorbachev's New Thinking," Gennady Gerasimov glibly responded: "Nineteen years."[299]

In Poland, the Soviet Union had effectively gained control over the "Polish corridor"[300] by sealing off the historic route of invasion from the West after World War II. Beginning with the Polish trade union movement Solidarity in 1981 and Poland's reemergence as the "main engine of change" in the spring of 1989, the political and military stakes were and remained enormous.[301] The presence of Pope John Paul II obviously added another important political dimension to Soviet relations with Poland. Serving as the spiritual voice of Catholics in Eastern Europe and as a symbol of Polish nationalism and independence, John Paul generated a thunderous response during his visits to his native land. Given his stature within the international community, his position suggested that as long as he remained pope, a portion of the road to Polish independence would now have to pass through Rome.

In addition to generating an unprecedented wave of popular euphoria, Gorbachev's policies and his message of change produced discord within the Eastern European leadership.[302] The pro-reform camp of Poland and Hungary greeted Gorbachev's "reforms . . . with official applause,"[303] while other Eastern European regimes found the implications of *glasnost* and democratization most unsettling.[304] Since Gorbachev had not fully considered the demoralizing impact his "gamble on liberalization" would have on the Eastern European regimes,[305] the split produced a dramatic role reversal in which Moscow suddenly found itself spearheading the liberalization drive, while Eastern European hardliners were dragging their feet. By the fall of 1989, the pace of change had become so rapid that it overwhelmed the entire empire. Solidarity triumphed in Poland. Church bells tolled in Budapest, as Hungarians peacefully overthrew the government and shouted "Russians go home!" and "Gorby! Gorby!" In November, the Berlin wall fell, Bulgaria's hardline regime collapsed, and Czechoslovakia's Velvet Revolution led to the formation of a new democratic government under Vaclav Havel,[306] who proved that, unlike the failed revolutions of 1848, it was possible for "a poet in politics" to emerge as the leader of his country. The fact that the Soviets issued "a nicely timed retrospective condemnation of the 1968 Warsaw Pact invasion" also served as heady encouragement for Prague reformers.[307] In Romania, however, a totally different form of poetic justice led to the summary execution of Nicolae Ceauşescu and his wife Elena on Christmas day.

But Gorbachev's intentions were most fully tested by the thorny question of German unification and the future of Berlin. In *Perestroika* Gorbachev had discussed the different social and political systems separating the two German states. In light of party chief Erich Honecker's declaration "that the path of perestroika did not suit East Germany,"[308] Gorbachev's own role in elevating the public consciousness of the German people was critical in transforming "a question for the distant future" into one of immediate significance.[309] Gorbachev's official state visit to Berlin in October 1989 to celebrate the fortieth anniversary of the founding of the DDR provoked a tense mood, as members of the crowd shouted "Freedom! Freedom!" while others chanted "Gorby! Gorby! Help Us!" Gorbachev tried to stay apart from the fray, although his cryptic remark in public that "Life itself punishes those who delay" was widely taken as a warning to Honecker.[310] The fact that Gorbachev also let it be known to the East German leadership that Soviet troops were not available for purposes of domestic repression obviously sent a signal and a chill up the old guard's spine.[311]

The euphoric celebration of tearing down the Berlin wall on November 9, 1989, however, did not solve the larger problem of German unification that boiled "uncomfortably on a diplomatic backburner."[312] In an effort to seize the diplomatic initiative, Gorbachev invited West German chancellor Helmut Kohl in the summer of 1990 to his native Stavropol to engage in some old-fashioned horsetrading. Here, in the shadow of his early successes, Gorbachev hoped to obtain German financial and technical aid in return for German unification and Germany's membership in NATO. Kohl eagerly accepted Gorbachev's terms, and for a relatively small sum of 21 billion deutsche marks Gorbachev relinquished the military gains of World War II and incurred the wrath of conservatives, who accused him of having almost singlehandedly reversed the verdict of the war.[313]

While Gorbachev's "New Thinking" had clearly set in motion the process of change in Eastern Europe,[314] his decision to permit the old regimes to crumble and let the changes in Eastern Europe take their course was pivotal in securing what was for the most part a bloodless people's victory in Eastern Europe. Conservative assessments of these changes, however, were far from magnanimous. Party hardliners derisively referred to Gorbachev and Shevardnadze as "the Knights of Malta," who had sold out Soviet foreign policy interests to the West,[315] and they blamed Gorbachev for the "collapse of the socialist system" and the needless sacrifice of the strategic "buffer zone" in Eastern Europe.[316]

When the debate shifted to superpower diplomacy, the importance of propaganda and television images in forming political impressions dominated a series of high-profile summits with Reagan and enabled Gorbachev to showcase his public relations skills. As the friendly rivalry unfolded between the two men for the prize in international communication, the summits also revealed that Reagan, "the Great Communicator," had met his public relations match in Gorbachev, "The Great Persuader."[317] Gorbachev's ability to seize "the imagination of the world" and set the East–West agenda created a major problem for the Reagan White House,[318] since it was "the leader of the Western alliance who now appeared as a tired old man"[319] in contrast to his more youthful Soviet rival.

In the case of the Geneva summit, the perception that the outcome might "be 'won' or 'lost' on the p.r. front"[320] led advance teams from both sides to set the stage for the two leaders to display their mediagenic personalities while chatting informally during their impromptu walks or friendly fireside chats. In fact, the Geneva summit was perhaps more significant for "its atmosphere than for its accomplishments."[321] The relaxed, captivating ambience of the poolhouse on the grounds of the American delegation's villa in Geneva created a perfect setting for Reagan and Gorbachev to confer and register their differences over strategic nuclear weapons policy.[322] But despite their profound disagreements on policy issues, particularly SDI, the summit made clear that both men obviously felt comfortable in one another's presence, and they eagerly agreed to a new round of meetings in Washington and Moscow. In fact, the seemingly spontaneous nature of the interaction between the two men contributed more than anything else to the optimism surrounding the summit.

As a public-relations vehicle, Gorbachev's performance in Geneva also played well in Moscow, where the press conference he conducted before his departure from Geneva was broadcast on Soviet television.[323] Gorbachev described the atmosphere at the summit and his confidential meetings with Reagan as "frank talk"[324] and criticized the Americans for wanting to deploy nuclear weapons in space.[325] He labeled as naïve Reagan's proposal to share Star Wars technologies and berated Reagan for underestimating the Soviet Union's technical and economic capabilities[326] and belaboring the notion that the arms race would wear down the Soviet Union economically.[327] Yet despite what appeared as nothing more than political posturing, the summit euphoria easily carried over for some months, as both Reagan and Gorbachev extended the warmth of the Geneva summit via televised addresses to one another's population at the New Year. Gorbachev, who viewed the televised exchange of messages as a "good omen" for the future of Soviet–American relations, skillfully referred in his remarks to Steinbeck's novel *The Winter of Our Discontent* and expressed his desire to view the present moment as "the winter of our hope."[328]

Unlike Geneva, the location, the haste with which it was arranged, and the mysterious nature of the proceedings transformed Reykjavik, or the SDI summit, in October 1986 into a surrealistic encounter. Fearful that the steps required to respond to SDI would be enormously taxing on the Soviet Union's economy and technological resources, Gorbachev invited Reagan to meet in Reykjavik, where he proposed dramatic cuts in Soviet ICBMs in return for significant restrictions on the future testing and development of the SDI program[329] in an attempt to prevent the Americans from obtaining a destabilizing "first strike capability."[330] But Gorbachev's maneuver, though bold in its conception, proved to be "a breathtaking gamble" that failed,[331] since Reagan refused to alter his position on SDI. As had now become his custom, Gorbachev immediately went on the offensive during a press conference in Reykjavik and attributed the failure of the summit to Reagan's unwillingness to give up research and testing on SDI in outer space.[332] He mused that "America must long for the 'good ole days'" following World War II, when the United States was strong and militarily superior and the Soviet Union was economically weakened. And he struck at the very heart of the ideological vision of Reagan's presidency by exposing what he puckishly identified as "nostalgia for the past in America."[333] For the most part Gorbachev's performance at Reykjavik played well among Europeans. And as part of his propaganda offensive, he even asserted in *Perestroika* that Reykjavik could make it possible for humanity to "regain the immortality it lost when nuclear arms incinerated Hiroshima and Nagasaki."[334]

If Reykjavik was the SDI summit in the cold north Atlantic, Washington could be described as the up-tempo INF summit that created good feelings among Soviets and Americans alike. In many ways the Washington summit was Gorbachev's finest hour. Press coverage of the event was extensive, and in a matter of days he managed singlehandedly to win over normally skeptical Washingtonians and capture the hearts and minds of a broad section of the American public, as Americans suddenly discovered for themselves what Europeans had already experienced of the new political phenomenon called Gorbymania.[335] From the moment he arrived in December, Gorbachev engaged in an extraordinary performance of personal diplomacy.[336] Moving from one reception to another, Gorbachev quickly became the toast of a town that lives and dies on political power. His busy schedule also included an uncomfortable meeting with powerful and influential executives in American publishing, print, and broadcast journalism, when in response to a question on "human rights," he castigated the press "for its fascination with rumor and scandal." When Gorbachev realized what was happening, he curbed his anger and apologized: "Maybe I was a little emotional, but I was sincere."[337] In a press conference held at the Soviet embassy the next day, Gorbachev attempted to right himself by explaining that despite his enjoyment of "exchanges" with the press, he believed the media had to undergo its own *"perestroika"* and "master a new way of thinking."[338]

Throughout the summit Gorbachev also took advantage of every opportunity to press his peace and disarmament offensive. At the White House ceremony opening the summit, he hearkened back to the U.S.–Soviet alliance during World War II and their "common path to victory over the forces of evil."[339] He also applauded the INF treaty to eliminate intermediate-range nuclear weapons and cited the agreement as an important precedent, because it demonstrated for the first time "that it was possible to restrain and reverse the arms race."[340] But the most memorable moment of the summit occurred when Gorbachev was making his way to the White House to meet with Reagan. To the surprise of everyone, including his traveling companion Vice President George Bush, Gorbachev suddenly ordered the limousine to stop at the corner of Connecticut Avenue and K Street, so that he could step out on the pavement and press the flesh with the people. It was a rare event, a spontaneous, highly unorthodox encounter with Washingtonians, as crowds rushed to greet him excitedly in what suddenly became the American reincarnation of "Gorby fever." "'The guy is a p.r. genius,' gushed one woman. 'I'm still shaking,' said another,"[341] as television cameras captured the moment.[342] Milking the moment for all it was worth, Gorbachev used the press conference at the end of the summit to describe being greeted by Americans, who were suddenly in good spirits and waving their hands in Washington's streets. He knew he had been a big hit, and he loved it.[343]

The White House state dinner given in honor of the Gorbachevs was "one of the most glittering . . . events of Reagan's presidency."[344] Americans in black tie mingled with their Soviet guests in business suits, disregarding the purported political significance of their sartorial attire. The evening combined the mistiness of a college reunion with the elegance of a state dinner; as guests, their faces illuminated in the soft glow of candlelight, spontaneously came to-gether—with Van Cliburn at the piano—to sing *Moscow Nights* and create an image of warmth, humanity, and, above all, hope. In his farewell speech at the White House the next day, Gorbachev worked to sustain the mood of the previous evening and keep the newly opened channels active and friendly. Care-fully fashioning his words to appeal to a broad democratic audience, he welcomed the emergence of a growing desire in American society for improved Soviet–American relations, which reflected a similar mood that had long been prevalent among the Soviet people.[345]

In his welcoming speech to the American delegation at the Moscow Sum-mit on May 29, 1988, Gorbachev cited the progress of past summits in curb-ing the use of "habitual stereotypes" and "enemy images"[346] and later praised Reagan's "realism," while expressing his own belief that "we do not need weapons" that run the risk of "endangering our own lives—and the rest of hu-manity."[347] But the Moscow summit also provided Reagan with a high-profile occasion to bury his earlier views about the Soviet Union as an "evil empire." The fact that he publicly discarded this notion while he was in the Kremlin, the very center of that empire, was obviously a source of great pleasure to Gor-bachev.[348] In the eyes of Soviet citizens, the very presence in Moscow of such a staunch anticommunist figure as Reagan was a major propaganda victory for Gorbachev and testimony to his success in "taming American reactionaries."[349] Moreover, the fact that one of "the most conservative of postwar U.S. Presi-dents" had spoken of "the Kremlin leader as 'a friend' seemed . . . to symbolize the end of the Cold War and [establish] the framework of future relations."[350]

Despite all the international publicity, the summits never fulfilled the promise that began in Geneva and ended in Moscow. In December 1989, the ill-fated Malta summit between Bush and Gorbachev, which some described as the "storm-tossed"[351] or "seasick summit,"[352] did little to crystallize a new, ro-bust political partnership, although the diplomatic passage from Yalta to Malta did mark the symbolic end of the Cold War. In much the same way, the one-day Helsinki summit in August 1990 hardly measured up to the significance of its predecessors, although it did achieve one important diplomatic objective by obtaining the Soviet Union's formal endorsement of UN policy in the Gulf in response to Iraq's invasion of Kuwait and making it possible for the leaders of the world's two nuclear powers to come together for the first time during a world crisis.[353]

In the early days of *perestroika* and *glasnost,* Gorbachev had made his mark as an internationalist by promoting international security, the importance of the UN as "a mechanism" for peace,[354] and a policy of nuclear restraint. Gorbachev used the 40th commemoration of the bombing of Hiroshima and Nagasaki to declare a unilateral moratorium on the underground testing of nuclear weapons[355] and compromise the United States in the eyes of world opinion because of U.S. refusal to join in the moratorium. Forming an alliance with antiwar groups, intellectuals, and officials, who shared a similar vision for the future, Gorbachev also launched an international peace offensive to reverse the spread of nuclear weapons. The July 1986 Moscow meeting of the International Forum of Scientists for a Nuclear Test Ban provided him with an opportunity to make his case. Speaking at the forum, Gorbachev defended his decision to extend the moratorium on nuclear testing against those who dismissed it as "utopian." He also condemned the inflexible mentality of the American "military-industrial complex," while reassuring his audience that many Americans did not share their government's narrow outlook on the future of space.[356] In an address broadcast on Soviet television on August 18, 1986, Gorbachev continued to press the offensive and argue that "prenuclear thinking essentially lost its significance on August 6, 1945," because America's decision to drop the bomb on Hiroshima had made it clear that any attempt to "ensure one's own security" must consider "the security of other states and peoples."[357] He also accused right-wing militarists and nationalists in the United States of having "gone mad with the arms race" to achieve "military superiority" and weaken the Soviet Union politically and economically.[358]

In keeping with the spirit of "New Thinking," the meeting of the "glitterati" who gathered in Moscow in February 1987 to participate in the International Forum for a Nuclear-Free World was undoubtedly the crown jewel of Gorbachev's public diplomacy. More than a thousand participants, including international celebrities such as Gregory Peck, Peter Ustinov, Claudia Cardinale, Andrei Sakharov, Norman Mailer, Armand Hammer, "millionaire businessman" Donald Kendall, Yoko Ono, and Pierre Trudeau[359] had been carefully selected to enhance the international visibility of the event. "Moscow had never seen anything like it"; and it was a credit to Gorbachev's own star quality that so many responded to him as the main attraction.[360] In his address to the forum, Gorbachev outlined his views on "New Thinking" and condemned "the militarization of the mind" for threatening to destroy the "moral inhibitions" that prevent the human race from committing "nuclear suicide."[361]

On December 7, 1988, Gorbachev took his disarmament message directly to the United Nations and seized his "dramatic moment on the world stage"[362] to appear before the UN as an "energetic and eloquent" world statesman.[363] He chose this occasion to cite advances in the mass media and international communication under *glasnost* and emphasize the need for an "internationalizing dialogue"[364] that would promote unity within multinational diversity.[365] Included in his presentation were measures to promote Third World development,[366] protect the international environment, and create "a world space organization" to oversee the peaceful use of outer space. He then called for a "complete cease-fire" in Afghanistan[367] and surprised his audience in the form of a "'Christmas gift' to the world,"[368] when he announced that the Soviet Union would "unilaterally" cut the size of its standing army by 500,000 troops and withdraw 50,000 troops stationed in Eastern Europe.[369]

Gorbachev's "New Thinking" also enabled him to address the issues of global peace and human suffering. He targeted the burdensome debt in Third World countries imposed by the West in the form of "neocolonialist 'tribute'"[370] and the "hypocrisy" of preventing the peoples of Asia, Africa, and Latin America from seeking an alternative to the capitalist system.[371] As a spokesman for international peace, arms control, and reconciliation, Gorbachev also sought to reach other political capitals and publics to enhance his image as an international statesman around the globe. Nor did he hesitate to comment on the explosive topics of racism and international terrorism in Africa and the Middle East, supporting the political and territorial claims of Yasser Arafat and the PLO and accusing the racist regime in South Africa of wanting "to perpetuate . . . colonialism . . . and apartheid" with the support of "its Western patrons."[372] In *Perestroika* he would later reiterate his support for "national liberation" movements throughout Africa[373] and for the native population in South Africa in their bloody struggle against an increasingly isolated and oppressive racist regime. He also rebuked the West for accusing the Soviet Union of having organized a "communist plot" in South Africa to foment popular unrest.[374]

Gorbachev continued to play the ideological card in Central and Latin America when he beat the drum loudly and criticized the United States for falling into the familiar pattern of blaming Moscow for fomenting revolution in other parts of the world. He also dismissed accusations that the Soviet Union was attempting "to engineer a series of socialist revolutions" in the region and reminded Reagan that it was the United States "who [had] planted a bomb in Latin America in the form of its mammoth foreign debt."[375] He also defended the Sandinistas for overthrowing the unpopular Somoza regime and denied that the revolution was the "work of Moscow and Cuba." He even advised the United States to leave Nicaragua in peace,[376] and in a distinctively Russian accent he echoed the familiar message of "U.S. Out" and "Yankee, Go Home." Of course, the most nettlesome problem in Central America and the Caribbean was Cuba. Despite the legitimate indigenous nature of the Cuban revolution, no one could deny that Soviet subsidies had kept Castro's land revolution afloat for over two decades.[377] Castro, in return, had rendered a great service to the Soviet Union by providing troops to serve as "Soviet proxies" in Angola and in the war between Ethiopia and Somalia in the 1970s,[378] which enabled Cuba to establish itself as a factor in Third World politics.[379]

But in addition to a roster of unresolved multilateral issues, Gorbachev also had to face the obdurate problem of bilateral relations with China. Ideological divisions, military clashes, and border disputes dating back to the 1960s had poisoned Sino–Soviet relations. Gorbachev resolved the territorial problem in one bold stroke when he unilaterally accepted the Chinese position that the Ussuri River channel was the border between the two countries.[380] Gorbachev's initiative also created a new window of opportunity for China's Deng Xiaoping, who acknowledged the tortured past of Sino–Soviet relations but also believed that "Knowledge of the past must have limits."[381] In this new spirit of reconciliation, Gorbachev arrived in Beijing in May 1989 as the first Soviet leader to visit China in thirty years,[382] only to have the prodemocracy student demonstrations disrupt his welcoming ceremony. Although his presence in Beijing may have been viewed by some as a harbinger of democratic change, the timing of the protests totally eclipsed the purpose of his visit and obviously put him in an awkward situation vis-à-vis his Chinese hosts.

Of all the foreign policy issues that Gorbachev encountered, none was more important than Afghanistan, which had remained a painful "bleeding wound"[383] afflicting every part of the Soviet body politic. Soviet intervention dated back to December 1979, when Soviet troops liquidated sitting president Hafizullah Amin and installed "a hastily resurrected and repatriated Babrak Karmal" as their client in Kabul.[384] As the death toll mounted in Afghanistan, the Soviet public grew increasingly disenchanted with the government's "one-sided treatment of the war."[385] When confronted with the loss of more Soviet soldiers, the enormous financial burden of the war, and the burden of "world opinion,"[386] Gorbachev signaled a change in Soviet policy by emphasizing that the Soviet people wanted their "soldiers home as soon as possible."[387] To achieve his political objectives on the home front, he decided on a well-organized effort to prepare the population for withdrawal by encouraging the press to "portray the grim reality of war."[388] He then unveiled a new hands-off policy when he ordered Soviet troops to begin their withdrawal on February 15, 1989. By extricating the Soviet Union from Afghanistan by the target date of May 15, Gorbachev also managed to use his statesmanlike approach and communication skills to turn a bleak political situation into a momentary public-relations success.[389]

Despite his many setbacks and disappointments, Gorbachev's work in international affairs earned him the Nobel Peace Prize in 1990 for his contributions to *glasnost* and foreign policy. Once again Gorbachev was a victim of bad timing, however, since the political turmoil within the USSR had become so tense that he had to postpone his trip to Oslo in favor of a special award ceremony "to avoid an angry reaction at home—where the awarding of the prize provoked as much puzzlement as praise."[390] In his Nobel speech, Gorbachev described the troubling times that had been inflicted upon the Soviet Union and "the obligation of the West to help the USSR [pursue] its peaceful policies."[391] He also exhibited real moments of reflective insight when he admitted some of his "own shortcomings" in having underestimated the magnitude of the problems facing the Soviet Union and having "imprudently" raised such "great expectations."[392]

THE DEMISE OF THE GREAT MASTER OF IMPROVISATION

As the political and economic situation continued to deteriorate in 1989, and sensing that his customary surefootedness was beginning to desert him, Gorbachev attempted to shed his ideological allegiance to the past and restore his ties with the people. In the spring of 1990, he even called for "an end to the absurd idolization of Lenin."[393] And when *Time* magazine asked Gorbachev what it meant in this new context "to be a communist today," he eschewed any reference to class conflict and focused upon more abstract "democratic and . . . universal human values."[394] But all his attempts to reposition himself politically could not regain the people's confidence. His "anxieties about public opinion were validated on May Day," 1990, when he and other members of the august Soviet leadership, standing atop Lenin's tomb, were vilified by the "jeers and catcalls" of those marching in "the free parade" that followed the official parade. Some of the participants carried signs and banners proclaiming: "MARXISM-LENINISM IS ON THE RUBBISH HEAP OF HISTORY"[395] and "DOWN WITH THE POLITBURO! RESIGN!"[396] while a Russian Orthodox priest carried an enormous crucifix and shouted, "Mikhail Sergeyevich, Christ is risen!"[397] When a visibly incensed Gorbachev led the "sheeplike and stonyfaced" members of the party leadership from atop the mausoleum, "a wave of jubilation came over the crowd."[398] The unthinkable had suddenly occurred. Gorbachev, who had at the outset capitalized upon his mediagenic personality, now stood rebuked and politically naked atop Lenin's tomb during one of the most symbolic and highly celebrated of Soviet secular holidays.

Stunned by recent events, Gorbachev realized that he now stood at a crossroads. Before choosing his path, however, he sought refuge in a trip to Canada and the United States at the end of May. Unlike his earlier visits, Gorbachev now traveled with a great deal of new baggage, including Yeltsin's recent election as president of the Russian Republic and the desire among members of the international news media to chronicle Gorbachev's demise. The new mood was also reflected in a *Newsweek* cover story titled "Why Gorbachev Is Failing." North American crowds, however, continued to respond enthusiastically to Gorbachev's "celebrity status," as Bush did everything he could "to boost Gorbachev's morale."[399] The high point of the trip occurred during Gorbachev's visit to Stanford University, where Gorbachev "gave a graceful loser's speech about the Cold War."[400] At one poignant moment during the proceedings, George Shultz, in an attempt to buttress Gorbachev's position at home, deviated from his prepared text and hailed Gorbachev as "a great leader" whose standing in the international community entitled him to play a key role "in this drama—*we need you, Mr. Gorbachev.*"[401]

Gorbachev's efforts to present a modern, sophisticated image abroad had, in fact, backfired. As he grew increasingly attached to the glamor of international diplomacy, he began to lose the common touch that had marked his early days as a trailblazing reformer. Soviets had grown tired and resentful of the elegant international lifestyle he and Raisa enjoyed, particularly as economic conditions at home continued to deteriorate.[402] Opinion polls, which had been introduced amidst great public fanfare to herald the beginning of a more democratic process and serve as an ally of the government, now began to chronicle the dramatic decline in Gorbachev's popularity. Results of polls published in *Argumenty i Fakty*,[403] *Moscow News*, and *Ogonyok*[404] all indicated a precipitous drop in public support for Gorbachev and his programs between 1989 and 1990. Not even the Nobel Prize could produce a momentary bounce in Gorbachev's favor.[405] A highly unusual poll conducted near the end of 1990 created an even darker picture. The poll asked respondents to rate individuals who they believed would make a difference to the Soviet Union by the year 2000. At the head of the list stood Jesus Christ, with 58 percent; followed by Sakharov, with 48 percent; Lenin, with 36 percent; and Gorbachev with only 26 percent.[406] Another poll conducted in January 1991, comparing the character and leadership qualities of Yeltsin and Gorbachev, showed Yeltsin clearly outdistancing his rival.[407]

Given the "personal animus" that had developed between the two men, Yeltsin's sudden rise in popularity and his election as president of the Russian Republic constituted a difficult cross for Gorbachev to bear. From the very beginning, the Gorbachev-Yeltsin tandem had always been a shaky proposition. Ironically, Gorbachev actually contributed to his own paranoia concerning Yeltsin's challenge, since "the more [he] sought to block Yeltsin's emergence as a rival leader, the more popular Yeltsin became."[408] What made Yeltsin's "political resurrection" so compelling was his image as a burly political figure, "a typical Bolshevik, . . . straight out of central casting. Stubborn, overbearing, . . . a human engine without brakes."[409] He also possessed superb political instincts. When rumors of a coup began to circulate, Yeltsin made it clear that he would "fight for" Gorbachev, the same Gorbachev whom Yeltsin described as "the lover of half-measures and half-steps [that] will eventually be his downfall."[410] To make matters worse, an "angry, almost hysterical" Gorbachev began to behave like "a leader at the end of a tether." As his position continued to weaken, Gorbachev denounced Vladislav Starkov, the editor of *Argumenty i Fakty,* for having published a survey showing that Sakharov and Yeltsin among others had surpassed Gorbachev in popularity.[411] How ironic it was that suddenly Gorbachev, the populist champion of the press polls and surveys as a means of providing "major 'feedback' linking" the people and the government,[412] now condemned these vehicles as "divisive" and disruptive.[413]

Once Gorbachev had set the pot to boil, he also discovered that he could not keep it from boiling over. In an inflammatory fit of rage, he declaimed that "Reading the press, you get the feeling that you are standing knee-deep in gasoline. The only thing lacking is a spark."[414] In February 1990 his frustration erupted in angry malediction when he attacked his critics in the Supreme Soviet. The sight of his "hysterical outburst" shocked the Soviet audience, making it appear as if "the Godhead" had "crack[ed]."[415] As the magic escaped him, he also "became the butt of jokes" and the bearer of the title "'Baltoon'—the chatterbox" on account of his "garrulous" style and lengthy speeches.[416] Fearful of Yeltsin's challenge, sensing that the political process was eluding his grasp, and infuriated by the idea of the media's contributing to his political demise, Gorbachev installed "hard-liner Leonid Kravchenko as TV czar" in November 1990 to crack down on Gostel (the government television station).[417]

Media politics, however, could not solve the Soviet Union's pressing social and economic problems. And when the time came in the summer of 1990 for Gorbachev to honor his commitment to Yeltsin to support the more radical Shatalin 500 Day Plan for economic reform, Gorbachev waffled. Unlike the more conservative government plan put forward by Nikolai Ryzhkov, Shatalin's plan emphasized decentralization, privatization, and price reforms as a means of rejuvenating the stagnant Soviet economy.[418] When Gorbachev attempted to merge the best features of both plans, Yeltsin accused him of "want[ing] to cross a hedgehog with a grass snake."[419] As events continued to spin out of control,[420] a once jaunty, but now chastened, Gorbachev realized that while it had been "easy" during the early days of *perestroika* and *glasnost* to determine "what was wrong," it had been far more difficult to determine "what was right."[421] Given the mounting "political fragmentation" and sense of impending crisis, "the specter of dictatorship . . . loom[ed] large" on the Soviet horizon.[422] When Gorbachev's rhetoric failed to fill the shops with food and consumer goods,[423] his critics began to portray him as a weak and indecisive leader, accusing him of "no longer leading the country but merely . . . creating an illusion of leadership."[424]

Critics also accused Gorbachev of not "paying attention to the Party" and of being ineffective "at organizational politics."[425] Critics questioned his authority and asked him, "Why don't you stop travelling abroad and concern yourself with the country?" Gorbachev immediately rose to his own defense, citing his travels abroad as a means of securing "reliable, peaceful conditions" that would enable the Soviet Union to concentrate on resolving its domestic problems. But he did not stop there. He also engaged in his own brand of intellectual one-upmanship, sardonically describing what a "disaster" it would be to place diplomatic travel in the hands of those who were "incompetent in politics [and] unable to analyze processes."[426] Unfortunately, his spirited self-defense was flawed by his intellectual arrogance, godlike assumptions, and theatrical excess.

In late September Gorbachev continued to consolidate his authority, at least on paper. When the USSR Supreme Soviet gave him the "extraordinary powers" he requested, Sobchak asked what came next, the "emperor's crown or the generalissimo's epaulets."[427] Vested with new powers, Gorbachev promised during the Congress of People's Deputies in December to introduce "resolute measures" to stem the crisis, resolve the nationalities question, and preserve the Union.[428] The immediate crisis dated back to March 1990, when Lithuania had declared its independence from the Union. In December Gorbachev personally entered the fray when he visited Vilnius "to beard the lion in its den." For three days he provided a momentary glimpse of the old Gorbachev, as he exuded "boundless self-confidence . . . in his ability to convince people . . . [that] 'We are all tied together now.'" But when the Lithuanians impudently rejected his arguments[429] and he returned home empty-handed, he ordered troops to Lithuania and six other republics under the pretext of defending the territorial integrity of the Union. At 2:00 A.M. on January 13, 1991, Soviet troops moved on Vilnius and seized the communications network composed of the city's television tower and the republic's main printing facilities. As tanks rolled through a chain of human protesters who surrounded the tower as a symbol of national independence, paratroopers fired and clubbed their way with AK-47s through the civilian crowd. When the violence had subsided, fourteen Lithuanians had been killed, and dozens more were injured.[430]

From a political standpoint the attack "was a botched job."[431] What had been designed as a reassertion of central authority turned into a public-relations disaster and inflamed popular discontent. As foreign journalists and correspondents filed reports from Lithuania[432] and as a shocking film of the Vilnius attack was relayed from one television station to another within the Soviet Union, the public airing of the events "caught . . . the Kremlin's censors . . . off guard" and blew into thin air the state's monopoly of a single, sanitized version of what had occurred.[433] As Muscovites marched on the Kremlin, carrying posters that read MR. GORBACHEV—ENOUGH EXECUTIONS AND KILLINGS and COMRADES THIS IS YOUR END,[434] the media broadcast and printed "gory scenes of the beating and killing." At one point Gorbachev even considered suspending "the new law [on] freedom of the press," but he backed down when challenged by liberal members of the Supreme Soviet. The media assault had clearly taken its toll, and Gorbachev realized that "the revolution [he] had initiated . . . had taken on a life of its own."[435]

Faced with the prospect of a popular revolt, Gorbachev quickly tacked in a new direction and opted in favor of a shift to the right. In another ill-advised maneuver, Gorbachev attempted to engineer Yeltsin's expulsion from Soviet political life. When word of Gorbachev's plan spread throughout Moscow, 500,000 demonstrators converged in protest on the Kremlin. In an attempt to flex his political muscle and intimidate the protesters, Gorbachev summoned 50,000 troops to the capital to stand at the ready and await further commands from the Kremlin. But at the critical moment Gorbachev hesitated.[436] When he blinked, Yeltsin had won. One of Gorbachev's aides dubbed March 28, 1991, "*the* turning point for Mikhail Sergeyevich. He went to the . . . edge [of the] abyss . . . and backed away." Suddenly fearful of "the right-wing menace," he again abruptly "reversed direction" and sought an alliance with Yeltsin, who seemed to alternate in Gorbachev's mind between the roles of populist ally and political nemesis.[437]

In the spirit of this new alliance, Gorbachev enlisted Yeltsin's support for an administrative solution to curb the interethnic violence and bloodshed in the form of a new union treaty and went to the people in March 1991 with a referendum that posed the following question: "Do you consider it necessary to preserve the Union of Soviet Socialist Republics as a renewed federation of equal sovereign republics in which human rights and freedoms of nationality will be fully guaranteed?" Although the vague wording and uneven turnout at the polls among the various republics called into question the significance of the vote—80 percent of Soviet citizens voted with 76.4 percent in favor—

Gorbachev hailed the results as a popular mandate to draft "a new constitution."[438] It would be a mistake, however, to conclude that Gorbachev was simply skimming off a momentary political advantage, since the referendum did represent an expression of the mood and sentiment of the Soviet people. Realizing that "his hardline strategy was bankrupt," Gorbachev hoped he could transform the results of the referendum into a new vote of confidence and the new Union Treaty into "a way out of his impasse."[439]

As unprecedented criticism from the press continued to mount, however, the implementation of a solution to the nationalities question remained elusive. When Ivan Polozkov as head of the Russian party organization attacked Gorbachev publicly during the Moscow Party Committee's Plenum in April 1991 for "tak[ing] [his] hands off the wheel" and leaving the "government machine . . . leaderless," a furious Gorbachev seized the floor and delivered what must have been one of the shortest but most effective speeches of his career. "Okay, that's enough," he declared and called upon those present to resolve the issue of the general secretary's authority, since "neither the man, nor the party can remain in such a situation." Citing factionalism within the Party ranks, he boldly announced his resignation and abruptly left the hall, which erupted into a state of confusion. In a gesture that was symptomatic of the indecisiveness that now permeated the entire Soviet political system, the delegates, when faced with the reality of a leadership void, acted quickly to remove the question of Gorbachev's resignation from the agenda. Gorbachev's ploy had succeeded, if only temporarily, to reaffirm his authority within the Party and postpone the final reckoning. But by publicly savoring his victory over the conservatives, he was also loading the cannon of conservative resentment and pointing it directly at himself. Still, at a time when his grip on the levers of power was slipping and his standing in the eyes of the people was sinking, his nimble political maneuvering had enabled him to survive another intramural test of strength and confront a new and different political calculus.[440]

The next attempt to usurp Gorbachev's power occurred in June 1991 on the floor of the Supreme Soviet. Conservatives, fearing the implications of the new Union Treaty and the dissolution of the empire, put forward Prime Minister Valentin Pavlov as the ideal point man to assume more of Gorbachev's everyday political and administrative duties. Informed of the machinations, Gorbachev arrived at the meeting at just the right time to derail the conservative express and "mock the reactionaries as 'hurrah patriots' trying to 'usurp democracy.'" With a chastised Vladimir Kryuchkov, Dmitri Yazov, and Boris Pugo at his side, he blithely quipped into the television cameras that "the coup is over."[441] While his breezy reassertion of political authority was designed for public consumption at home and abroad, his impromptu decision to dress down senior government officials in plain view of the media begs explanation. It revealed his political naïveté, narcissism, and belief that he had, indeed, become the grand chess master of Soviet politics. Prominent officials such as Kryuchkov, Yazov, and Pugo, however, who resented sitting in a hallway and

being publicly upbraided by Gorbachev, would wait for the time to exact political revenge, which they did as leaders of the August coup.

Gorbachev, however, enjoyed playing the role of martinet and burnishing
the image of his own true grit and determination, but his failure to act force-
fully against the conspirators and dismiss them from office exposed his lack of
the killer instinct that was necessary for survival at the summit of Soviet politics. Ever the man in the middle, he continued to engage in his delicate "bal-
ancing act"[442] and tried to remain politically relevant, while conservative anger
and popular frustration were swirling around him. When warnings of a coup
surfaced both from within and outside the Soviet Union, Gorbachev chose to
deny the danger of a conspiratorial threat to his power. With that fateful decision he sacrificed everything and lost.

Perhaps the most unsettling aspect about the August coup was Gorbachev's
failure to take advantage of the information revolution he had set in motion to
position himself on the side of the people. Equally damaging was his decision
to ignore the warnings that an impending coup was coming from political in-
timates such as Alexsandr Yakovlev, party stalwarts such as Yegor Ligachev, and
even President Bush, who had shared intelligence information with Gorbachev
in June that pointed in the direction of a coup.[443] Gorbachev, however, was less
interested in dire predictions concerning his political future than in signing the
START agreement to control and reduce strategic nuclear weapons, which he
and Bush concluded during the Moscow summit in late July. In view of his ela-
tion over START, his decision to go on television and announce that the new
Union Treaty would be ready for signing on August 20 reflected his hope that
the two agreements would resurrect his standing in the eyes of the people.

Thinking himself secure, he departed in August for a vacation in the Crimea.
Much to his surprise, however, he discovered that the response to the Union
Treaty was not what he expected. On August 18 party conservatives, in "a des-
perate attempt to turn back the flow of history,"[444] staged a coup to preserve
their powers and the power of the Soviet state. Their immediate "goal was to
persuade Gorbachev to drop the Union Treaty and declare a state of emergency." Should Gorbachev be unwilling to cooperate, the conservatives de-
manded that he would have "to resign" and make way for his hand-picked
vice-president, Gennady Yanayev.[445]

What followed was a theatrical piece of political intrigue, ineptitude, and
heroism, broadcast around the world.[446] From the outset the "coup was a
fools' folly," perpetrated by "*apparatchiks,* not politicians," who had no idea
what it meant to manage the flow of information and take control of the Soviet Union.[447] During a hastily assembled and poorly planned press conference,[448] the leaders of the coup, with Yanayev as the principal spokesman, sat
on stage behind a large table, faced the cameras, and made public their political intentions. The "shadow government"[449] had emerged from behind the
curtain. But their performance was a public-relations disaster.[450] In full view of
the Soviet public and the world, they seemed awkward, incoherent, and old, as

if they had come from another era and no longer fit into the contemporary context of Soviet politics. Moreover, the bizarre nature of the event created the impression that it was history's "first coup d'état to have been announced in advance"[451] at a press conference.[452] Yet despite their amateurish behavior, the aims of the conspirators became "instantly transparent,"[453] when asserting Gorbachev's poor health, they proclaimed a state of emergency[454] and professed their commitment "to the preservation of a unitary Soviet state."[455]

The failure of the coup's leadership to gain control of the media and swiftly cut the communication links abroad and within the country[456] ultimately determined the outcome of the confrontation. In one of the more significant ironies of the moment, it was Nicholas Daniloff, the same American journalist who had been imprisoned and released on the eve of the Washington summit, who exposed the primary failure of the coup's leadership to "seize the press, shut down the opposing media, and pump out an 'authorized version,' of events over radio and television."[457] The conspirators' failure to muzzle the press and their misguided assumption that the people would rally to the call for order also revealed how "pathetically ignorant" they were of "the magnitude of the sea-change that had already taken place"[458] in the media and the political culture of the Soviet Union.

When the coup failed to trigger the anticipated political collapse, Yeltsin decided to make his stand at the White House, which represented the crucible of democracy and the dreams and aspirations of "Russian democrats."[459] Within the White House the presence of international celebrities such as Mstislav Rostropovich and prominent political figures such as Eduard Shevardnadze contributed to a communal bond of popular solidarity.[460] Against this backdrop the most dramatic image of the confrontation was framed when Yeltsin, "like Lenin on his armored car in 1917," climbed atop a tank to denounce the conspirators and call for a general strike.[461] To many, Yeltsin's bold stand "was an act of political genius"[462] that galvanized the resistance and led other voices, including that of Russian Orthodox patriarch Alexei II, to condemn the putsch and support Yeltsin's call for Gorbachev's release and safe passage back to Moscow.[463]

While the coup was unfolding, Gorbachev and his family were in Cape Foros relaxing in the "palatial villa" that, according to Robert Kaiser, "suited the czarist streak in [his] personality."[464] But the issue of Gorbachev's personality came back to haunt him in a different way during the coup, since his skill in "weaving a tricky path between reformers and reactionaries"[465] contributed to speculation that he might actually swing over in support of the coup, as he had during the crackdown in the Baltics. Simply introducing the possibility that Gorbachev might have had some contact with members of the coup also raises the question of what Gorbachev's stand might have been, had the coup succeeded. From the public record, however, it appears that Gorbachev never entertained such a notion. When confronted with a delegation of putschists, he conducted himself admirably and vehemently denied any involvement in the coup or attempts to "[save] his own skin."[466] Despite his bravado, however,

Gorbachev was fearful for his safety and that of his family.[467] In an obvious allusion to the Bolshevik execution of the Romanov imperial family in Ekaterinburg in 1918, Raisa Gorbachev later confided to a Soviet journalist that they were fully aware of Russian "history and its tragic episodes"[468] and that they might suffer the bloody fate that put an end to the Romanov dynasty.

As the coup fizzled in Moscow, a group led by Alexander Rutskoi arrived at Cape Foros to free the Gorbachevs and take the conspirators into custody. Returning to Moscow on Thursday, August 22, a "disheveled, . . . unsteady,"[469] and disoriented Gorbachev exited from his Aeroflot jet and deliberately made his way across the tarmac. In his first public remarks since the coup, he hailed the changes brought about in the Soviet people and society by *perestroika* and credited those changes with the defeat of the coup. He also expressed his respectful appreciation for Yeltsin's role during the recent events. But he made a costly "political mistake" when he decided to go directly home instead of to the White House to appear with Yeltsin and thank the people for their sacrifice and courageous display of support.[470] He repeated the mistake when he chose to bypass the victory celebration the next day.[471]

At a press conference on Friday, August 23, Gorbachev did little, if anything, to strengthen his case with the people. In fact, what he said probably did more harm than good, since instead of addressing the broader, epic significance of what had happened and the role of political reform, the people, and the press in saving the democratic movement and enabling him to return, he chose to detail the personal physical danger and terror that he and his family had experienced as victims of a terrible plot. His decision to focus more "on his personal experience" than on the "country['s] trauma"[472] also revealed a certain narcissistic side to his personality. At a major turning point in Russian history, his inability to comprehend the true dimensions of the seismic shift that had occurred within the Soviet Union prevented him from forging a new bond with the people.

The reviews of his press conference were not good. Alexander Yakovlev was furious at the spectacle of Gorbachev professing his "allegiance to . . . the Party's 'renewal.'" In a private conversation he told Gorbachev, "The Party is dead. . . . Talk about its 'renewal' is senseless. It's like offering first aid to a corpse!"[473] Given the perception that the coup might have succeeded "*had the people remained silent*,"[474] Gorbachev's failure to attack the sacrosanct institutions and "totalitarian icons" from the past[475] further distanced him from the new body politic. Gorbachev's lackluster return also made it clear that the coup, in fact, had been "his undoing" and that there was no room for "the . . . benign czar . . . [he] wanted to be,"[476] nor was there a role for him as a post-Soviet political figure.

Although Gorbachev "returned from his brief Crimean captivity a different man in a different country, . . . he had no idea how very different" things had actually become.[477] Within forty-eight hours of his arrival in Moscow, however, he received his first lesson in the new politics and some on-the-job training from none other than his archrival, Yeltsin. The occasion was a meeting of the Supreme Soviet of the Russian Republic, where the delegates greeted Gorbachev with a chorus of "Resign! Resign!"[478] "The televised confrontation" that ensued ranks among the highest moments of "political theatre."[479] Standing next to Gorbachev at the podium, Yeltsin repeatedly pointed to the text of a document and insisted that Gorbachev read a list of names that would reveal how "all but two of his ministers betrayed him."[480] Yeltsin obviously relished this moment to pay Gorbachev back for forcing him to leave the Kremlin hospital and face a well-orchestrated public humiliation at the hands of the Moscow Party Committee in 1987. But Yeltsin was not finished. With Gorbachev at his side, he insisted, despite Gorbachev's lame objections, that he "now sign a decree suspending the activities of the Russian Communist Party."[481] Faced with no alternative, Gorbachev matter-of-factly relented and signed. He realized that no one any longer paid attention to anything he said or did. Moreover, he suddenly found himself cast in a totally dependent, unenviable, and subordinate role to Yeltsin.[482] On August 24, only two days after his return to Moscow, Gorbachev resigned as general secretary of the Communist party, dissolved its Central Committee, and effectively proclaimed the end of the Bolshevik era.[483]

Gorbachev's decision to leave Moscow, shortly after dispensing with the Party, and write a book on the coup immediately raised questions about his priorities during a time of crisis. Given the enormous significance of the recent events, the self-referential focus of his book, *The August Coup: The Truth and the Lessons,* cast him in the role of the attorney pleading his case before the court of world public opinion. He insisted that "the coup did not come unexpectedly, like a bolt from the blue."[484] Had it not been for "the profound changes"[485] he had introduced through *perestroika*, democratization, and *glasnost*,[486] as well as "the new relationship" he had forged with the outside world, the coup, he maintained, would not have been defeated.[487] Despite his increasing isolation, Gorbachev continued to view himself as a voice from the political center who stood for moderate, democratic change and reform. But when he attempted to assume the mantle of chief of state and declare that he would not allow "any hesitation or any temporizing in carrying out reforms" as long as he remained president, the rhetoric was empty.[488] And when he claimed that "Now, when the future of our great country is being decided, I think least of all about myself,"[489] most Soviets scoffed at his empty posturing.

In search of a new political role, Gorbachev tried in his book to align himself with Yeltsin and other leaders of the various republics to create a "Union of Sovereign States"[490] that would retain the political center and the president as supreme commander-in-chief. In an effort to update his résumé and reposition himself as the new head of state, he reassured his audience that given his extensive foreign policy contacts and credentials, "no one should have any worries."[491] He also used the creation of the Union of Sovereign States to defend his foreign policy against critics, who had accused him of sacrificing the gains of World War II and weakening the international communist movement. Moreover, he described the Soviet Union as a superpower with an inefficient economy and an inferior standard of living that needed to discard its utopian commitment to a global expansion of communist revolutionary ideas in favor of a foreign policy that was designed to serve its "*own national interests* and . . . domestic development."[492]

Despite his diminished influence and lack of authority, Gorbachev continued to work to "preserve the concept of a Union"[493] and fashion a new role for himself in Soviet politics. Power, however, had clearly shifted to Yeltsin, who realized that in order "to crown his own ascendancy," he had to "finish off Gorbachev politically."[494] He did so when he excluded Gorbachev from the December 8 meeting constituting the Commonwealth of Independent States and shared the news of its creation with President Bush before informing Gorbachev of the outcome. Gorbachev was furious.[495] His deputy spokesman, Sergei Gregoriyev, concisely summed up the situation: "Yeltsin had Gorbachev by the balls."[496] Gorbachev was shrewd enough, however, to recognize the changing political reality. He quickly worked out the terms of his resignation with Yeltsin, including provisions for the creation of the Gorbachev Institute, which would serve as a combined think tank and presidential library.

Gorbachev's trials, however, were hardly over. Upon his return to the Kremlin to pick up his political effects, he suddenly discovered "a new name on the door and a new man behind the desk—Yeltsin," symbolically marking the end of the communist era and the Gorbachev period in Soviet history.[497] Though privately and publicly humiliated, Gorbachev nevertheless mustered the strength to bid his countrymen a proper farewell.[498] Televised around the world on Christmas Day 1991, his resignation speech was a moving example of eloquence in defeat and a touching reminder of his ability to use the media to reach his audience. His valedictory looked back to the beginnings of *perestroika*, when "things were not going well in the country" and major reform was a "risky endeavor." He candidly admitted that making radical changes had been far "more complex" than he had anticipated. But he was far from apologetic as he proudly cited the elimination of the totalitarian system, advances in personal freedoms and human rights, and the beginnings of a mixed economy. He also highlighted what he valued as his greatest accomplishments in foreign policy: putting "an end to the cold war and the arms race" and eliminating "the threat of a world war." While he shared his apprehension about the future, he also expressed faith in the "wisdom" of the people as "heirs to a great civilization" to sponsor its "rebirth."[499]

Despite all the political confusion and search for a new role, the one thing that remained firmly in place was Gorbachev's blood feud with Yeltsin. The intensity of the conflict manifested itself when Gorbachev tenaciously refused to participate in a court process inspired by Yeltsin that would have put him and the party on trial and forever discredited his leadership. The effort by Yeltsin's aides to revoke Gorbachev's privileges, including his use of a limousine, prompted one newspaper to quip "Soon, . . . Mikhail Sergeyevich will be going to work on a bicycle."[500] The government's decision to use his refusal to testify as reason to deny him permission to travel abroad "was a cruel and clever blow."[501] It also backfired, since the campaign of judicial harassment prompted Western statesmen, most notably German Chancellor Helmut Kohl, to intervene on Gorbachev's behalf and secure permission for him to travel to Berlin for Willy Brandt's funeral. Since Brandt represented the vision of a peaceful end to the Cold War between East and West, Gorbachev's presence at his funeral was living testament to the realization of Brandt's dream. Gorbachev also stood firm in his personal cold war with Yeltsin by comparing Yeltsin's government to "an insane asylum" and insisting that not "Even Stalin's sick mind" could have conjured up a comparable travesty of justice.[502]

His thwarted attempt to stage a political comeback in the spring 1996 presidential election, in which he received less than 2 percent of the vote, seems to have sealed his political fate. But according to Tatyana Tolstaya, even within Russia, where "no one will vote for him," he still had a role, since his image as a "nice, inoffensive, safe," and intelligent alternative to the use of force and violence had transformed him into something of a cult figure, "almost a holy fool," who continues to talk about "the truth [of] his own ideas."[503] Outside Russia, Gorbachev has burnished his image well by working on his foundation and globetrotting to give speeches and attend conferences. With one eye carefully fixed upon posterity, he has also cast himself in the liberal image of Jefferson, de Tocqueville, and other prominent political thinkers in the Western liberal tradition. He also reinforced his peaceful, democratic credentials by emphasizing that although he had possessed "emergency powers," he had chosen not to use them because "I simply could not betray myself."[504]

While Gorbachev may not have betrayed himself in his own eyes, questions concerning his consistency and competence have contributed to the controversy over his personality and leadership. Gorbachev's skills as a politician have also come under careful examination. Other aspects that weigh heavily in an assessment of Gorbachev's public life as a political leader and international statesman have centered upon his political and diplomatic perceptions as well as his ability to judge people. Despite his efforts to craft a highly cultivated image of international sophistication, Gorbachev was in many ways remarkably naïve in the world of diplomacy. At Reykjavik he had revealed his anxiety about the future of the Soviet Union's nuclear forces, while at home he had opened "a Pandora's box" for failing to comprehend the explosive impact of *glasnost* on the nationalities question.[505] By promoting to positions of political power individuals who ultimately betrayed him, Gorbachev also exhibited his ineptitude as a judge of character and further undermined his own position. Perhaps one of Gorbachev's greatest shortcomings was his inability to keep pace with the reform movement he had initiated. A more generous interpretation, however, argued that Gorbachev could "hardly be faulted for not having foreseen the elemental fury of the forces he had unleashed."[506] Nor could he realize his ambition of transforming his role as Russia's "last tsar" into his dream of becoming "Russia's first elected president."[507] In real terms, Gorbachev's failure also meant that he had to adjust to the transfer of political power to Yeltsin and forsake the comfort and style that came with his office—including a stable of limousines, a large detachment of staff and servants, and the glittering diplomatic receptions held in the grandeur of Saint Catherine's and Saint George's Halls.[508]

Gorbachev was the victim of an overweening self-confidence and impatience with institutions that did not respond to the call for change.[509] And though he may have tried to redefine his political identity, Gorbachev remained deeply rooted in the traditions of Soviet Marxism, which made it difficult for him to recognize "that communism was the problem, not the solution."[510] In the epilogue to his *Memoirs,* Gorbachev attempted to defend his record and rehabilitate himself in the eyes of posterity. He focused not on *perestroika*'s failure to provide prosperity but upon his personal commitment to democratic goals and his desire to "use this new-found freedom to create prosperity." He also defended himself against his critics' charges of Hamlet-like behavior, ironically emphasizing that he did "not know anyone against whom so many slings and arrows have been launched as against Gorbachev."[511] He specifically cited Yeltsin's "uncivilized"[512] behavior and Yeltsin's vain attempt to "clip [Gorbachev's] wings."[513] In his *Memoirs* he was also able to move beyond his personal pain and humiliation to stress the humanitarian work of his foundation, the importance of public life, the satisfactions derived from his travels and lectures abroad, and the need to address international issues on a global scale.[514] Here he was clearly in his element, with eyes facing West. Bearing witness to his own political odyssey and the weight of a larger political heritage, Gorbachev succinctly asserted in retrospect that "in its essence communism is a humanist ideology."[515]

In the world of politics, where leaders may not be able to see around corners, Gorbachev's intellectual tolerance, curiosity, and "openness to new ideas" reinforced the impression that he was cut from different political cloth than his predecessors and many of his contemporaries.[516] But despite the bright flashes of political insight, he was unable to transform his ideas into concrete programs and effective policies. As a reformer he had wanted to make the system work better, not scrap it. When the experiment failed, so did he, and the Soviet Union collapsed. But it is the sheer magnitude of the changes he initiated and their worldwide repercussions, irrespective of their success, that confer upon him the distinction of being the most consequential, and perhaps the single most significant, figure of the latter half of the twentieth century.

NOTES

1. Andrei Sakharov, *Moscow and Beyond: 1986–1989* (New York: Vantage Books, 1992), p. 10.

2. Isaac J. Tarasulo, "Personalities," in Isaac J. Tarasulo, ed., *Perils of Perestroika: Viewpoints from the Soviet Press, 1989–1991* (Wilmington, Del.: Scholarly Resources, 1992), p. 286.

3. Dusko Doder and Louise Branson, *Gorbachev: Heretic in the Kremlin* (New York: Penguin, 1991), p. 294.

4. *Time,* Sept. 9, 1985, p. 32.

5. Doder and Branson, *Heretic in the Kremlin,* p. 292.

6. Ibid., p. 31.

7. Robert G. Kaiser, *Why Gorbachev Happened: His Triumphs and His Failures* (New York: Simon & Schuster, 1991), p. 114.

8. Dev Murarka, *Gorbachov: The Limits of Power* (London: Hutchinson, 1988), p. 190.

9. Dusko Doder, *Shadows and Whispers: Power Politics inside the Kremlin from Brezhnev to Gorbachev* (New York: Penguin, 1988), p. 271.

10. Gail W. Lapidus, "Soviet Society in Transition," in Alexander Dallin and Condolezza Rice, eds., *The Gorbachev Era* (Stanford, Calif.: Stanford Alumni Association, 1986), p. 37.

11. Kaiser, *Why Gorbachev Happened,* p. 92.

12. Hedrick Smith, *The New Russians* (New York: Avon, 1991), p. 41.

13. Doder and Branson, *Heretic in the Kremlin,* pp. 5–7.

14. Michel Tatu, *Mikhail Gorbachev: The Origins of Perestroika,* translated from the French by A.P.M. Bradley (Boulder, N.Y.: East European Monographs No. CCC, distributed by Columbia University Press, 1991), p. 12.

15. Smith, *New Russians,* p. 44.

16. Donald Morrison et al., eds., *Mikhail S. Gorbachev: An Intimate Biography* (New York: Time, Inc., 1988), p. 50.

17. Smith, *New Russians,* p. 46.

18. Doder, *Shadows and Whispers,* p. 282.

19. Morrison et al., eds., *Mikhail S. Gorbachev,* p. 69.

20. Zhores A. Medvedev, *Gorbachev* (New York: W.W. Norton, 1986), p. 43.

21. Morrison et al., eds., *Mikhail S. Gorbachev,* pp. 83–95.

22. Doder and Branson, *Heretic in the Kremlin,* pp. 32–33.

23. Medvedev, *Gorbachev,* p. 57.

24. Robert V. Daniels, *The End of the Communist Revolution* (London: Routledge, 1993), p. 9.

25. Kaiser, *Why Gorbachev Happened* (1991 ed.), p. 51.

26. Doder, *Shadows and Whispers,* p. 295.

27. Thomas G. Butson, *Gorbachev: A Biography* (New York: Stein and Day, 1986) p. 15.

28. Kaiser, *Why Gorbachev Happened,* p. 52.

29. Smith, *New Russians,* p. 32.

30. Tatu, *Mikhail Gorbachev,* p. 69.

31. Doder and Branson, *Heretic in the Kremlin,* p. 65.

32. *Time,* Sept. 9, 1985, p. 21.

33. Seweryn Bialer, *The Soviet Paradox: External Expansion, Internal Decline* (New York: Alfred A. Knopf, 1986), p. 110.

34. Kaiser, *Why Gorbachev Happened,* p. 18.

35. Basile Kerblay, *Gorbachev's Russia* (New York: Pantheon, 1989), p. 19.

36. Medvedev, *Gorbachev*, p. 208.

37. Doder and Branson, *Heretic in the Kremlin*, pp. 247–48.

38. Stephen F. Cohen, "Introduction: Gorbachev and the Soviet Reformation," in Stephen F. Cohen and Katrina vanden Heuvel, eds., *Voices of Glasnost: Interviews with Gorbachev's Reformers* (New York: W.W. Norton, 1989), p. 16.

39. Tatu, *Mikhail Gorbachev*, pp. 73–75.

40. Doder, *Shadows and Whispers*, pp. 279, 308.

41. Kaiser, *Why Gorbachev Happened*, (1991 ed.) p. 172.

42. Ibid., p. 247.

43. Ibid., p. 253.

44. Butson, *Gorbachev*, p. 17.

45. Gail Sheehy, *The Man Who Changed the World: The Lives of Mikhail S. Gorbachev* (New York: Harper Collins, 1991), p. 210.

46. Kaiser, *Why Gorbachev Happened*, (1991 ed.) p. 415.

47. Tatu, *Mikhail Gorbachev*, p. 148.

48. Doder and Branson, *Heretic in the Kremlin*, p. 388.

49. Morrison et al., eds., *Mikhail S. Gorbachev*, p. 188.

50. Ibid., pp. 97–98.

51. Kaiser, *Why Gorbachev Happened*, (1991 ed.) p. 98.

52. Doder and Branson, *Heretic in the Kremlin*, pp. 88, 90.

53. Medvedev, *Gorbachev*, p. 185.

54. Morrison et al., eds., *Mikhail S. Gorbachev*, pp. 173–74.

55. Medvedev, *Gorbachev*, pp. 185–86.

56. Doder and Branson, *Heretic in the Kremlin*, p. 90.

57. Doder, *Shadows and Whispers*, p. 309.

58. Cohen, "Gorbachev and the Soviet Reformation," in Cohen and vanden Heuvel, eds., *Voices of Glasnost*, pp. 30–31.

59. Tatyana Zaslavskaya, "Socialism with a Human Face," in Cohen and vanden Heuvel, eds., *Voices of Glasnost*, p. 133.

60. Elem Klimov, "'Learning Democracy': The Filmmakers' Rebellion," in Cohen and vanden Heuvel, eds., *Voices of Glasnost*, p. 245.

61. Moshe Lewin, *The Gorbachev Phenomenon* (Berkeley: University of California Press, 1991), p. 152.

62. Ibid., p. 164.

63. Seweryn Bialer, "The Changing Soviet Political System," in Seweryn Bialer, ed., *Politics, Society, and Nationality Inside Gorbachev's Russia* (Boulder, Colo.: Westview Press, 1995), p. 205.

64. Doder, *Shadows and Whispers*, pp. 308–9.

65. Mikhail S. Gorbachev, *Perestroika: New Thinking for Our Country and the World* (New York: Harper & Row, 1987), pp. 54–55.

66. Anatolii Sobchak, *For a New Russia: The Mayor of Saint Petersburg's Own Story of the Struggle for Justice and Democracy* (New York: The Free Press, 1992), pp. 36–37.

67. Stuart H. Loory and Ann Imse, eds., *Seven Days That Shook the World: The Collapse of Soviet Communism* (Atlanta: Turner Publishing, 1991), p. 184.

68. Doder and Branson, *Heretic in the Kremlin*, p. 26.

69. Bialer, *Soviet Paradox*, p. 138.

70. Stephen White, *Gorbachev and After* (Cambridge, Eng.: Cambridge University Press, 1991), p. 219.

71. Tatu, *Mikhail Gorbachev*, pp. 71–72.

72. Doder, *Shadows and Whispers*, p. 307.

73. Butson, *Gorbachev*, p. 147.

74. Alexander Yakovlev, *The Fate of Marxism in Russia* (Binghamton, N.Y.: Vail-Ballou Press, 1993), pp. 20–21.

75. Walter Laqueur, *The Long Road to Freedom: Russia and Glasnost* (New York: Macmillan, 1989), pp. 284–85.

76. Gorbachev, *Perestroika*, p. 35.

77. Isaac J. Tarasulo, "Party Struggle and Political Reform," in Isaac J. Tarasulo, ed., *Gorbachev and Glasnost: Viewpoints from the Soviet Press* (Wilmington, Del.: Scholarly Resources, 1989), p. 275.

78. Lewin, *Gorbachev Phenomenon*, p. 85.

79. Ibid., pp. 98–99.

80. Daniels, *End of the Communist Revolution*, p. 15.

81. Aleksandr Bovin, in his role as journalist, critic, and reformer, described "democratization" as "the most important element of *perestroika*." Bovin, "Semi-Glasnost," in Cohen and vanden Heuvel, eds., *Voices of Glasnost*, p. 219.

82. Morrison et al., eds., *Mikhail S. Gorbachev*, p. 184.

83. Cohen, "Gorbachev and the Soviet Reformation," p. 14.

84. Len Karpinsky, "The Autobiography of a 'Half-Dissident,'" in Cohen and vanden Heuvel, eds., *Voices of Glasnost*, p. 301.

85. Ben Eklof, *Soviet Briefing: Gorbachev and the Reform Period* (Boulder, Colo.: Westview Press, 1989), p. 117.

86. Sobchak, *For a New Russia*, p. 27.

87. Robert Sharlet, "The Rule of Law," in Robert V. Daniels, ed., *Soviet Communism from Reform to Collapse* (Lexington, Ky.: D.C. Heath, 1995), p. 129.

88. Fyodor Burlatsky, "Democratization Is a Long March," in Cohen and vanden Heuvel, eds., *Voices of Glasnost*, p. 192.

89. For an extensive discussion of *zakonnost*, see Eklof, *Soviet Briefing*, pp. 66–85.

90. Ibid., pp. 72–74, 79–80.

91. Thomas Sherlock, "Politics and History under Gorbachev," in Alexander Dallin and Gail W. Lapidus, eds., *The Soviet System: From Crisis to Collapse* (Boulder, Colo.: Westview Press, 1995), pp. 248–49.

92. Nikolai Shmelyov, "The Rebirth of Common Sense," in Cohen and vanden Heuvel, eds., *Voices of Glasnost*, pp. 145–47.

93. Bialer, *Soviet Paradox*, p. 162.

94. Gorbachev, *Perestroika*, p. 57.

95. Ed. A. Hewett, "Is Soviet Socialism Reformable?" in Dallin and Lapidus, eds., *The Soviet System*, pp. 312–15.

96. Cornelius Castoriadis, "The Gorbachev Interlude," in Ferenc Feher and Andrew Arato, eds., *Gorbachev: The Debate* (Cambridge, Eng.: Polity Press, 1989), p. 80.

97. Ibid., pp. 74, 79–81.

98. Archie Brown, *The Gorbachev Factor* (Oxford, Eng.: Oxford University Press, 1996), p. 318.

99. Ibid., p. 127.

100. Murarka, *Gorbachov*, p. 14.

101. Tatu, *Mikhail Gorbachev*, pp. 84–85.

102. Boris Yeltsin, *Against the Grain* (New York: Simon & Schuster, 1990), p. 155.

103. Robert Maxwell, ed., *M. S. Gorbachov: Speeches and Writings,* vol. 2 (Oxford, Eng.: Pergamon Press, 1987), pp. 164–66, 168, 171, 174–76.

104. Marshall I. Goldman, *What Went Wrong with Perestroika* (New York: W.W. Norton, 1991), p. 18.

105. Ibid., p. 30.

106. Isaac J. Tarasulo, "Economic Reforms," in Tarasulo, ed., *Gorbachev and Glasnost,* p. 68.

107. Goldman, *What Went Wrong,* p. 126.

108. Ibid., p. 94.

109. Ibid., p. 98.

110. Kerblay, *Gorbachev's Russia,* p. 65.

111. Castoriadis, "Gorbachev Interlude," pp. 77–78.

112. Gorbachev, *Perestroika,* pp. 118–19.

113. Ibid., p. 122.

114. Ibid., pp. 120–21.

115. Laqueur, *Long Road to Freedom,* p. 186.

116. Adam Hochshild, *The Unquiet Ghost: Russians Remember Stalin* (New York: Penguin, 1994), p. 154.

117. Ibid., pp. xxii–xxiii.

118. Daniels, *End of the Communist Revolution,* p. 18.

119. Mikhail S. Gorbachev, *Memoirs* (New York: Doubleday, 1995), pp. 480–81.

120. Murarka, *Gorbachov,* p. 326.

121. Yuri Afanasyev, "The Agony of the Stalinist System," in Cohen and vanden Heuvel, eds., *Voices of Glasnost,* p. 97.

122. Hochschild, *Unquiet Ghost,* pp. 18–19.

123. Kaiser, *Why Gorbachev Happened* (1991 ed.) p. 247.

124. Ibid., p. 204.

125. Bialer, "Changing Soviet Political System," pp. 203–4.

126. Eklof, *Soviet Briefing,* p. 29.

127. Nina Andreyeva, "Polemics: I Cannot Waive Principles," in Tarasulo, ed., *Gorbachev and Glasnost,* pp. 278–79.

128. Ibid., pp. 286–87.

129. Ibid., pp. 280–81.

130. Ibid., p. 282.

131. Ibid., p. 285.

132. Bialer, "Changing Soviet Political System," p. 203.

133. Tarasulo, "Party Struggle and Political Reform" in Tarasulo, ed., *Gorbachev and Glasnost,* p. 270.

134. "Principles of *Perestroika*: The Revolutionary Nature of Thinking and Action," *Pravda,* Apr. 5, 1988, in Tarasulo, ed., *Gorbachev and Glasnost,* pp. 297–301.

135. Doder and Branson, *Heretic in the Kremlin,* pp. 311, 315.

136. Morrison et al., eds., *Mikhail S. Gorbachev,* p. 147.

137. Doder and Branson, *Heretic in the Kremlin,* p. 354.

138. Sakharov, *Moscow and Beyond,* p. 45.

139. Ibid., p. 131.

140. Andrei Sakharov, "Dimensions of Freedom," in Tarasulo, ed., *Perils of Perestroika,* pp. 344–45.

141. Sakharov, *Moscow and Beyond,* p. 115.
142. White, *Gorbachev and After,* p. 41.
143. Ibid., p. 64.
144. Kaiser, *Why Gorbachev Happened,* (1991 ed.) p. 268.
145. Smith, *The New Russians,* p. 463.
146. Kaiser, *Why Gorbachev Happened,* (1991 ed.) p. 282.
147. Sakharov, *Moscow and Beyond,* p. 120.
148. Yeltsin, *Against the Grain,* p. 245.
149. Kaiser, *Why Gorbachev Happened,* (1991 ed.) p. 278.
150. Ibid., p. 282.
151. Ibid., pp. 278–79.
152. Sobchak, *For a New Russia,* p. 103.
153. Kaiser, *Why Gorbachev Happened,* (1991 ed.) p. 280.
154. Smith, *The New Russians,* p. 471.
155. Bialer, "Changing Soviet Political System," p. 216.
156. Kaiser, *Why Gorbachev Happened,* (1991 ed.) p. 163.
157. Yeltsin, *Against the Grain,* p. 199.
158. Kaiser, *Why Gorbachev Happened,* (1991 ed.) p. 183.
159. Yeltsin, *Against the Grain,* p. 201.
160. Kaiser, *Why Gorbachev Happened,* (1991 ed.) p. 190.
161. Yeltsin, *Against the Grain,* p. 199.
162. Ibid., p. 201.
163. Kaiser, *Why Gorbachev Happened* (1991 ed.) p. 230.
164. Kerblay, *Gorbachev's Russia,* p. 131.
165. Doder and Branson, *Heretic in the Kremlin,* p. 326.
166. Ibid., p. 277.
167. Kaiser, *Why Gorbachev Happened,* (1991 ed.) p. 193.
168. Laqueur, *Long Road to Freedom,* p. 296.
169. Doder and Branson, *Heretic in the Kremlin,* p. 278.
170. Laqueur, *Long Road to Freedom,* p. 258.
171. John Morrison and Boris Yeltsin, "The Renaissance of Boris Yeltsin," in Daniels, ed., *Soviet Communism from Reform to Collapse,* p. 185.
172. Yeltsin, *Against the Grain,* p. 151.
173. Ibid., p. 261.
174. Ibid., pp. 179–80.
175. Ibid., p. 188.
176. Ibid., p. 165.
177. Ibid., p. 139.
178. Ellen Mickiewicz, *Split Signals: Television and Politics in the Soviet Union* (Oxford, Eng.: Oxford University Press, 1988), pp. 207–9.
179. Sheehy, *The Man Who Changed the World,* p. 4.
180. Mickiewicz, *Split Signals,* p. 213.
181. Ibid., p. 226.
182. Sheehy, *The Man Who Changed the World,* p. 243.
183. Mickiewicz, *Split Signals,* p. 225.
184. Butson, *Gorbachev,* p. 144.
185. Tatu, *Mikhail Gorbachev,* p. 89.
186. Kerblay, *Gorbachev's Russia,* p. 23.

187. White, *Gorbachev and After,* p. 91.

188. Sobchak, *For a New Russia,* p. 17.

189. White, *Gorbachev and After,* p. 91.

190. For an extended discussion of the historical evolution of the term *glasnost,* see Laqueur, *Long Road to Freedom,* pp. 48–50, 313–15.

191. Tatu, *Mikhail Gorbachev,* pp. 89–90.

192. Eklof, *Soviet Briefing,* p. 44.

193. Kerblay, *Gorbachev's Russia,* p. 24.

194. Laqueur, *Long Road to Freedom,* p. 253.

195. Kaiser, *Why Gorbachev Happened,* (1991 ed.) p. 159.

196. Goldman, *What Went Wrong,* p. 187.

197. Doder, *Shadows and Whispers,* p. 301.

198. Anders Aslund, *Gorbachev's Struggle for Economic Reform: The Soviet Reform Process, 1985–1988* (Ithaca, N.Y.: Cornell University Press, 1989), p. 6.

199. Morrison et al., eds., *Mikhail S. Gorbachev,* p. 150.

200. Walter Laqueur, *The Dream That Failed: Reflections on the Soviet Union* (Oxford, Eng.: Oxford University Press, 1989) p. 61.

201. Ibid., p. 27.

202. Doder, *Shadows and Whispers,* p. 301.

203. Wilson P. Dizard and S. Blake Swensrud, *Gorbachev's Information Revolution: Controlling Glasnost in the New Electronic Era* (Washington, D.C.: The Center for Strategic and International Studies, 1987), p. 66.

204. Kerblay, *Gorbachev's Russia,* pp. 97–98.

205. Gorbachev, *Perestroika,* p. 66.

206. Ibid., pp. 78–79.

207. White, *Gorbachev and After,* p. 90.

208. Smith, *New Russians,* pp. 576–77.

209. Mickiewicz, *Split Signals,* p. 33.

210. Ibid., p. 203.

211. Tatu, *Mikhail Gorbachev,* p. 88.

212. Kerblay, *Gorbachev's Russia,* p. 23.

213. Mickiewicz, *Split Signals,* p. 224.

214. Jerry Hough, *Russia and the West: Gorbachev and the Politics of Reform* (New York: Simon & Schuster, 1990), pp. 203–4.

215. Laqueur, *Long Road to Freedom,* p. 299.

216. Kendall Bailes, "Science and Technology in the Soviet Union: Historical Background and Contemporary Problems," in Dallin and Rice, eds., *The Gorbachev Era,* pp. 70–71.

217. Bialer, *Soviet Paradox,* p. 160.

218. Doder, *Shadows and Whispers,* p. 330.

219. Dizard and Swensrud, *Gorbachev's Information Revolution,* p. 7.

220. Medvedev, *Gorbachev,* p. 259.

221. Ibid., p. 266.

222. Ibid., pp. 262–63.

223. Murarka, *Gorbachov,* p. 200.

224. Morrison et al., eds., *Mikhail S. Gorbachev,* p. 146.

225. Mikhail S. Gorbachev, *Toward a Better World* (New York: Richardson & Steirman, 1987), p. 235.

226. Ibid., p. 234.

227. Murarka, *Gorbachov,* p. 206.

228. Medvedev, *Gorbachev,* p. 265.

229. Doder, *Shadows and Whispers,* p. 320.

230. White, *Gorbachev and After,* p. 94.

231. Mary Dejevsky, "*Glasnost'* and the Soviet Press," in Julian Graffy and Geoffrey A. Hosking, eds., *Culture and the Media in the USSR Today* (New York: St. Martin's Press, 1989), p. 35.

232. Mickiewicz, *Split Signals,* p. 56.

233. Doder, *Shadows and Whispers,* p. 319.

234. Doder and Branson, *Heretic in the Kremlin,* p. 132.

235. Gorbachev, *Perestroika,* p. 235.

236. Smith, *New Russians,* p. 81.

237. White, *Gorbachev and After,* pp. 86–87.

238. Julian Graffy, "The Literary Press," in Graffy and Hosking, eds., *Culture and the Media in the USSR Today*, p. 133.

239. Gorbachev, *Memoirs,* p. 206.

240. White, *Gorbachev and After,* p. 87.

241. Anatoli Rybakov, *Children of the Arbat* (New York: Dell, 1988), p. 477.

242. For Rybakov's portrait of Stalin, see Rybakov, *Children of the Arbat,* pp. 599–604.

243. Morrison et al., eds., *Mikhail S. Gorbachev,* p. 152.

244. Sheehy, *The Man Who Changed the World,* p. 246.

245. Klimov, "Learning Democracy," p. 237.

246. Ibid., p. 233.

247. Ian Christie, "The Cinema," in Graffy and Hosking, eds. *Culture and the Media in the U.S.S.R. Today,* pp. 46–47.

248. Klimov, "Learning Democracy," p. 234.

249. Smith, *New Russians,* p. 558.

250. Ibid., p. 111.

251. Murarka compared Varlam's character to Stalin's henchman, Lavrenti Beria. See Murarka, *Gorbachov,* p. 282.

252. David Ioravsky, "Glasnost Theater," *New York Review of Books,* Nov. 10, 1988, p. 36.

253. Ibid., pp. 38–39.

254. Michael Glenny, "Soviet Theatre: *Glasnost'* in Action—with Difficulty," in Graffy and Hosking, eds., *Culture and the Media in the USSR Today,* pp. 86–87.

255. Ioravsky, "Glasnost Theater," pp. 36–37.

256. Mikhail Ulyanov, "The Preaching Theater," in Cohen and vanden Heuvel, eds., *Voices of Glasnost,* p. 246.

257. Ibid., pp. 258–59.

258. Bovin, "Semi-Glasnost," p. 216.

259. Ulyanov, "Preaching Theater," p. 246.

260. Ibid., p. 248.

261. Christopher Rice, "Soviet Music in the Era of *Perestroika*," in Graffy and Hosking, eds., *Culture and the Media in the USSR Today,* pp. 100–1.

262. Ibid., p. 93.

263. "Rock Music? Subculture? Lifestyle," Editorial Roundtable Discussion, "Sotsiologicheskie Issledovaniya" (June 1987) in Tarasulo, ed., *Gorbachev and Glasnost,* p. 158.

264. Laqueur, *Long Road to Freedom,* p. 104.

265. Graffy, "Literary Press," pp. 130–31.

266. Lewin, *Gorbachev Phenomenon,* pp. 78–79.

267. Georgi Arbatov, "America Also Needs Perestroika," in Cohen and vanden Heuvel, eds., *Voices of Glasnost,* p. 313.

268. See Hough, *Russia and the West,* p. 225, and Doder and Branson, *Heretic in the Kremlin,* p. 216.

269. Gorbachev, *Perestroika,* p. 17.

270. Ibid., pp. 158–59.

271. Ibid., p. 147.

272. Ibid., p. 189.

273. Ibid., p. 145.

274. Ibid., p. 13.

275. Ibid., p. 128.

276. Ibid., p. 132.

277. Doder and Branson, *Heretic in the Kremlin,* p. 215.

278. Gorbachev, *Perestroika,* p. 149.

279. Ibid., pp. 138–42.

280. Ibid., p. 222.

281. Ibid., p. 215. For Arbatov's views on these issues, see Arbatov, "America Also Needs Perestroika," p. 323.

282. Bialer, *Soviet Paradox,* p. 370.

283. Hough, *Russia and the West,* p. 227.

284. Eduard Shevardnadze, *The Future Belongs to Freedom* (London: Sinclair-Stevenson, 1991), pp. 92–93.

285. Laqueur, *Long Road to Freedom,* p. 221.

286. Doder and Branson, *Heretic in the Kremlin,* pp. 218–19.

287. White, *Gorbachev and After,* pp. 210–11.

288. Gorbachev, *Perestroika,* p. 208.

289. Ibid.

290. Mikhail S. Gorbachev, *At the Summit* (New York: Richardson, Steirman, & Black, 1988), pp. 69–74.

291. Laqueur, *Long Road to Freedom,* p. 222.

292. Henry Kissinger, *Diplomacy* (New York: Simon and Schuster, 1994) p. 791.

293. Robin F. Laird, "Introduction: The Changing Soviet Environment," in Susan L. Clark, ed., *Gorbachev's Agenda: Changes in Soviet Domestic and Foreign Policy* (Boulder, Colo.: Westview Press, 1989), pp. 1–2.

294. *Time,* Sept. 9, 1985, p. 21.

295. Sheehy, *The Man Who Changed the World,* p. 201.

296. Condoleeza Rice, "The Soviet Alliance System," in Dallin and Rice, eds., *The Gorbachev Era,* p. 162.

297. Doder and Branson, *Heretic in the Kremlin,* p. 377.

298. Morrison et al., eds., *Mikhail S. Gorbachev,* p. 183.

299. Doder and Branson, *Heretic in the Kremlin,* p. 229.

300. Condoleeza Rice, "The Development of Soviet Military Power," in Dallin and Rice, eds., *The Gorbachev Era*, p. 131.

301. Kaiser, *Why Gorbachev Happened*, (1991 ed.) p. 297.

302. Laqueur, *Long Road to Freedom*, p. 247.

303. Doder and Branson, *Heretic in the Kremlin*, p. 230.

304. Laqueur, *Long Road to Freedom*, p. 246.

305. Kissinger, *Diplomacy*, p. 794.

306. Sheehy, *The Man Who Changed the World*, p. 218.

307. Timothy Garton Ash, *The Magic Lantern: The Revolution of '89 Witnessed in Warsaw, Budapest, Berlin and Prague* (New York: Vantage, 1993), p. 141.

308. Gorbachev, *Memoirs*, p. 484.

309. Bialer, *Soviet Paradox*, p. 341.

310. Kaiser, *Why Gorbachev Happened* (1991 ed.) p. 302, and Hannes Adomeit, "Gorbachev and German Unification: Revision of Thinking, Realignment of Power," in Dallin and Lapidus, eds., *The Soviet System*, pp. 471–72.

311. Ash, *Magic Lantern*, p. 141.

312. Kaiser, *Why Gorbachev Happened* (1991 ed.), p. 356.

313. Doder and Branson, *Heretic in the Kremlin*, pp. 434–35.

314. Sheehy, *The Man Who Changed the World*, p. 218.

315. Shevardnadze, *Future Belongs to Freedom*, p. 217.

316. Georgi Arbatov, *The System: An Insider's Life in Soviet Politics* (New York: Random House, 1992), p. 58.

317. Sheehy, *The Man Who Changed the World*, p. 165.

318. Ibid., p. 215.

319. Murarka, *Gorbachov*, p. 377.

320. *Time*, Sept. 9, 1985, p. 32.

321. Morrison et al., eds., *Mikhail S. Gorbachev*, p. 143.

322. Butson, *Gorbachev*, pp. 153–54.

323. Murarka, *Gorbachov*, p. 381.

324. Mikhail S. Gorbachev, *The Coming Century of Peace* (New York: Richardson & Steirman, 1986) p. 48.

325. Ibid., p. 45.

326. Murarka, *Gorbachov*, p. 380.

327. Gorbachev, *Coming Century of Peace*, p. 55. See also Murarka, *Gorbachov*, pp. 380–381.

328. Maxwell, ed., *M. S. Gorbachev*, vol. 1, pp. 328–30.

329. Medvedev, *Gorbachev*, pp. 279–81.

330. Ibid., p. 239.

331. Sheehy, *The Man Who Changed the World*, p. 197.

332. Gorbachev, *Toward a Better World*, p. 30.

333. Ibid., p. 41.

334. Gorbachev, *Perestroika*, p. 240.

335. Doder and Branson, *Heretic in the Kremlin*, p. 286.

336. Morrison et al., eds., *Mikhail S. Gorbachev*, pp. 222–23.

337. Ibid., pp. 231–32.

338. Gorbachev, *At the Summit*, pp. 153–54.

339. Ibid., p. 97

340. White, *Gorbachev and After*, p. 196.

341. Morrison et al., eds., *Mikhail S. Gorbachev*, pp. 232–33.

342. Sheehy, *The Man Who Changed the World*, p. 208.

343. Gorbachev, *At the Summit*, p. 152.

344. For an overview of the event, see Morrison et al., eds., *Mikhail S. Gorbachev*, pp. 225–27.

345. Gorbachev, *At the Summit*, p. 166.

346. Ibid., p. 229.

347. Ibid., p. 233.

348. Ibid., pp. 252–53.

349. Kaiser, *Why Gorbachev Happened* (1991 ed.), p. 227.

350. Doder and Branson, *Heretic in the Kremlin*, pp. 318–19.

351. White, *Gorbachev and After*, p. 197.

352. Sheehy, *The Man Who Changed the World*, p. 221.

353. Ibid., p. 354.

354. Gorbachev, *At the Summit*, pp. 24–25.

355. Morrison et al., eds., *Mikhail S. Gorbachev*, p. 142.

356. Gorbachev, *Toward a Better World*, pp. 311–12, 321–25.

357. Ibid., pp. 364–65.

358. Ibid., p. 368.

359. For a discussion of the significance of those in attendance, see Doder and Branson, *Heretic in the Kremlin*, p. 209, and White, *Gorbachev and After*, p. 188.

360. Doder and Branson, *Heretic in the Kremlin*, p. 209.

361. Gorbachev, *At the Summit*, pp. 4–6.

362. Kaiser, *Why Gorbachev Happened* (1991 ed.), p. 249.

363. Isaac J. Tarasulo, introductory remarks to "Mikhail Gorbachev Addresses the United Nations," in Tarasulo, ed., *Gorbachev and Glasnost*, p. 329.

364. Ibid., p. 338.

365. Ibid., p. 335.

366. White, *Gorbachev and After*, p. 190.

367. Mikhail S. Gorbachev, "Mikhail Gorbachev Addresses the United Nations," in Tarasulo, ed., *Gorbachev and Glasnost*, pp. 341–43.

368. Doder and Branson, *Heretic in the Kremlin*, p. 356.

369. Gorbachev, "Mikhail Gorbachev Addresses the United Nations," in Tarasulo, ed., *Gorbachev and Glasnost*, p. 347.

370. Gorbachev, *Perestroika*, pp. 171–72.

371. Maxwell, ed., *M. S. Gorbachov*, vol. 2, p. 186.

372. Gorbachev, *Coming Century of Peace*, pp. 95–96.

373. Gorbachev, *Perestroika*, p. 187.

374. Ibid., p. 176.

375. Ibid., pp. 187–88.

376. Ibid., pp. 175–76.

377. Rice, "Soviet Alliance System," p. 164.

378. White, *Gorbachev and After*, p. 206.

379. Rice, "Soviet Alliance System," p. 164.

380. Hough, *Russia and the West*, p. 229.

381. Shevardnadze, *Future Belongs to Freedom*, p. 160.

382. White, *Gorbachev and After*, p. 202.

383. Smith, *New Russians*, p. 104.

384. Butson, *Gorbachev,* p. 52.

385. White, *Gorbachev and After,* p. 205.

386. Ibid.

387. Gorbachev, *Perestroika,* p. 177.

388. Isaac J. Tarasulo, "Foreign and Military Issues," in Tarasulo, ed., *Gorbachev and Glasnost,* p. 220.

389. Smith, *New Russians,* p. 104.

390. Kaiser, *Why Gorbachev Happened* (Touchstone edition, 1992), p. 412.

391. Tarasulo, "Personalities," p. 286.

392. Kaiser, *Why Gorbachev Happened* (Touchstone ed., 1992), p. 412.

393. Kaiser, *Why Gorbachev Happened* (1991 ed.), p. 411.

394. Ibid., p. 409.

395. Ibid., pp. 330–31.

396. David Remnick, *Lenin's Tomb: The Last Days of the Soviet Empire* (New York: Random House, 1993), p. 327.

397. Kaiser, *Why Gorbachev Happened* (1991 ed.), p. 331.

398. Sheehy, *The Man Who Changed the World,* p. 339.

399. Kaiser, *Why Gorbachev Happened* (1991 ed.), pp. 334–35.

400. Sheehy, *The Man Who Changed the World,* p. 350. Boldin, however, questioned Gorbachev's generous interpretation of "the term 'victory in the Cold War,'" since it failed "to convey" that it was "a total rout" for the USSR. Valery Boldin, *Ten Years that Shook the World: The Gorbachev Era as Witnessed by His Chief of Staff* (New York: Basic Books, 1994), p. 296.

401. Sheehy, *The Man Who Changed the World,* p. 350.

402. Ibid., p. 224.

403. White, *Gorbachev and After,* p. 247.

404. Kaiser, *Why Gorbachev Happened* (1991 ed.), p. 325.

405. Ibid., p. 367.

406. White, *Gorbachev and After,* p. 239.

407. Ibid., p. 247.

408. Doder and Branson, *Heretic in the Kremlin,* p. 424.

409. Daniels, *End of the Communist Revolution,* p. 37.

410. Yeltsin, *Against the Grain,* p. 262.

411. Kaiser, *Why Gorbachev Happened* (1991 ed.), pp. 303–4.

412. White, *Gorbachev and After,* p. 235.

413. Kaiser, *Why Gorbachev Happened* (1991 ed.), p. 304.

414. Smith, *New Russians,* p. 503.

415. Sheehy, *The Man Who Changed the World,* pp. 306–9.

416. Kaiser, *Why Gorbachev Happened* (1991 ed.), p. 305. See also Doder and Branson, *Heretic in the Kremlin,* p. 75.

417. Smith, *New Russians,* p. 566.

418. Stanislav Shatalin, "The Radical Alternative," in Daniels, ed., *Soviet Communism from Reform to Collapse,* pp. 206–16.

419. Gorbachev, *Memoirs,* p. 382.

420. Kaiser, *Why Gorbachev Happened* (1991 ed.), pp. 370–71.

421. Kissinger, *Diplomacy,* p. 798.

422. Lewin, *Gorbachev Phenomenon,* p. 174.

423. Doder and Branson, *Heretic in the Kremlin,* p. 247.

424. Ibid., p. 353.

425. Smith, *New Russians,* p. 520.

426. Kaiser, *Why Gorbachev Happened* (1991 ed.), p. 352.

427. Sobchak, *For a New Russia,* p. 163.

428. Kaiser, *Why Gorbachev Happened* (1991 ed.), pp. 381–82.

429. Ibid., pp. 315–16.

430. Ibid., pp. 392–94.

431. Remnick, *Lenin's Tomb,* p. 387.

432. Goldman, *What Went Wrong,* p. 225.

433. Smith, *New Russians,* pp. 557–65.

434. Doder and Branson, *Heretic in the Kremlin,* p. 437.

435. Kaiser, *Why Gorbachev Happened* (1991 ed.), pp. 396–400.

436. Smith, *New Russians,* pp. 613–14.

437. Daniels, *End of the Communist Revolution,* p. 50.

438. White, *Gorbachev and After,* pp. 174–75.

439. Smith, *New Russians,* p. 616.

440. Kaiser, *Why Gorbachev Happened* (Touchstone ed.), pp. 410–11.

441. Smith, *New Russians,* pp. 618–19.

442. Hough, *Russia and the West,* p. 181.

443. Kaiser, *Why Gorbachev Happened* (Touchstone ed.), pp. 422–23.

444. Daniels, *End of the Communist Revolution,* p. 51.

445. Loory and Imse, *Seven Days That Shook the World,* pp. 57–61.

446. For a spirited discussion of the personal dynamics and theatrical components of the coup, see Martin Sixsmith, "The August Coup," in Daniels, ed., *Soviet Communism from Reform to Collapse,* pp. 253–68.

447. Kaiser, *Why Gorbachev Happened* (Touchstone ed., 1992), p. 423.

448. For a discussion of the indecisive nature of the press conference, see Loory and Imse, *Seven Days That Shook the World,* pp. 97–99.

449. Shevardnadze, *Future Belongs to Freedom,* p. 219.

450. Nicholas Daniloff, "Media Coverage," in Loory and Imse, *Seven Days That Shook the World,* p. 235.

451. Remnick, *Lenin's Tomb,* p. 435.

452. Daniels, *End of the Communist Revolution,* pp. 29–30.

453. Daniloff, "Media Coverage," p. 235.

454. Ibid., p. 76.

455. John B. Dunlop, "Anatomy of a Failed Coup," in Dallin and Lapidus, eds., *The Soviet System,* p. 596.

456. Giulietto Chiesa, *Cronaca del Golpe Rosso* (Milan: Baldin & Castoldi, 1991), p. 22.

457. Daniloff, "Media Coverage," p. 233.

458. Hedrick Smith, "Introduction," in Loory and Imse, *Seven Days That Shook the World,* p. 29.

459. Smith, *New Russians,* p. 632.

460. Shevardnadze, *Future Belongs to Freedom,* pp. 209–10.

461. Daniels, *End of the Communist Revolution,* p. 32.

462. Kaiser, *Why Gorbachev Happened* (Touchstone ed.), p. 427.

463. Smith, *New Russians,* p. 639.

464. Kaiser, *Why Gorbachev Happened* (Touchstone ed.), pp. 424–25.

465. Ibid., p. 457.

466. Mikhail S. Gorbachev, *The August Coup: The Truth and the Issues* (New York: HarperCollins, 1991), p. 27.

467. Loory and Imse, *Seven Days That Shook the World*, p. 94.

468. Ibid., p. 52.

469. Sixsmith, "August Coup," p. 260.

470. Loory and Imse, *Seven Days That Shook the World*, p. 153.

471. Chiesa, *Cronaca del Golpe Rosso*, p. 90.

472. Kaiser, *Why Gorbachev Happened* (Touchstone ed.), p. 429.

473. Remnick, *Lenin's Tomb*, pp. 494–95.

474. Sobchak's italics. Sobchak, *For a New Russia*, p. 173.

475. Goldman, *What Went Wrong*, p. 237.

476. Kaiser, *Why Gorbachev Happened* (Touchstone ed.), p. 426.

477. Loory and Imse, *Seven Days That Shook the World*, p. 154.

478. Kaiser, *Why Gorbachev Happened* (Touchstone ed.), p. 430.

479. Sixsmith, "August Coup," p. 266.

480. Loory and Imse, *Seven Days That Shook the World*, p. 158.

481. Chiesa, *Cronaca del Golpe Rosso*, pp. 113–14.

482. Ibid., pp. 112ff, 131. For more on Chiesa's discussion of how power shifted quickly from Gorbachev to Yeltsin, see pp. 48–49, 67, 78, 84, 87, 120.

483. Remnick, *Lenin's Tomb*, p. 495.

484. Gorbachev, *August Coup*, p. 11.

485. Ibid., pp. 56–57.

486. Ibid., p. 41.

487. Ibid., p. 32.

488. Ibid., p. 38.

489. Ibid., p. 89.

490. Ibid., p. 53.

491. Ibid., p. 73.

492. Gorbachev's italics. Ibid., pp. 118–19.

493. Kaiser, *Why Gorbachev Happened* (Touchstone ed.), p. 435.

494. Daniels, *End of the Communist Revolution*, p. 52.

495. Kaiser, *Why Gorbachev Happened* (Touchstone ed.), p. 436.

496. Remnick, *Lenin's Tomb*, p. 499.

497. Daniels, *End of Communist Revolution*, p. 52.

498. Kaiser, *Why Gorbachev Happened* (Touchstone ed.), pp. 436–37.

499. For the text of Gorbachev's speech, see "Statement by the Heads of State of the Republic of Belarus, The Russian SFSR, and Ukraine" in Daniels, ed., *Soviet Communism from Reform to Collapse*, pp. 315–19.

500. Remnick, *Lenin's Tomb*, p. 526.

501. Ibid., p. 529.

502. Ibid., pp. 526–27.

503. Tatyana Tolstaya, "The Way They Live Now" (a review of *Resurrection: The Struggle for a New Russia* by David Remnick) translated from the Russian by Jamey Gambrell, *New York Review of Books*, Apr. 24, 1997, pp. 14–15.

504. Remnick, *Lenin's Tomb*, p. 503.

505. Doder and Branson, *Heretic in the Kremlin*, p. 409.

506. Abraham Brumberg, "Introduction," in Abraham Brumberg, ed., *Chronicle of a Revolution: A Western-Soviet Inquiry into Perestroika* (New York: Pantheon, 1990), pp. 12–13.

507. Doder and Branson, *Heretic in the Kremlin,* p. 410.

508. Ibid., p. 294.

509. Ibid., pp. 127–28.

510. Kissinger, *Diplomacy,* p. 795

511. Gorbachev, *Memoirs,* pp. 673–74.

512. Ibid., p. 673.

513. Ibid., p. 680.

514. Ibid., pp. 674–78.

515. Ibid., p. 680.

516. Daniels, *End of the Communist Revolution*, p. 27.

CONCLUSION

In attempting to assess the impact of these four figures on the political makeup of the contemporary world, a number of important questions immediately come to mind. For example, in the case of Gandhi, Mao, and Mandela, issues of identity represent a major consideration in an analysis of their political development. As members of local elites who aspired to leadership roles, they found themselves attracted to the West through European education, social habits, foreign lifestyles, and political power. In some instances this attraction created an unsettling ambiguity, as many anticolonial figures who labored under the desire to advance within the structures of colonial rule came to the uneasy realization that the acquisition of European mores and values was also part of a much larger desire to gain respect from the ruling elite. At the same time, they were reluctant to break with their cultural past and continued to draw politically from their membership and standing within the native community. For others, the commitment was to remain thoroughly true to one's own background and identity and defiantly opposed to the westernization of their native cultures.

Of course, there was also a third way, as expressed in the careers of Gandhi and Mandela, which combined a deep interest in the Western world with preservation of native traditions. Yet, despite their educational opportunities as members of the British empire and their genuine respect for the values of an English education, both Gandhi and Mandela broke with the British model and proceeded to create political movements that identified with the native cultural traditions of India and South Africa. Though similar, they did, however, move in different political directions. Gandhi, for example, was free to travel as a young man to England and South Africa and chart the course of his own professional development. His experiences abroad, however, extended beyond the narrow pursuit of his career goals as a lawyer to include greater contact with English culture, London dress and manners, and the bearing and self-confidence of the British elite. His decision to move to South Africa and establish a legal practice in that country set the stage for his political conversion and the development of his theories of communal development. His discovery of the fate of brown-skinned Indians, who were deprived of their legal rights and political freedom in the face of British repression, inspired Gandhi to develop his theory of civil disobedience as a means of challenging British attitudes through examples of individual integrity, moral conviction, and personal determination. His creation of a communal farm with its emphasis on simplicity and self-sufficiency not only provided an immediate example to the Indians of South Africa on how to construct and shape an alternative social model; it also served as a model for a larger visionary concept of human sharing and caring, which extended beyond the reaches of South Africa and India and embraced the entire world.

Gandhi, however, eventually rejected Western ways in favor of native Hindu culture and traditions and made it a point to craft his movement out of Hindu cultural practices, values, and historical traditions. His militancy was, in fact, nonmilitant, but, nonetheless, politically effective in enabling the people of India to force the British to leave their most prized colonial possession. But the discipline that eschewed violence actually represented a total rejection of violence in favor of a broader commitment to the more accepting virtues of Indian culture. The net result was to provide the Indian population with a sense of pride of place and a new appreciation for their common cultural identity and values. It was this contribution that, more than any other, served as Gandhi's most elemental lesson to his people and the world.

Gandhi also emerged as an intensely religious man, who used his religion to preach love, humility, and self-sacrifice. This created a dynamic tension between Gandhi the holy man and Gandhi the political figure. And while spiritual rectitude won him much international acclaim and recognition, it also called into question his credentials as a strong political leader during the struggle for independence and his capacity to prevent the partition of India into the separate states of India and Pakistan. But the true dimensions of his personal sacrifice can be measured by nothing less than the loss of his life, as he became the victim of sectarian passions and attitudes when he was killed at point-blank range by an assassin's bullet on his way to a prayer service. Though tragic and sad in its manifold dimensions, the act also pays a disturbingly ironic tribute to the stature of an exceptional man who fought to preserve life, only to fall by the wayside in a violent act of political and religious excess.

Mandela's relationship with the elements of British culture took a different turn. By all accounts, including his own, he was impressed with British culture and studied to become a lawyer in British South Africa. Like Gandhi, who also trained as an English barrister, Mandela too wore Western suits and was drawn to the lights of the city. In his case, the primary attraction was the vibrant, urban culture of Johannesburg. But he never lost the recollections of his youth, of his tribal upbringing, of his ritualistic passage into manhood, and of his having been trained to serve someday as a chief to his people. In Mandela's case, the trials of his political passage weighed so heavily upon the man that his political leadership and his struggle to obtain justice for his people bore the joint insignia of pride and prejudice. More than any of the other personalities discussed in this book, it is the sheer strength of Mandela's personality and the power of his convictions that provide the deepest form of inspiration. This becomes particularly apparent when reading the sections on his seemingly interminable years of imprisonment. These passages, in which he faithfully describes his own ordeal, poignantly reveal the depth of his own pride and humility and his enormous reservoirs of personal strength. One realizes immediately that one is in the presence of a truly unique historical figure who was able to transform the strengths of his personality into a rare and charismatic political personna.

It should also be clear that it was the power of his intelligence and his ability to outwit and withstand his British and Afrikaans opponents—not to mention his ability to outlast them after a grueling twenty-seven years in prison—that gave shape to his remarkable personality and conferred upon him the title of the leader of a movement for a free South Africa rooted in human justice and tolerance. Nor, however, is it at all surprising to confront the ambiguities of his personal ordeal, as he often vacillated between the inclinations of his innate gregarious personality and an arresting aloofness, which at times bordered on arrogance and seemed to reflect his years of imprisonment, isolation, and solitary introspection. But, like Gandhi, he too managed to merge the world of two different cultures. Where they differed, however, was in the style of the two mergers. Gandhi's represented the strength of passive, nonviolent resistance, whereas Mandela avowed the use of force against the political establishment as a means of overcoming tyranny and racism and providing the vast majority of South Africans with an opportunity to live in peace, dignity, and freedom.

Although his term of office has come to an end, the debates concerning his presidency will continue. One thing is clear, and that is that the assessment of Mandela's career as an underground revolutionary and political prisoner differs significantly from the assessment of his years as South Africa's first black president. There can be no doubt that the political atmosphere of the first appealed more directly to the cast of his character and psychological makeup. As a moral leader he was without rival. But as a head of state and of the government of South Africa, he suddenly had to face the more practical side of administrative affairs. This is not to suggest that despite a seemingly chronic economic slump, scant capital investment, high unemployment, and continued violence that Mandela did not leave his mark. From his support of the Truth and Reconciliation Commission to his government's ability to expand both the scope and the quality of public services in many areas of South Africa, Mandela demonstrated qualities of presidential leadership.

For the most part, however, Mandela was concerned with the symbolic and ceremonial aspects of his office, and not with the day-to-day administration of things. And as had been the case during the struggle for freedom, it was Mandela's charismatic presence that served as the indispensable link during the period of political transition. For example, when he openly entered the public arena, he brought with him the same independence and legendary self-control that had served him for nearly three decades as the silent but legendary victim of South Africa's cruel and inhumane system of *apartheid*. Once again, his moral rectitude, his capacity for forgiveness, and his ability to listen to friend and foe alike made him the indispensable man, the only figure who was capable of bridging the gap between black and white South Africans.

As a leader, Mandela was tall and splendid in his appearance. He was a powerful speaker who inspired his listeners with unwavering conviction and a real sense of purpose. He also possessed the rare and wonderful gift of being able to listen patiently to the fears and anxieties of his white opponents and address those concerns with sincerity and compassion. Throughout it all, he somehow managed to emerge with his sense of humor and his aristocratic demeanor intact. He also provided his people with an extraordinary model of cultural, individual and national pride. His courage and ability to set a moral example in the face of overwhelming odds also served as a symbol for the struggle to overcome personal humiliation through political activism and honor a commitment to the demands of one's own individual conscience. It also endowed him with his political legacy and enabled him to leave his ultimate gift to his countrymen in the form of a nation-maker, who was above all else committed to justice and the construction of a new South Africa.

Mao's progress along the path of westernization raises a number of different political issues, most of which resulted from a conflict between the weight of China's cultural legacy and the promise of Marxist revolution. In Mao's case, his ties to the countryside went deep, as evidenced by his frequent return to rural China to seek shelter and political renewal. These experiences reinforced his commitment to revolutionary ideas, albeit imported from abroad, and prompted him to engage in what seemed to be an endless process of ideological development in pursuit of a revolutionary message that was tailor-made to the needs of a backward, yet politically explosive, China. In fact, the appeal of that message, as applied during the wars of national liberation, was founded upon the principles of simultaneous domestic revolution and a total popular commitment to a fierce and determined struggle against colonial domination. It was so commanding and wide in its revolutionary scope that it inspired wars of national liberation throughout Southeast Asia, including the eventual triumph of North Vietnam first over the French and later over American military forces, followed by the virtually uncontested unification of all Vietnam.

Much of Mao's success can be attributed to his "Sinification of Marxism." Like the others, he too was a political hybrid, and he drew heavily from the longstanding tradition of Chinese peasant rebellion. At the center of Mao's revolutionary thinking stood the role of the peasantry, which he cast in the mold of the agricultural proletariat within a larger imported version of Marxist revolution. Lenin had accomplished a similar goal through his "Russification of Marxism," when he adapted the Russian proletariat to the requirements of Marxism and assigned a place to the peasantry in the forthcoming revolution. Mao's initiative, however, clearly moved beyond the contours of Lenin's revolutionary calculus, because it institutionalized the emergence of the peasantry as the central focus of the revolution. It is likewise interesting to note the differences in revolutionary strategy that accompanied the two men, as well as the composition of each country at the time of its revolution. China, for example, lagged behind Russia in the process of modernization and industrialization, although it must be noted that Russia also lagged behind Europe in that same process. Nonetheless, given the urban nature of Lenin's revolution, the Bolsheviks first seized power in the capital of Saint Petersburg (then Petrograd) before fanning out into the countryside, where it took four years for the Reds to defeat the Whites and secure the fate of the revolution. In Mao's case, the process was reversed, as the Reds took twenty-two years to defeat the Nationalist forces of Chiang Kai-shek by winning over the countryside, encircling the cities and eventually forcing the Nationalist army to surrender and Chiang Kai-shek and his government to flee to Taiwan.

After his military and political victory in the field, Mao concentrated his efforts and that of the party on the construction of a new communist society in China. Forever experimenting with alternative modes of government centralization and peasant self-sufficiency, Mao earned a reputation as a maverick, whose initiatives ranged from Soviet-style central planning to the upheaval of the Cultural Revolution. In what eventually developed into the Sino–Soviet conflict dating from the early 1960s, Mao came out boldly and condemned the political sin of revisionism, which led to the creation of a new class in the Soviet Union and the betrayal of the principles of the revolution. To combat this danger, Mao called for totalism, or total revolution, in which each individual would go through a rigorous process of psychological reconstruction and concentrate on purging his or her political identity of the cultural bonds and pre-revolutionary attitudes of the past. Through such a process of radical individual transformation, Mao believed that it would be possible to reconstruct Chinese society and achieve complete and unswerving loyalty to the revolution and its historical destiny. Since Mao's death, the tone and tenor of the revolution has taken a dramatic turn away from the tenets of total revolution in favor of a new, more pragmatic, approach to economic development and the conduct of foreign policy. China's economic upswing has truly been remarkable over the past two decades, as has its less confrontational foreign policy alignment and style. And while Mao's legacy may still loom large in the rhetoric of revolutionary politics, the world has changed even more dramatically. For example, unlike the 1960s and 1970s, when Maoists around the world proclaimed their commitment to Mao and their devotion to the revolution, Mao's image has steadily faded into the background, while the number of his followers has continued to decline.

When addressing the familiar issues of political and economic modernization, Gorbachev occupies a rather unique position within the group. In the strict sense of the term, Gorbachev did not make a revolution. He inherited one. As a result, he was a product of the Bolshevik revolution and of Soviet Marxism's fervent adherence to modernization and the unchallenged authority of the state. But as the new head of state, he also inherited a weak and dispirited country and tried to use Western models of reform to change the existing system. His transformational efforts, however, created a peculiar anomaly in which liberal reforms would be introduced to save a system based upon the model of state capitalism, which had for half a century been the exclusive doctrinal preserve and ideological showpiece of Soviet communism.

In many ways Soviet communism had become something less of a benign anachronism, insofar as the methods of centralized planning were unable to keep pace with the demands for greater economic growth. But the system did provide the people with a sense of security, knowing that basic goods and services would be provided. This does not mean that Soviet citizens were unaware of the more desirable social and economic conditions that prevailed in the West or that they failed to express their disappointment at not being able to experience a more comfortable lifestyle. But while they were willing to countenance Gorbachev's calls for change, they were for the most part unwilling to jeopardize the security they valued as an essential part of their daily existence. The moment Gorbachev's reforms undermined that system of social and economic security, Soviet citizens began to recoil at the shortages in material goods and services. This dichotomy between rising expectations and apprehensive concerns about the future underlay the dilemma facing Gorbachev, as he set to change Soviet thinking and experiment with changes in the political and economic system.

It is within this context that the timing and nature of Gorbachev's reform process takes on additional meaning. For the most part individuals outside the Soviet Union were unaware of the scope and depth of the Soviet problem. Though admittedly bureaucratic and elephantine in its ways, the Soviet Union seemed to benefit on its own terms from stolid institutional procedures and its own peculiar brand of administrative rigor. Moreover, while criticism on both sides failed to assign style points to the Soviet regime, the system itself appeared indestructible, and it tended to project an image of reassuring purpose and certainty emanating from within the Kremlin's stately walls. It was precisely this atmosphere of institutional authority that rendered Gorbachev such an attractive figure when he emerged on the international political scene.

As has been frequently noted, it was Gorbachev's youth and energy that contributed to so much of his appeal both at home and abroad. Wherever he went, particularly in the early years, Gorbachev loved to press the flesh and mingle with the people. Be it in the streets of Leningrad or the sidewalks of northwest Washington, Gorbachev gravitated almost automatically to the public; and they alertly and enthusiastically responded in kind. His extroverted ways and winning demeanor reinforced his image as an international states-man and political magician. They also suggested the beginnings of a new pe-riod in foreign policy and a new approach in international relations. But despite grumblings from within the ranks by disaffected members of the con-servative *apparat* concerning Gorbachev's international celebrity status, Gor-bachev's problem was not one of image. In fact, he came by his image honestly, and it served him well during his early days in office. What became more diffi-cult, however, was the attempt to transfer the promise of that image into pro-grams of political and economic change. The task was by no means an easy one. Nonetheless, in an effort to initiate a process of change, Gorbachev adopted *perestroika* and *glasnost* as the key phrases to serve as watchwords for reform.

The first, *perestroika*, spoke to the need for restructuring Soviet politics and the Soviet economy. The new approach emphasized the introduction of the human factor in Soviet society and the need to free the people to participate more directly in the economic process. The same manner of thinking also ad-dressed the *zastoi* or stagnation of the Soviet political system and the need to bring new blood into the party and the government. Gorbachev did not hesi-tate to call for these changes in party meetings and public gatherings. But the call, though inspirational to some, was hardly cause for riotous jubilation within the ranks of the party cadres. In this instance the occupiers of the privi-leged positions within the Soviet elite were not about to comply in meek sub-mission to Gorbachev's call. Instead, they formed a political nucleus that would work to obstruct Gorbachev's reforms and preserve their ranks and privileges. As the traditional party rank and file, they combined with their gov-ernment counterparts, the military, the police, and security forces to form an "iron triangle" and thwart Gorbachev's reforms. At first, their resistance ex-pressed itself through rumblings of disaffection with Gorbachev's new initia-tives, reflected in the more traditional forms of political opposition that emerged from within the party and the government apparatus. But as the sen-timent surrounding Gorbachev grew increasingly negative and conditions within the Soviet Union continued to deteriorate rather than improve, it was from within these same circles that the failed leadership of the August coup fi-nally emerged.

Glasnost was the other celebrated component in Gorbachev's recipe for in-spirational, political, social, and economic change. *Glasnost* was immensely popular among Soviet intellectuals and their Western counterparts, because it appealed directly to their self-image and to the desire of Gorbachev and his closest advisers to overcome decades of bureaucratic hostility toward members of the intellectual elite. The courting of the *intelligentsia* and the energy it gen-erated among writers, filmmakers, journalists, artists, actors, and so many oth-ers was a fitting tribute to Gorbachev's social sensitivity, his political creativity, and his desire to participate more directly in the creation of a new, dynamic So-viet society. It is also important to note that by virtually all responsible accounts his interest was genuine, as was his belief that such an approach was not mere window-dressing, but was, in fact, essential if the Soviet Union were to rouse itself from its torpor and passivity. It is true that Gorbachev became increasingly nervous as events began to spin out of control. And he did in some instances turn against the voices of change when they seemed to contribute to the opposition forces that were about to orchestrate his undoing. But of the many faces that he wore during his six years in office, none seemed to suit him better than his official role as defender of Russia's intellectual elite and its role as a moral compass for Russian society.

Despite his many colorful triumphs, Gorbachev was unable to remain in control of the political process both at home and abroad. Without doubt, the single most explosive political issue within the Soviet Union escaped his comprehension and eluded his grasp. That issue was the nationalities questions, as he naïvely, and unfortunately, sincerely believed that the Soviet Union could serve as a big tent where minority nationalities prized their membership in the Union and, in his view, appreciated the use of Russian as the common language of its citizens. Of course, events quickly belied such a benign scenario, as the flames of national independence movements eventually extended from Nagorno-Karabakh and the Baltic states to the Muslim parts of Soviet Central Asia. The rapidity with which the Union disintegrated in many ways reflected, for obvious reasons, the collapse of the Soviet state, which had for so long held such a disparate ethnic tapestry together through its political and military presence and seeming invincibility. In fact, once that invincibility was tested, it was truly remarkable how what was once regarded as the epitome of centralized state power in the twentieth century managed to disappear so quickly and decisively. The collapse also seemed at the time to mark an unexpected reversal of Marxist historiography. The very manner of the Soviet demise and the shock surrounding the sudden withering away of the state did not, of course, conform to Soviet thinking. The collapse also contributed to the Soviet Union's being so decisively and unceremoniously relegated to the dustbin of history.

The other great area of Gorbachev's public notoriety was his foray into foreign policy and his elaboration of "New Thinking," which he hoped would chart a more peaceful course for the international future. His texts and speeches on this topic clearly qualify as diplomatic thinking for a new age. The emphasis on internationalism, on the role of the United Nations, and on the future of disarmament are thoughtful and engaging. They made one want to follow his ideas and participate in a larger collective effort to turn the world away from its predatory past in the direction of a saner and more humane international environment. Though splendid in its presentation, however, Gorbachev's vision could not singlehandedly redefine the jagged contours of the contemporary world and will into existence a new era of global reform. That is not to say that Gorbachev's message failed to inspire others. Witness, for example, the overall peaceful transformation of Eastern Europe, which would not have occurred had it not been for Gorbachev's presence and his permission to let things unfold as they did in 1989.

His diplomatic presence, however, did not bring about the desired effect, particularly in a confrontation where the images of an "Evil Empire" and the proposed deployment in space of "Star Wars" technology stubbornly collided. Regarding the Cold War and the nuclear confrontation between the Soviet Union and the United States, Gorbachev's attempts to secure radical reductions in the size of the nuclear arsenals of both states proved for the most part illusory, as Reagan, his partner in summitry, was unwilling to sign away America's technological advantage in the face of Gorbachev's persistent attempts to chart an alternative course for the future. What did emerge, however, was the striking combination of an unreconstructed cold warrior finding himself at ease with a youthful and dynamic Soviet leader, as they both engaged in a political duet that was the talk of Moscow, Washington, and beyond. For these and many similar reasons, Gorbachev, though flawed and ultimately driven from office, remains a worthy example for those who pursue alternative modes of diplomatic discourse and negotiation and who seek solutions outside the well-worn paths of conventional politics.

SUGGESTIONS FOR FURTHER READING

GANDHI

A sensible place to begin reading on Gandhi is Mohandas K. Gandhi's *Autobiography: The Story of My Experiments with Truth,* translated by Mahadev Desai (New York: Dover Publications, 1983). The book provides a nice compendium of the development of Gandhi's thought as well as valuable insights into his personality and sense of deep personal commitment. Also worth reading are the sections in *Gandhi: All Men Are Brothers: Autobiographical Reflections,* edited by Krishna Kripalani (New York: Continuum, 1992), which follows a similar format but contains additional material from Gandhi's writings and speeches. The best introductory biography of Gandhi is Louis Fischer, *Gandhi: His Life and Message for the World* (New York: Mentor, 1982). Fischer's book is highly readable and thoroughly engaging, as it combines a well-structured narrative of Gandhi's life with a stimulating account of his emergence as a world political figure.

Ved Mehta's *Mahatma Gandhi and His Apostles* (New Haven, Conn.: Yale University Press, 1993) provides excellent insights into the significance of Gandhi's life, his spiritual and political struggles, the breadth of his humanity, and the formation of his political ideas as expressed through his own words and those of his followers. An interesting work of a totally different nature is Erik H. Erikson's *Gandhi's Truth: On the Origins of Militant Nonviolence* (New York: W.W. Norton, 1993). In this work Erikson applies his psychological theories of identity formation to Gandhi's personal development as a son, husband, religious figure, and political leader. Though seemingly reductionist, Erikson's work does provide valuable insights into Gandhi's psychological makeup. It also makes a legitimate case for the application of Western psychological techniques to the study of other cultures. B. R. Nanda's *Gandhi and His Critics* (Oxford, Eng.: Oxford University Press, 1996) is a spirited response by one of Gandhi's loyal supporters to those who disparaged Gandhi's religious bearing and beliefs, his economic theories of village life, and the impact of his political career. Dennis Dalton's *Mahatma Gandhi: Nonviolent Power in Action* (New York: Columbia University Press, 1993) provides an excellent bridge for an American audience between Gandhi's struggle for liberation and Martin Luther King's adoption of nonviolent action in his campaign of civil disobedience.

MAO

An excellent overview of Mao's life and the making of the communist revolution in China remains Stuart Schram's *Mao Tse-tung* (Baltimore, Md.: Penguin, 1967) in the Pelican series on political leaders of the twentieth century. Two classic works—one by Benjamin Schwartz, *Chinese Communism and the Rise of Mao* (Cambridge, Mass.: Harvard University Press, 1951), the other by Jerome Ch'en, *Mao and the Chinese Revolution* (London: Oxford University Press, 1965)—also deserve special mention as landmark studies in the field.

For sheer readability, verve, and insight into Mao the man and the early days of the movement, the portrait that emerges from Edgar Snow's *Red Star over China* (New York: Random House, 1938 [1961]) is still without peer. Representing the best in political journalism, Snow provides valuable insights into Mao's youth, the clarity of his political instincts, the depth of his political convictions, and his rather unassuming personal style, while at the same time capturing the dramatic significance of the communist movement, the vicissitudes of the civil war, and such heroic events as the Long March. Of course, nothing captures the color of Maoism better than the Little Red Book, or *Quotations from Chairman Mao Tse-tung* (Peking: Foreign Languages Press, 1966), which became the bible of the Cultural Revolution and a reflection of Mao's campaign to keep the original revolutionary spirit alive. Robert Jay Lifton's *Revolutionary Immortality: Mao Tse-tung and the Chinese Cultural Revolution* (New York: W.W. Norton, 1976) also serves as an excellent companion work to the Little Red Book because of Lifton's portrayal of Mao's desire not to let the revolution die but have it and him transcend the political present and define the political future.

Maurice Meisner's *Mao's China and After: A History of the People's Republic* (New York: Free Press, 1986) provides a sound overview of Maoism by discussing both the domestic context of the movement and the protean demands of a larger international environment. At a more introductory level, Albert Marrin's *Mao Tse-tung and His China* (New York: Penguin, 1989) provides readers with a well-paced introduction to Mao's life and the controversies that surround his political career.

MANDELA

Containing excerpts from his speeches, writings, and courtroom appearances, Mandela's *No Easy Walk to Freedom* (London: Heinemann, 1989) serves as a good introduction to his political views and outlook and the challenges posed by the freedom struggle in South Africa. His autobiography, *Long Walk to Freedom* (Boston: Little, Brown, 1994), is even more powerful, as it describes his trials and suffering without a sense of bitterness or regret. The work also brings together the dynamics of Mandela's personal life and his courage and integrity as a leader, public figure, and government official.

Mary Benson's *Nelson Mandela: The Man and the Movement* (New York: W.W. Norton, 1994) is a touching biography by a Mandela loyalist. Benson, who participated in the struggle and understood it well, was also able to capture the essence of Mandela's charismatic personality and his ability to inspire hope among his followers. Martin Meredith's *Nelson Mandela: A Biography* (New York: St. Martin's Press, 1998) is broad in scope and detailed in its analysis. It also provides a comprehensive overview of Mandela's life history, beginning with his village youth and extending up to and beyond his election as president of South Africa. By providing valuable insights into Mandela's political and personal relationships with other prominent black South African leaders, Tim J. Juckes's *Opposition in South Africa: The Leadership of Z. K. Matthews, Nelson Mandela, and Stephen Biko* (Westport, Conn.: Praeger, 1995) provides a more comparative, multigenerational view of the dynamics of the opposition movement and the significance of Mandela's political career.

GORBACHEV

The material on Gorbachev is extensive. For a compilation of much of that material see the bibliography in my *Politics, Diplomacy, and the Media: Gorbachev's Legacy in the West* (Westport, Conn.: Praeger, 1998). In many ways the best way to encounter Gorbachev is through his own words. His book *Perestroika: New Thinking for Our Country and the World* (New York: Harper & Row, 1987), which caused such a stir when it appeared, remains a lively and thought-provoking introduction to Gorbachev and the claims of *perestroika*. His *Memoirs* (New York: Doubleday, 1995) are well written and provide a sense of coherence to the Gorbachev years. Numerous speeches, including other political works by Gorbachev, have also been published. Of course, another important voice, in the form of Boris Yeltsin's *Against the Grain: An Autobiography* (New York: Simon & Schuster, 1990), provides a totally different and highly critical point of view.

There are many insightful and informative accounts of the Gorbachev period. Two excellent ones have been done by journalists: The first is Hedrick Smith's *The New Russians* (New York: Avon, 1991); the second is Robert G.

Kaiser's *Why Gorbachev Happened: His Triumphs and His Failures* (New York: Simon & Schuster, 1991) (revised Touchstone edition, 1992). Another early and distinctive perspective on the Gorbachev phenomenon is provided by the Soviet dissident Zhores A. Medvedev in *Gorbachev* (New York: W.W. Norton, 1986). For an excellent discussion of the economic dimensions and problems of *perestroika,* see Marshall I. Goldman's *What Went Wrong with Perestroika* (New York: W.W. Norton, 1991). On the subject of *glasnost,* the anthology of interviews of prominent Soviet reformers presented in Stephen F. Cohen and Katrina vanden Heuvel, eds., *Voices of Glasnost: Interviews with Gorbachev's Reformers* (New York: W.W. Norton, 1989), is highly informative. An engaging, illuminating, and highly literate account of *glasnost* also appears in Walter Laqueur's *The Long Road to Freedom: Russia and Glasnost* (New York: Macmillan, 1989).

INDEX

Act for the Better Government of India, 3

Addis Ababa, 76

Afghanistan, 122, 133, 135

African National Congress, 66

Afrikaans University of Witwatersrand, 67

Afrikaner, 63, 67, 73, 81, 86

Afrikaner Volksfront, 86

Against the Grain, 116

agrarian, 35, 48, 54

ahimsa, 17, 20

Alexei II, Patriarch, 142

Amin, Hafizullah, 135

Amritsar, 4, 13

ANC, 68, 77, 78, 79, 89; in Addis Ababa, 76; African National Congress, 66; Indians and communists, joined forces with, 69; Leaders, 70, 73, 82, 87, 91; outlawed, 74; Transvaal conference of the, 71; violence with Inkhata, 87; Youth League, 67

Andreyeva, Nina, 112, 113

Andropov, Yuri, 103

Angola, 134

anti-Semitic, 118

apartheid, 74, 84, 90, 91, 134, 166; crimes under, 79; criticism of, 86; introduction of, 68; policy, 72, 74; victims of, 83, 84

apparat, 106, 107, 118, 169

apparatchik, 104, 107

Arafat, Yasser, 134

Aristotle, 102

Armenians, 109

Asiatic Registration Act, The, 9

assegais, 86

baasskap, 68

Badenhorst, Colonel Piet, 81, 82

Baltic States, 142

Bantu, 71, 82

"bantustans," 72

Benson, Mary, 74

Bhagavad Gita, 13

Biko, Stephen, 82

"black assertiveness," 82

Black Consciousness Movement, 82

Black Pimpernel, 75

Boer War, 63

Bolshevik, 106, 107, 137, 143, 144

Bolshevik movement, 33, 34, 168

bourgeois, 34, 44

brahmacharya, 8, 16

Brezhnev, Leonid, 80, 103, 117

British Commonwealth of Nations, 84

British Parliament, 79

Brzezinski, Zbigniew, 118

Bush, George, 131, 132, 136, 141, 145

Buthelezi, Chief Mangosutha, 86

Castro, Fidel, 75, 92, 134
Ceauşescu, Nicolae, 128
Chagall, Marc, 125
Chernenko, Konstantin, 103
Chernobyl, 120
Chiang Kai-shek, 35, 36, 39–44, 52, 167
Children of the Arbat, 112, 121, 124
China, 134, 135, 166, 167
Chinese Republic, 32
Churchill, Winston, 15, 79
Clarkebury, 64
CODESA, 87, 88, 89
Coetsee, Kobie, 84
collectivization, 48, 111
colonialism, 23, 134
colour bar, 7, 63
Comintern, 34
Communist Manifesto, The, 33
Communist Party, 66, 68, 69, 87, 115, 144
Congress of the People, 71
Congress Party, 14
Copernicus, Nicolas, 105
Crawnpore, 3
Crimea, 114, 141
Cuba, 92, 134
Cultural Revolution, The, 167

Dalai Lama, 51
Dalton, Dennis, 13, 22, 173
Daniloff, Nicholas, 142
Darwin, Charles, 105
DDR, 128
de Kiewiet, Cornelius, 63
de Klerk, F. W., 84–89, 91
de Tocqueville, Alexis, 146
de Wet, Judge Quartus, 79
Defiance Campaign, 69, 70
demokratizatsiya, 108
Deng Xiaoping, 52, 54, 134
de-Stalinization, 109, 112
Dole, Robert, 118
Dutch Reformed Church, 68
Dyer, Reginald, General, 4

eGoli, 66
Eie volk, eie taal, eie land, 68

Engels, Friedrich, 69
Erikson, Erik, 6
Ethiopia, 76, 77, 134

Fabian Socialism, 69
faction, 38
Financial Times, 118
Fischer, Bram, 67, 89
Fischer, Louis, 10, 22, 173
Fort Hare, University College of, 65–67, 82
Freedom Day, 69
freedom of speech, 117
Freud, Sigmund, 105

Gandhi, Indira, 22
Gandhi, Mahatma: ascetic lifestyle, 9, 11, 15, 22; caste system, views on, 18; civil disobedience, 12; his death, 21; fasting, 11, 20; Hind Swaraj by, 10; in London, 6; nonviolence, use of, 8, 9, 11–13, 17, 18, 19; prison, 11, 12, 14, 18, 20; in South Africa, 7
Gang of Four, 52, 53
Garvey, Marcus, 78
Geneva, 129, 130, 132
Gerasimov, Gennady, 127
Godse, Nathuram Vinayak, 21
Gokhale, Gopal Krishna, 3
Gorbachev, Mikhail: Andreyeva, reply to, 113; *The August Coup: The Truth and the Lessons*, 144; in Beijing, 135; Berlin, visit to, 128; Central Committee Plenum, speech at, 108; China, relations with, 134; communication media, 106–108, 114, 117, 118, 131, 133; decline in popularity, 136–138; on diversity, 111; during crisis, 120; education, 102; Geneva summit, 129, 130; Helmut Kohl, meeting with, 129; Leningrad, speech in, 106; *Memoirs*, 147; Moscow City Party Committee, meeting with, 115; Moscow, return to, 103; Moscow summit, 132; Murmansk, speech in, 127; Nobel Peace Prize, 135; nuclear weapons, view of, 126, 133; *Perestroika: New Thinking*

for Our Country and World, 108, 125; Prague, visit to, 127; Reagan, meeting with, 130; resignation, 144, 145; rise to power, 101, 103; Stalinism, views on, 109, 111, 123; in Stavropol, 102; Twenty-seventh Party Congress, address to, 110; United Nations, appearance before, 133, 134; Washington summit, 131; Western capitals, visit to, 119; Western press, in the, 103, 105, 125; Yeltsin, rivalry with, 114–116, 136, 137, 139, 142, 145, 146
Gordimer, Nadine, 83
Gostel, 137
Grand Reformation, 103
Great Trek, 63
Gregory, James, 81, 133
Gromyko, Andrei, 103
Guardian, 118
gulag, 112
Gulag Archipelago, 121

Hani, Chris, 87
Harilal, 5
Harris, Reverend, 65
hartal, 12
Havel, Vaclav, 128
Healdtown, 65
Hegel, Georg W. F., 102
Helsinki accords, 109
high treason, 73, 79
Hindus, 3, 20, 21, 22
Hiroshima, 126, 130, 132, 133
hunger strike, 8

ICBMs, 130
Imperialism, 31, 74
Indian Civil Service, 1, 3
Indian Congress, 68
Indian National Congress, 3
inertia, 109, 110
INF, 131
infanticide, 47
Inkhata Freedom Party, 87
International Herald Tribune, 118
Iraq, 132
Izvestia, 119

Jefferson, Thomas, 146
Jesus Christ, 137
Jews, 109
Jiangxi, 38, 39
Jinnah, Mohammed Ali, 20
Johannesburg, 66, 70, 73, 76, 78, 164

Kaganovich, Lazar, 118
Kaiser, Robert, 101, 142
Kandinsky, Wasily, 125
Karmal, Babrak, 135
Kasturbai, 5
KGB, 119
Khadafi, Moammar, 92
Khrushchev, Nikita, 47
King, Coretta Scott, 83, 89
King, Martin Luther, Jr., 22, 76, 84
Klimov, Elim, 106, 122, 124
Kohl, Helmut, 129, 146
Komsomol, 102
Korean War, 44
Koumintang, 34, 36, 38, 39, 42
Kravchenko, Leonid, 137
Kryuchkov, Vladimir, 140
Kulakov, Fyodor, 102, 103
Kuwait, 132

Latin America, 51, 134
Leipzig option, 87
Lenin, Vladimir, 38, 54, 69, 102, 108, 109, 112, 119, 137, 136, 142; diplomacy, 125; use of *Glasnost*, 117; leadership, 34, 106; Liberation of Labor, 11; in plays, 124; thought, 35, 55, 107, 167
Liberal Party, 72
liberalism, 33
Liberation, 72
Libya, 92
Lifton, Robert Jay, 53
Ligachev, Yegor, 115, 141
Lincoln, Abraham, 65, 75
Lithuania, 138, 139
Lolita, 121
Long March, 39, 40, 50

Machiavelli, 102
Malan, Dr. Daniel, 68

Mandela, Nelson: in Algeria, 76, 77; All African Conference, at the, 75; arrest, 70, 73, 74; death of mother and son, 80; Eminent Persons Group, meeting with, 84; entry into politics, 67; marriage, 73, 88, 91; M-plan, 70; prison, 77, 78, 80, 81, 83; return to Robben Island, 80; return to South Africa, 77; Rivonia Trial, at the, 78, 79; University College of Fort Hare, at the, 65, 66; view of his warders, 81, 82; Walter Sisulu, meeting with, 66; youth, 64, 65; Youth League President, 71
Mandela United Football Club, 88
Mao Zedong, 69, 75, 163, 166, 167; in Beijing, 33; Chairman of Politburo, 40; Director of Peasant Movement Training Institute, 35; Great Helmsman, as the, 52, 54; Hundred Flowers Speech, 47, 48; Marxism, view on, 33–35; masses, view of the, 39, 48; military strategy, 37, 38, 50, 55; Nixon, meeting with, 54; political education, 32; propaganda, use of, 43, 45, 47; rise to power, 38, 39; Tien An'Mien Square, in, 44; youth, 32
martial law, 4, 74
Marx, Karl, 69, 108, 118
Mase, Evelyn, 67
Matthews, Z. K., 64, 65, 68
Maximova, Raisa, 102, 105, 114, 116, 136, 143
May Day, 136
mayor of Europe, 127
Medvedev, 102
memoirs, 82
Memoirs, 147
Memorial Society, 112
Meredith, Martin, 89
Methodist, 64, 65
Military Intelligence, Department of, 87
Mill, John Stuart, 102
Minister of Justice, 84
modernist, 36
moral authority, 92
moratorium, 132, 133
Moscow News, 119, 136
Moscow State University, 101

Moslem League, 20
M-Plan, 70
Mughal, 1
Muscovites, 105, 116, 139
Muslims, 3, 14, 20, 21, 22
Mussolini, Benito, 122

Nagasaki, 126, 130, 132
Napoleon, 32, 114
narod, 105
National Day of Protest, 69
Nationalism, 15, 67, 78, 111, 118, 128
nationalist, 35, 36, 45, 84
NATO, 129
Nazi invasion of the Soviet Union (1941), 111
Nehru, Jawaharal, 13, 71
New Economic Policy, 109
Newsweek, 136
nihilism, 112
Nixon, Richard M., 54
Nobel Peace Prize, 88, 135
nomenklatura, 107
Nomzano, Winnie, 73
nuclear war, 125, 126

Ogonyok, 119, 136
Operation Mayibuye, 78
operativnost, 120
opium, 31, 37, 45

PAC, 74, 87
Pakistan, 20, 21, 164
Pamyat, 118
Pan African Freedom Movement, 76
Paris Exhibition, 6
Parliament, 77, 81
Party Conference, 114, 115
Party Congress, 107, 110
Pavlov, Valentin, 140
Peasant Movement Training Institute, 35
Perestroika, 111, 115, 120, 122, 124, 128, 131, 143, 147; criticism of, 108, 110, 112, 116; early days of, 104, 106, 117, 132, 138, 145, 169; Gorbachev's use of, 126, 130, 131, 134, 144, 169; implementation of, 109, 116

Peter the Great, 32
Pipes, Richard, 119
Plato, 102
PLO, 134
Politburo, 40, 102, 103, 113, 115, 119
Pollsmoor Prison, 83
Pravda, 107, 113, 118, 119
Privolnoe, 101
Protocols of the Elders of Zion, 118
psychism, 53
Pugo, Boris, 140
Punjab, 4
Purges, 111

Queen Victoria, 3
Qunu, 64

Radio Liberty, 119
rationing cards, 44
Reagan, Ronald, 103, 126, 129–132,
    134, 171
Record of Understanding, 89
Red Army, 37, 38, 39, 42, 43, 44
Red Banner of Labor, 101
Red Guards, 51, 52
Red Star over China, 75
refuseniks, 112
Repentance, 112, 121, 122, 124
Reykjavik, 130, 131, 146
Rivonia, 76, 78, 90
Robben Island, 78, 80, 82, 83
Rolihala, 64
Romanov Imperial family, 143
Roosevelt, Franklin Delano, 79
Rostropovich, Mstislav, 142
Round Table Conference, 15
Rousseau, Henri, 102
Rowlatt Acts (1919), 4
Rutskoi, Alexander, 143
Rybakov, Anatoli, 112, 121, 124

Sakharov, Andrei, 99, 113, 114, 133, 137
Sandinistas, 134
SASO, 82
Satyagraha, 11, 13
saviour of India, 4
SDI, 126, 129, 130, 131
Sepoy Mutiny, 1, 4

Shanghai, 34, 35, 36
Shervardnadze, Eduard, 106
Siberia, 121
"Sinification of Marxism," 166
Sisulu, Albertina, 66
Sisulu, Walter, 66
skromny, 105
Slavophile, 115
Smith, Hedrick, 103
Smolny Institute, 106
Snow, Edgar, 41
Sobchak, Anatoli, 109, 138
Somalia, 134
Somoza, Anastasio, 134
Sophiatown, 71
South African Student Organization, 82
Sovetskaya Rossiya, 112
Soweto, 66, 82, 86, 88
Stalin, Josef, 34, 48, 54, 69, 79, 118,
    123, 124, 126, 146; criticism of, 113,
    118; era of, 111; Mao, rivalry be-
    tween, 46, 57; thought, 107; victims
    of, 112, 121
Stalinism, 109, 112, 124
Starkov, Vladislav, 137
START, 141
Stavropol, 101, 102, 103, 129
Steinbeck, John, 83, 130
Stevenson, Adlai, 80
Sun Zu, 38
Supreme Court, 7
Supreme Soviet, 114, 137–140, 144
swart gevaar, 68
swastika, 81

Taiwan, 44, 167
Tambo, Oliver, 70, 87, 89
Tatu, Michel, 105
Tatu river bridge, 40
Thatcher, Margaret, 127
Thembu, 64
Third Force, 87
Third International, The, 34
Third World, 133, 134
Thoreau, Henry David, 9
Tibet, 50–51
Tilak, 3
Time, 88, 136

Togliatti, 110
Tolstaya, Tatyana, 146
Tolstoy, Leo, 9, 83
Transkei, 64
Transvaal, 71
Trotsky, Leon, 102, 118, 124
tsar liberator, 105
Tutu, Archbishop Desmond, 85, 86, 91

Ulyanov, Mikhail, 124
Umkhonto we Sizwe, 75
UN Security Council, 74, 79
Union Act, The, 63
University of London, 79, 83
University of South Africa, 67
untouchability, 11, 18

Van Rensburg, 81
Versailles, 33
Verwoerd, Dr. Hendrick, 71
Viceroy of India, 15
Vilnius, 138–139
Voice of America, 119
volkstaat, 86

Warsaw Pact, 128
Washington, George, 32
Washington Times, 84
Whitehall, 3
Wilson, Woodrow, 125
Winter of Our Discontent, The, 130
Witwatersrand, 66

Xhosa, 64, 65, 77, 87
Xuma, Dr. A. B., 68, 77

Yakovlev, Alexander, 106, 113, 141,
    143
Yazov, 140
Yeltsin, Boris, 110, 114–116, 138, 143,
    144, 147; Gorbachev, rivalry with,
    136, 137, 139, 142, 145, 146
Yenan, 40–41
Youth League, 67, 68, 69
Yutar, Percy, 90

Zaslavskaya, Tatyana, 106, 108
zastoi, 169
Zulu, 63, 86, 87, 89

ABOUT THE AUTHOR

ANTHONY R. DeLUCA is Professor of History at Emerson College. He is also the author of *Politics, Diplomacy, and the Media: Gorbachev's Legacy in the West* (Praeger, 1998).

ISBN 0-275-95969-4

90000>

HARDCOVER BAR CODE